Money in Politics

In politics, money is often the name of the game. Politicians enrich themselves while in office, spend campaign money to finance their reelection, and accept lucrative "golden parachute" jobs after leaving office. *Money in Politics* argues that these different forms of capital are part of a common system and should be analyzed in a single framework. The book advances a comparative theory that shows how self-enrichment, campaign spending, and golden parachute jobs are connected to each other. This theory explains when and how money enters politics, ultimately illuminating that a change in one form affects the other types and revealing the consequences this has for democracy. The book uses a wide range of evidence from countries around the world, including causally identified quantitative studies, qualitative cross-national comparisons, and original survey experiments. Enlightening and instructive, this book shows that we can only fully comprehend the role of money in politics when we view it as a common system to be analyzed and critiqued.

SIMON WESCHLE is an Assistant Professor in Political Science at Syracuse University. His research focuses on democratic representation and accountability, and factors that impede it.

Money in Politics

Self-Enrichment, Campaign Spending, and Golden Parachutes

SIMON WESCHLE

Syracuse University

CAMBRIDGE
UNIVERSITY PRESS

CAMBRIDGE
UNIVERSITY PRESS

University Printing House, Cambridge CB2 8BS, United Kingdom

One Liberty Plaza, 20th Floor, New York, NY 10006, USA

477 Williamstown Road, Port Melbourne, VIC 3207, Australia

314–321, 3rd Floor, Plot 3, Splendor Forum, Jasola District Centre, New Delhi – 110025, India

103 Penang Road, #05–06/07, Visioncrest Commercial, Singapore 238467

Cambridge University Press is part of the University of Cambridge.

It furthers the University's mission by disseminating knowledge in the pursuit of education, learning, and research at the highest international levels of excellence.

www.cambridge.org
Information on this title: www.cambridge.org/9781316511848
DOI: 10.1017/9781009053952

First published 2022

A catalogue record for this publication is available from the British Library.

Library of Congress Cataloging-in-Publication Data
Names: Weschle, Simon, 1984- author.
Title: Money in politics : self-enrichment, campaign spending, and golden parachutes / Simon Weschle.
Description: New York : Cambridge University Press, 2022. | Includes bibliographical references and index.
Identifiers: LCCN 2021062479 (print) | LCCN 2021062480 (ebook) | ISBN 9781316511848 (hardback) | ISBN 9781009053952 (ebook)
Subjects: LCSH: Campaign funds. | Campaign funds–Corrupt aspects. | Political corruption–Economic aspects. | Politicians–Salaries, etc. | Politicians–Pensions.
Classification: LCC JF2112.C28 W47 2022 (print) | LCC JF2112.C28 (ebook) | DDC 324.7/8–dc23/eng/20220213
LC record available at https://lccn.loc.gov/2021062479
LC ebook record available at https://lccn.loc.gov/2021062480

ISBN 978-1-316-51184-8 Hardback
ISBN 978-1-009-05471-3 Paperback

Für meine Eltern

Contents

Figures

Tables

Acknowledgments

It has been a long journey since I had what I now recognize to be the first inkling of the idea behind this book's argument during my first year in Graduate School. The journey since then was often difficult and always challenging. But, at the end of the process, I am hopeful and optimistic that the book achieves some of the things that I set out to do many years ago. However, this is only the case because a large number of people have helped me along the way.

This means, first of all, my dissertation adviser Karen Remmer. She always managed to find just the right balance between pushing me and giving me space to develop the project at my own pace while being encouraging and supportive throughout. She is an ideal adviser. The same is true for the other members of my dissertation committee. Erik Wibbels' probing questions and sharp comments have improved the book greatly, and his guidance during the publication process has been invaluable. Pablo Beramendi's advice on everything ranging from this book to Galician vacations has been essential. I benefited greatly from the substantial and technical expertise of Daniel Gingerich. Addressing the comments and suggestions he made at my dissertation defense kept me busy for a long time. Finally, Michael Ward has supported me in more ways than I can count, and the generosity he displayed as a mentor sets the example that I try to emulate in my own career. Mike, I wish you could read these lines, but trust that you are in a better place now.

I spent time at three different institutions while working on this book. At each of them, I have been extremely fortunate to have had colleagues who read parts or all of the manuscript, who engaged in conversations about it, who provided constructive feedback, or who were (and still are) great friends. At Duke, I thank John Aldrich, Melina Altamirano, Laia Balcells, Andy Ballard, Ben Barber, Kyle Beardsley, Andy Beger, Tim Büthe, Cindy Cheng, Scott de Marchi, Chris DeSante, Cassy Dorff, Idil Edes Gallop, Max Gallop, Ana Guzman, Florian Hollenbach, Aaron Houck, Libby Jenke, Bill Keech, Aaron King, Herbert Kitschelt, Dan Krcmaric, Anh Le, Howard Liu, Fengming Lu, Bahar Leventoglu, Eddy Malesky, Nils Metternich, Shahryar Minhas, Michael Munger, Noa On, Frank Orlando, Vicky Paniagua, Brittany Perry, Jan Pierskalla, Guadalupe Rojo, Arturas Rozenas, Greg Schober, Anna Schultz, David Soskice, Danielle Thomsen, Will Wittels, and Sean Zeigler.

At the Carlos III-Juan March Institute, I am grateful to Diana Dakhlallah, Pablo Fernández-Vázquez, Robert Fishman, Gema García Albacete, Sebastián Lavezzolo, Mark Manger, Luis Fernando Medina, Magdalena Nebreda, Lluís Orriols, Javier Polavieja, Jonas Radl, Andrew Richards, Pedro Riera, Ignacio Sánchez-Cuenca, Pablo Simón, and Marga Torre.

At Syracuse, I benefited from comments and advice by Lamis Abdelaaty, David Arceneaux, Matt Cleary, Margarita Estevez-Abe, Chris Faricy, Shana Gadarian, Ryan Griffiths, Dimitar Gueorguiev, Erin Hern, Seth Jolly, Audie Klotz, Sarah Mawhorter, Dan McDowell, Kathy Michelmore, Glyn Morgan, Tessa Murphy, Elise Roberts, Michah Rothbart, Brian Taylor, Danielle Thomsen (again), Emily Thorson, Steven White, Matt Young, and Yael Zeira.

Miriam Golden and David Samuels were gracious enough to participate in my book manuscript workshop at Syracuse University. They both read the entire draft and provided detailed comments, which improved the book in many, many ways.

During my fieldwork in India, I benefited from interactions with, among others, Sanjeer Alam, Anil Bairwal and his team at the Association for Democratic Reforms, Laveesh Bhandari, Prasana Dash, Dhananjai Joshi, Nimah Mazaheri, Jesim Pais, Seema Sahai, E. Sridharan, Paranjoy Guha Thakurta, and Yogendra Yadav.

Over the course of the years, I've been lucky to receive feedback on parts of the book from many people in the discipline, including Ben Ansell, Lorena Becerra, Cristina Bodea, Julie Browne, Jennifer Bussell, Simon Chauchard, Ray Duch, Benjamin Egerod, Andrew Eggers, Alexander Fouirnaies, Nikhar Gaikwad, Jessica Gottlieb, Kenneth Greene, Charles Hankla, Alex Hirsch, James Hollyer, Francesca Jensenius, Paul Kellstedt, Marko Klašnja, Kendra Koivu, Avital Livny, Ana Luiza Melo Aranha, Didac Queralt, David Rueda, Luis Schiumerini, Joel Simmons,

Alberto Simpser, Abby Wood, Hye Young You, and Thomas Zeitzoff. I also thank conference participants at various editions of the annual meetings of the American Political Science Association, the European Political Science Association, and the Midwest Political Science Association, and seminar participants at Duke University, New York University, University of Konstanz, and Nuffield College/University of Oxford.

Parts of this book are revisions of published material. Portions of Chapter 5 appeared in Weschle, Simon. 2021. "Campaign Finance Legislation and the Supply-Side of the Revolving Door." *Political Science Research and Methods*, 9(2): 365–379 (Cambridge University Press). Parts of Chapter 7 were published in Weschle, Simon. 2016. "Punishing Personal and Electoral Corruption: Experimental Evidence from India." *Research and Politics*, 3(2): 1–6 (Sage Journals).

I am thankful to the anonymous reviewers at Cambridge University Press for their suggestions, Robert Dreesen and Sara Doskow for their editorial guidance, as well as Cameron Daddis and Jadyn Fauconier-Herry for their editorial assistance. Kelley Friel copy-edited this book, and her 9,339 revisions and suggestions vastly improved its readability. Many thanks also to the Longform podcast, which has been a weekly companion throughout the writing process. Hearing much better writers struggle with many of the same issues as I did was reassuring.

On a personal note, I would like to thank my parents. They are my biggest champions and have supported me enthusiastically and unwaveringly, even if that meant that their son lives more than 4,000 miles away. As a small token of gratitude, this book is dedicated to them. Finally, I can't put into words how grateful I am to my wife Allison and my daughter Nina, so I won't even try. They have had to put up with me the most while I was writing this book; they are the most important people in my life; and my greatest thank you of all goes to them.

Introduction

Andimuthu Raja's arrest came on February 2, 2011. After being called in for questioning by India's Central Bureau of Investigation in the morning, he was detained later that day and placed in Delhi's notorious Tihar Prison. This marked the apex of a scandal that one journalist described as setting "a new national benchmark for corruption caused by the nexus between politics and business."[1] As India's communications minister, Raja had overseen the sale of 2G mobile spectrum licenses in 2008. Auditors accused the ministry of a plethora of violations: The implementation of the sale deviated from the procedure approved by the cabinet, and licenses were significantly undervalued. Deadlines were arbitrarily changed on short notice, eliminating companies without prior knowledge. Applications by others were processed even though documents were fake or missing.[2] Auditors concluded that the losses to the state, and the gains for telecommunications companies, were as high as $40 billion. But the corporations were not the only one's who received a windfall: Raja is suspected of having pocketed millions for himself.[3]

Former US Congressman Walt Minnick also had a close relationship with the business sector and received a lot of money from it. He admitted that he spent "two or three hours a day as a congressman trying to raise money" because he "needed to raise $10,000 to $15,000 a day."[4] Minnick

---

[1] "Spectrum Shadiness," *Caravan Magazine*, December 1, 2010.
[2] "Performance Audit of Issue of Licences and Allocation of 2G Spectrum of Union Government, Ministry of Communications and Information Technology," *Comptroller and Auditor General of India*, November 16, 2010.
[3] "A Raja Made Rs 3,000cr in Bribes," *Times of India*, February 11, 2011; "Indian Authorities Arrest Ex-Telecoms Minister A Raja," *BBC News*, February 2, 2011.
[4] "461: Take the Money and Run for Office," *This American Life*, March 30, 2012.

did not even wait to take office before he tried to capitalize on it. Only five days after he won his election in 2010, a couple of months before being sworn in, he was already busy making calls asking people to pay up. Two years later, the first-term representative with little clout in the legislature had amassed more than $2.6 million.[5] The major difference between Raja and Minnick is that whereas the former enriched himself personally, the latter spent the millions he raised on his reelection campaign to try to stay in office.

Finally, in September 2005, the heads of Russian and German energy companies signed an agreement to build a new gas pipeline through the Baltic Sea that was large enough to deliver almost 70 percent of Germany's annual gas supplies. Construction costs were estimated to exceed €4 billion (about $4.9 billion given the exchange rate at the time). Both German Chancellor Gerhard Schröder and Russian President Vladimir Putin signed off on the project. Schröder did so despite considerable opposition at home and abroad. For example, the Polish prime minister lamented that "we were not able to convince the Germans that this is bad for them."[6] Schröder left office two months later. Only seventeen days thereafter, he accepted the position of chairman of the board of Nord Stream, the consortium building the pipeline, with an estimated salary of several hundred thousand dollars per year.[7]

All three cases are examples of elected politicians taking large sums of money. They all illustrate the potential for such money to influence policy in a way that runs counter to the preferences of the majority of voters, thus highlighting a fundamental tension in democratic politics. But they differ in *how* the politicians used the money. Raja enriched himself while in office, Minnick financed his reelection campaign, and Schröder accepted a lucrative "golden parachute" job after leaving office.

Why did these politicians use the money they had access to in different ways? Is it because of their arbitrary personal preferences, or are there more systematic underlying reasons? If there is a pattern, is the presence or absence of these different types of money in politics independent of each other and driven by separate causes? Or, if the forms are connected, can they be explained by common factors? Under what conditions is each type present, and does having less of one form mean there is more of another?

What does this imply for the effectiveness of regulation designed to limit money in politics? And what difference does it make for a democracy if politicians enrich themselves while in office, raise money to try to stay there, or cash in on their position after leaving it?

1.1 ARGUMENT: THE SYSTEM OF MONEY IN POLITICS

In this book, I answer these questions by arguing that the most common ways in which politicians use money – for self-enrichment, to fund campaigns, and by accepting golden parachute jobs – are all part of a *common system* and should therefore be analyzed in a *single framework*. My approach is distinct from most prior studies, which tend to either examine money in politics in a comparative manner, but without distinguishing between different types, or explore one form of money while ignoring the others, typically in a single country. Here, I look at *several* types of money in politics *together* while taking an explicitly *comparative* perspective. I develop and test a theoretical framework that: (1) shows how the different forms are connected to each other; (2) explains when money enters politics in what way; (3) illuminates how a change in one form affects the other types; and (4) reveals the consequences this has for democracy.

This analysis provides a string of novel, and often surprising, insights. It reveals that the different types of money are partially *fungible*, so a change in one form leads to important *second-order changes* in the opposite direction for the other types. For example, it is somewhat obvious that regulating campaign finance more strictly leads to less campaign spending. Yet it is less straightforward that the downstream effects of such regulation are *more* self-enrichment in office and *more* golden parachute employment. It is only once we examine the different forms of money as elements of a common *system* that we see how a change in one type leads to opposite effects in other types. Furthermore, various types of money in politics have different effects on numerous facets of democratic politics, such as voters' view of politicians or who wins elections. Thus, a change in one type of money leads not only to second-order changes in other forms; it also has *third-order effects* on the quality of democracy.

The connections between the different forms of money in politics, and the second- and third-order effects this implies, have received little attention in prior studies. Nor do they play a part in public discussion. I show that ignoring these connections leads to an incomplete, and possibly misleading, understanding of the topic. The central implication of this book is therefore that we can only fully understand the role of money in politics if we think of it as a *system*. The rest of this section provides a brief overview of my argument, which I make in three steps.

The Connection between the Types of Money in Politics

In a first step, I argue that self-enrichment, campaign spending, and golden parachute jobs should neither be treated as equivalent nor as entirely separate. Instead, they are part of a *system* and should be analyzed in a common framework.

The link that connects all three is that they are crucial in advancing politicians' career goals. As Mayhew (1974) famously argued, one of politicians' central aims is to get reelected. But extensive research shows that they are also interested in improving their personal financial situation. Money furthers both of these goals. As utility-maximizing actors, politicians will seek to use money in the ways that best suit their needs, given the conditions they operate in. In other words, the different forms of money are partially *fungible*. This highlights the need to develop a framework that gives us an idea when each form is more or less prevalent, and what downstream effects an increase or decrease in one type has on the others.

How Money Enters Politics

Second, I develop a theoretical framework that clarifies when money enters politics for self-enrichment, for campaign spending, or comes in the form of golden parachute jobs, and how a change in one form affects the others. I examine the impact of two macro-level factors that systematically shape how much of each type there is.

The first is the *legal environment*. Different laws govern the three forms of money, and some are more strictly regulated than others. I argue that politicians arbitrage these disparities, which generates important *second-order effects*. If one type of money is subject to more rigid laws, it is – unsurprisingly – likely to become less prevalent. However, this does not necessarily mean that money simply disappears from politics: because the different forms are partially fungible, less of one type generally leads to more of the others.

The second factor that determines how money enters politics is the *electoral campaign environment*. While self-enrichment and golden parachute jobs benefit politicians directly, campaign spending has an indirect effect – increasing their chances of getting elected. How much politicians spend on a campaign depends on how demanding the campaign environment is, in particular how competitive the race is likely to be and how effective the prevalent campaign strategies and technologies are. Because the different forms of money are part of a common system, this again has second-order consequences: politicians who spend less on elections are more likely to use the other types of money.

These two factors jointly determine how money enters politics. They help us predict whether politicians use the money they have access to for self-enrichment, as campaign spending, or in the form of a golden parachute job. Mapping the landscape in this way helps us understand the interconnected system of money in politics, and to explain why we see different types in different contexts. The map also offers insights into the downstream effects that an increase or decrease in one form of money is likely to have on other types. If we only look at one type in isolation, we miss these opposing second-order effects; they instead show up as unintended consequences.

Consequences for Democracy

In a final step, I argue that different forms of money have different repercussions for important aspects of *democratic politics*. The second-order consequences highlighted earlier are therefore followed by important *third-order effects*.

First, I show that voters react differently depending on whether politicians use the same amount of money for campaign spending, self-enrichment in office, or golden parachute employment. If, for whatever reason, one form becomes less common and causes another to become more prevalent, it changes how voters view their representatives. This has significant implications for the public's confidence in politics.

Second, how money enters politics influences who wins elections. Since campaign spending helps candidates win votes, conditions that lead to more of that type of money affect election outcomes. This is especially true when, as is usually the case, some candidates or parties have access to more money than others. And since changes in campaign spending can be brought about by changes in the other forms, *any* event that alters one form of money in politics potentially affects who wins elections, which has far-reaching consequences for democratic competition.

Evolving the Conversation about Money in Politics

Studying a single form of money in isolation thus overlooks crucial insights. This book highlights the need to move the conversation about money in politics forward by treating the different forms as part of an interdependent *system*. This allows us to examine how they are linked and to anticipate the knock-on effects that a change to one of them may generate. This will improve our understanding of money in politics, and inform the implementation of policies that can more successfully keep its influence in check.

1.2 TESTING: CHALLENGES, EMPIRICAL APPROACH, AND CASE SELECTION

To test the argument that the different types of money in politics are part of a common system, and investigate the second- and third-order effects it generates, I must overcome a series of challenges.

The first and most obvious difficulty is what *data* to use, given that money in politics is often hidden from public view. A common solution to this challenge has been to use perception-based indicators. However, existing measures do not sufficiently differentiate between different forms of money, so they are not suitable for my purpose. Instead, I follow an increasing number of studies that make use of laws requiring the disclosure of relevant information, or use "forensic" approaches to indirectly infer the quantities of interest (cf. Golden and Picci, 2005; Di Tella and Weinschelbaum, 2008; Djankov et al., 2010; Fisman and Golden, 2017a). However, such studies typically focus on a single form of money, which obviously would not allow me to test an argument about the connections between the different types. In contrast to nearly all prior research, I need to study situations in which there is data on *several forms of money* at the same time.

A second challenge for the empirical sections of the book is the issue of *causality*. I argue that the legal and electoral campaign environments shape how money enters politics. However, the latter is also likely to affect the former. For example, campaign finance reforms tend to be passed in response to increases in campaign spending, and stricter regulation of enrichment in office often follows revelations of egregious self-dealing (see e.g. Pinto-Duschinsky, 2002; Fisman and Golden, 2017a).[8] I therefore have to carefully identify situations that provide *plausibly exogenous variation* in the legal or electoral campaign

---

[8] For discussions of reverse causality in the study of money and politics, see Lambsdorff (2006); Treisman (2007).

environments that should affect the relative prevalence of the three types of money in politics.

It is difficult – but not impossible – to obtain data on several types of money in situations that allow me to get a handle on the direction of the causal arrow. Several of the world's largest democracies – India, Brazil, and the United States – make available the kind of information that permits me to study the connection between the different forms of money. I therefore use microlevel data from these contexts to conduct a series of within-country studies.

For India, I analyze detailed mandatory asset disclosure affidavits that politicians have to submit before each election. They enable me to assess how much their personal assets have grown over the course of a legislative period and how much resources they have accumulated for their reelection campaign. In the Brazilian case, I also assemble data on politicians' asset development, as well as on their campaign spending. Finally, for the United States, I analyze the information provided in candidates' campaign finance disclosure forms and assemble new data that tracks if (and when) thousands of state legislators left office and took up a golden parachute job.

In each instance, I use detailed case knowledge to identify situations that allow me to study the second-order consequences of a change in one form of money. Where possible, I exploit plausibly exogenous modifications to politicians' legal and electoral campaign environments, for example as a result of redistricting, discontinuities in laws, or court rulings. Where it is not possible to exploit exogenous interventions, I carefully try to ensure that I am analyzing comparable cases. Finally, to test the third-order effects on voters' attitudes and election outcomes, I conduct original survey experiments in India and the United States and exploit the staggered introduction of laws that regulate money in the US states.

Of course, these three countries are not a representative sample of democracies. Decisions about whether to make information publicly available are strategic (Hollyer, Rosendorff, and Vreeland, 2011; Berliner, 2014), and the demand for information on politicians is more pronounced in systems with an individualistic vision of representation (Carey, 2009). It is thus no accident that data mainly exists for first-past-the-post legislative or executive positions, which is what I examine in my three cases. Nevertheless, these countries are insightful to study. They all are large democracies in which money in politics plays an important role in public debate. They are also central to the academic study of the issue, so I am able to connect my findings to existing scholarship.

Nevertheless, the within-country examinations raise a third challenge: Do the patterns identified *within* these three democracies also hold when looking *between* countries? To address this question, I complement the single-country examinations with a series of shorter case studies to test my argument cross-nationally. This approach has a long tradition in the literature on money in politics (e.g. Scott, 1972; Johnston, 2005, 2014). I use sources such as previous academic studies, official statistics, and reports by anti-corruption groups and news organizations to analyze the connections between the different forms of money in various countries. The cases I examine vary along the two explanatory dimensions and show that my argument also explains why some forms of money are more common in some countries than in others.

This book thus takes a two-pronged empirical approach, using within-country quantitative as well as between-country qualitative analyses. It therefore combines attention to the broader cross-national patterns of how money enters politics with the within-country identification of the marginal effects of the explanatory variables. This approach allows me to provide a comprehensive set of empirical tests of my argument.

1.3   CONTRIBUTIONS OF THE BOOK

A contemporary review article of research on money in politics argues that "[a]sking how different forms of corruption accompany or substitute one another is perhaps the most important topic in … corruption studies" (Mistree, 2015, 367). In this book, I seek to do just that. Focusing on *politicians*, my account combines the three most common ways they use money in a unifying framework. My argument and evidence demonstrate the benefits of treating self-enrichment, campaign financing, and golden parachute employment as parts of a single system. This study advances the academic literature on money in politics on several fronts. It also has important policy implications for how to think about and address the impact of money on the functioning of our democracies.

Understanding Money in Politics

Legal scholar Matthew Stephenson has made it his mission to maintain a constantly updated bibliography of research that studies corruption. As of May 2021, it is more than 700 pages long and has almost 8,800 entries (Stephenson, 2021). The role of money in politics is thus by no means an understudied area. Broadly speaking, modern empirical studies of the flow of money to politicians fall into two camps.

The first camp took off when indicators such as Transparency International's Corruption Perceptions Index (CPI) became available. Such measures provided researchers with annual quantitative data to employ in large-n comparative studies. This literature has been successful at providing an overview of corruption, broadly conceived, around the world. We now have a much better idea of which countries have more or less of it, what drives these differences, and what the consequences are (for overviews see Treisman, 2000, 2007).

Studies in the second camp take a narrower approach. They typically focus on one or a small number of countries and use microlevel data on one form of money in politics. One such literature evaluates campaign contributions, mostly focusing on the United States, while another studies politicians' enrichment in office. And a small but growing literature assesses politicians' moves to the private sector. These studies have refined our understanding by examining in detail how politicians use money.

Despite the considerable scientific advances made by each of these two camps, the resulting bifurcation of the literature has limited our understanding of money in politics. Imagine each approach represents a different type of map (cf. Giere, 1990; Clarke and Primo, 2012). The first camp would comprise world maps that show all countries; they would have a high level of abstraction and display only broad shapes. The second camp would be depicted by maps that provide detailed pictures of single countries, but only with respect to a particular characteristic: one map might limit itself to displaying a country's highways, and another only its train tracks.

Both approaches are very useful, and have improved our understanding of money in politics. But they have also led to a number of blind spots. This book represents a step toward addressing those blind spots. I combine the strengths of each camp by studying the *mechanisms* of how money enters politics in a *comparative* framework. We can gain many additional insights this way, and we can solve a number of puzzles that the current approaches to studying money in politics pose.

Solving Puzzles of the "Black Box" Approach

Studies that use large-n cross-country research designs provide a large, but abstract, world map that often lacks depth. Cross-national indicators such as the CPI aggregate many different forms of money at various levels, ranging from bribe-extorting policemen to government ministers who embezzle millions or illegally finance their campaigns. They thus have a *black box* quality to them.[9]

Such studies identify broad reasons why some countries are, on aggregate, more corrupt than others, but cannot examine the causes and consequences of the specific ways in which money enters politics. If a country, for instance, experiences a change in one of the determinants, then its corruption score will increase or decrease. This implicitly conveys that different forms of money in politics go together. However, even a cursory look at the three countries that Andimuthu Raja, Walt Minnick, and Gerhard Schröder hail from reveals this not to be the case.

The United States is well known for its expensive election campaigns. Upwards of $14 billion was spent in the 2020 elections on federal races alone[10] – more than the annual GDP of Armenia, Nicaragua, or Namibia. At the same time, the majority of members of Congress become lobbyists or join corporate boards after leaving office.[11] However, US lawmakers rarely enrich themselves while in office.[12]

Elections in India are also expensive. The 2019 campaign was estimated to have cost more than $8.5 billion.[13] And Andimuthu Raja is only one of many Indian politicians suspected of having enriched themselves in office. Yet the phenomenon of politicians leaving office to take up lucrative private sector jobs is unknown in India. In fact, observers often lament the opposite problem – that the country's politicians hardly ever see the necessity to exit politics.

Finally, Gerhard Schröder is not the only German politician to have taken up a private sector job after leaving office: More than a third of his cabinet did as well, as do many members of parliament.[14] Yet parties in Germany spend less on their entire national election campaigns than some US senators do on a single race, and enrichment while in office is practically unheard of in German politics.[15]

---

[9] The Varieties of Democracy project (Lindberg et al., 2014) has developed a number of indicators that distinguish between the arenas in which corruption occurs, such as the legislative or the executive. However, these measures do not distinguish between different forms of money.

[10] "2020 Election to Cost $14 Billion, Blowing Away Spending Records," *Center for Responsive Politics*, October 28, 2020.

[11] Lazarus, McKay, and Herbel (2016); Palmer and Schneer (2016, 2019).

[12] Eggers and Hainmueller (2013, 2014).

[13] "India's Election Spending Surges Past US to Record High," *CNN*, June 8, 2019.

[14] See Klein and Höntzsch (2007); Edinger and Schwarz (2009); Dörrenbächer (2016).

[15] McKay (2003); "Why Germany's Politics Are Much Saner, Cheaper, and Nicer Than Ours," *The Atlantic*, September 30, 2013.

Thus, it is decidedly *not* the case that different forms of money in politics go together, or that a given determinant has the same effect on all three types. The black box approach cannot explain why different forms of money are common in different countries; nor can it tell us why the different types apparently respond in different ways to a common factor.

This book solves these puzzles. It provides a map of how money enters politics that shows which characteristics determine whether the dominant form in a given context is self-enrichment, campaign spending, or golden parachute employment. This explains whether (and why) a typical politician in a country is like Andimuthu Raja, Walt Minnick, or Gerhard Schröder. By highlighting that the various forms are part of a common system and thus connected to each other because of their partial fungibility, the book also shows that decreasing one form often leads to increases in other types.

The latter helps resolve another puzzle in the literature, as it makes clear why there is considerable continuity in overall levels of money in politics, despite a great many reforms designed to limit it (see e.g. Lambsdorff, 2007; Warner, 2007; Persson, Rothstein, and Teorell, 2013; Mungiu-Pippidi, 2015, 2017; Rothstein, 2018). Such reform efforts typically target only *one* form of money, and leave the door open for others, which invites arbitrage efforts. Therefore, reforms often have only a limited effect on how much money enters politics.

Solving Puzzles of the "Partial Equilibrium" Approach

Studies that focus on one form of money, typically in a single context, are akin to detailed maps of specific features in one country. Just as having a map of a country's highways is vital, but only does so much to help us understand its entire infrastructure, the focus on one type of money in politics is important, but only provides a partial understanding. The piecewise approach makes it difficult to combine the findings to build a comparative picture. Studies in this *partial equilibrium* research tradition have therefore generated a somewhat fragmented understanding of the role of money in politics, which has resulted in some puzzling findings. Studying the different forms in a common framework helps make sense of them.

One characteristic of partial equilibrium studies is that they explain the prevalence of personal enrichment, campaign spending, and golden parachute employment independently of each other. For example, the most widely accepted explanation for golden parachute jobs is the private sector's "need" for the connections that politicians provide (cf. de Figueiredo and Richter, 2014). But it seems unlikely that companies in, say, India have no need for better political connections. In fact, one study characterizes an "Indian business model in which cultivating political connections in Delhi became the core competence and the most important survival imperative for businesses" (Khatri and Ojha, 2016, 63). Yet Indian companies do not tend to hire former politicians.

My framework explains why this is the case by highlighting that a country's legal and electoral campaign environments determine how money enters politics. In India, these environments are such that self-enrichment in office is widespread and politicians see no need to leave politics for the private sector to earn money. More broadly, this book explains why Andimuthu Raja, Walt Minnick, and Gerhard Schröder are typical cases for their countries.

Another puzzle emerges when looking at the effect sizes of different partial equilibrium analyses. A series of recent studies use regression discontinuity designs that compare winners and losers of close elections to estimate the effect of holding office on different forms of money. Those that examine personal enrichment generally find that after a few years, narrow winners have only slightly more assets than narrow losers (e.g. Bhavnani, 2012; Querubin and Snyder, 2013; Fisman, Schulz, and Vig, 2014). Yet winners of close elections have been found to raise *much* more campaign money than losers of such elections (Fouirnaies and Hall, 2014). These findings are especially puzzling given that the first set of studies use data from the high-corruption environments of the historical United States or contemporary India, whereas the latter examine the comparatively low-corruption United States in recent times. Why does holding office have a lesser effect on money where levels of corruption are high?

Looking at the different forms of money as part of a common system helps solve this puzzle. I show that the electoral campaign environment, particularly its level of competitiveness, plays an important role in how money enters politics. Because they compare the winners and losers of close elections, regression discontinuity designs by definition focus on electorally vulnerable candidates. These incumbents have reason to prioritize campaign spending. As a second-order effect, they then have less leeway to enrich themselves. This helps explain why studies find a large effect of being in office on campaign spending and a small effect on self-enrichment.

Finally, there is a curious disconnect regarding the consequences of changes to one type of money in politics. For instance, prior studies have found that stricter campaign finance legislation limits campaign spending and affects various election characteristics (e.g. Milligan and Rekkas, 2008; Avis et al., 2021; Fouirnaies, 2021). However, such reforms have little effect on the influence of money in politics. For example, Pinto-Duschinsky (2002) observes that "[t]he frequency with which new laws concerning campaign and party finance are enacted is testimony to the failure of many existing systems of regulations" (Pinto-Duschinsky, 2002, 69). Systematic examinations of the consequences of stricter laws regulating money in politics have also produced a string of null results (e.g. Issacharoff and Karlan, 1998; Werner, 2011; Law and Long, 2012; Norris and Abel van Es, 2016; Abdul-Razzak, Prato, and Wolton, 2020).

Again, this book helps solve that puzzle and explains why such reforms are often so ineffective, and why money in politics is so persistent. Because the different types of money form part of an interconnected system, a change in one form leads to opposing trends in the other forms, which weakens the impact of reforms designed to reduce the impact of money on politics. Due to the siloed nature of the micro-mechanism literature, this important context has been missing from past studies.

Toward a General Equilibrium Analysis of Money in Politics
All of this means that this book contributes to a growing literature on the *connections between different avenues via which money enters politics*. Past research in this area has focused on the links between legal and illegal forms of influence (Kaufmann and Vicente, 2011), between grand and petty corruption (Bussell, 2012), between different forms of the same type of money in politics (Issacharoff and Karlan, 1998; La Raja and Schaffner, 2015; Ang, 2020), or between the political arena and the bureaucracy (Boehmke, Gailmard, and Patty, 2005; Campos and Giovannoni, 2007; Bennedsen, Feldmann, and Lassen, 2009; Naoi and Krauss, 2009; Harstad and Svensson, 2011; You, 2017). The current book furthers this line of inquiry by studying the choice between the different ways in which money flows to elected politicians.[16]

This moves us closer to a *general equilibrium analysis of money in politics*. By providing a framework that situates different forms of money within a common system, the book highlights the second-order consequences that result from the responses of politicians affected by various legal or electoral campaign environments. This helps us better anticipate

---

[16] A few (mostly theoretical) studies distinguish between money used for personal versus electoral gain (e.g. Nyblade and Reed, 2008; Golden, 2012; Gingerich, 2014*b*).

what have so far been unintended consequences (cf. Fisman and Golden, 2017*b*). What is more, it becomes clear that the way money enters politics has profound third-order effects on important aspects of democratic competition, which have rarely been studied in the literature.

Implications for Policy

The findings in this book also have implications for how the policy community approaches the issue of money in politics. The bifurcated thinking that is prevalent in the academic literature is also found in advocacy work and public debate. On the one hand, a black-box approach tries to tackle money in politics writ large by combating its nonspecific determinants. For example, greater transparency is widely promoted as a potent weapon against the undue influence of all forms of money. Indeed, the best-known anti-corruption organization is called Transparency International. But as my argument and evidence make clear, different factors often have different effects on different forms of money in politics. While nonspecific determinants may decrease some types, they may also increase others, resulting in an ambiguous overall effect. And indeed, the evidence on the effect of transparency on corruption writ large is mixed (e.g. Rothstein, 2011; Hollyer, Rosendorff, and Vreeland, 2014; Kosack and Fung, 2014; Corbacho et al., 2016; Bauhr and Grimes, 2017).

On the other hand, partial equilibrium thinking is also widespread among activists seeking to limit the influence of money in politics. For example, one of the central demands of India's anti-corruption Aam Aadmi Party was an independent ombudsman who monitors politicians' assets and punishes those found to have illicitly enriched themselves.[17] In Britain, the High Pay Centre think tank instead worries that politicians give preferential treatment to companies that may employ them in the future and demands the regulation of post-politics jobs.[18] And in the United States, groups with names like Americans for Campaign Reform and Citizens for Clean Elections advocate limitations on election spending.

Thus, when not focusing on nonspecific determinants, efforts to curb money in politics target a single type, whichever is most common in a given context. The hope is that doing so will limit the total amount of

---

[17] "National Manifesto 2014," *Aam Aadmi Party*, April 4, 2014.
[18] "The Revolving Door and the Corporate Colonisation of UK Politics," *High Pay Centre*, March 25, 2015.

money that flows into politics. The system perspective I take in this book highlights the weaknesses of this argument. Because the different forms of money are partially fungible, a decrease in one form will have the second-order effect of increasing others. Efforts to "get money out of politics" are thus often unsuccessful, or less successful than hoped.

An important implication of this book is therefore that policies should be coordinated to address several forms of money simultaneously.[19] However, this is easier said than done. Wide-reaching reforms that restrict several forms of money require concerted efforts by a broad coalition of stakeholders over an extended period of time. In most contexts, this is unattainable. Furthermore, money in the form of golden parachute employment for now-again private citizens is difficult to restrict in societies that value individuals' freedom to choose their occupation.

If comprehensive reforms are not possible, this book demonstrates that stakeholders should not just think about the immediate consequences of restricting one form of money. Instead, it is important to try to anticipate second-order increases in other forms, as well as the associated third-order implications for democratic politics, such as electoral competitiveness or citizens' views of politicians. Reforms are more likely to be successful if they take such downstream effects into account, weigh their positive and negative normative consequences *ex ante*, and make an informed prediction about whether the reform and its knock-on effects will truly improve the quality of democracy. This book offers the theory and evidence needed to inform such deliberations.

Theory-Driven Causal Empiricism

Finally, the book advances an ongoing debate about how to study social phenomena. While the old adage that correlation does not imply causation has been a staple of introductory political science courses for decades, the discipline has become much more serious about establishing causality in recent years (for overviews, see e.g. Angrist and Pischke, 2010; Dunning, 2012; Samii, 2016). One concern associated with this "causal empiricism" approach is that it does not always use theory to motivate the study of specific cases and to situate the results within a larger context (Huber, 2013). Indeed, some have argued that synthesis studies that review a body of causally identified case studies are the appropriate venue for theory development (Samii, 2016).

---

[19] See also Fisman and Golden (2017*b*).

But theory development can take place alongside the careful empirical study of situations that allow for causal identification. I begin this book by laying out a general theory of how the different forms of money in politics are part of an interconnected system. The theoretical framework's predictions are then tested using a series of well-identified research designs. Thus, rather than engaging in post hoc theorizing based on known empirical results, I use a general equilibrium theoretical account to motivate and situate the empirical studies that test different components of the argument. Finally, I employ a series of qualitative case studies to test whether the within-country findings generalize to a broader context. This proves to be a fruitful approach and can be one way to balance theoretical and empirical rigor in the field.

1.4 A NOTE ON SCOPE

My goal in this book is to examine the connection between different forms of money in politics. However, money plays a role in so many ways, and at so many levels of government, that it is impossible to investigate all of them in a single study. It is therefore necessary to clearly delineate what falls within the scope of my argument, and what does not.

The book's theoretical and empirical focus is on the behavior of elected *politicians*. I do *not* examine people who are tasked with implementing laws, such as bureaucrats in ministries or agencies, state administrators in government offices, or police officers; nor do I examine the judicial branch (see instead e.g. Banerjee, Hanna, and Mullainathan, 2012; Bussell, 2012; Olken and Pande, 2012; Gingerich, 2013; Brierley, 2020). The politicians that my theory applies to can be elected members of the executive or legislative who have access to money, either from special interest groups or through appropriating state resources. While I discuss the sources of that money, I argue that it is politicians who have agency over their career and thus decide how money enters politics.

Because electoral competition plays a major role in my argument, I concentrate on *democracies*. Money is important for politicians in authoritarian regimes as well, but the context is so different that my theoretical argument does not apply (see instead e.g. Chang and Golden, 2010; Truex, 2014; Hollyer and Wantchekon, 2015; Yadav and Mukherjee, 2016; Hou, 2019; Szakonyi, 2020).

I focus on instances in which money or material goods go *to* politicians (either directly or through intermediaries such as their campaign). As the next chapter makes clear, the main ways in which this happens are self-enrichment, campaign money, and golden parachute jobs. The book thus concentrates on these three forms. It does not discuss lobbying (see instead e.g. Baumgartner et al., 2009; Yadav, 2011; Klüver, 2013; de Figueiredo and Richter, 2014) since this money is not directly channeled to politicians. Instead, money is paid to lobbyists, who in turn provide (selective) information to lawmakers.[20] Lobbying complements the transfer of money to politicians in its various forms, allowing special interests to communicate their policy preferences (cf. Kim, Stuckatz, and Wolters, 2020).

Finally, throughout the book I use the term money in politics rather than corruption. The latter is commonly defined as the (illegal) abuse of public office for private or electoral gain. Thus, corruption focuses on the illegal use of money in politics. I examine both legal and illicit uses, and argue that the legal environment plays an important role in determining how money enters politics. This makes money in politics rather than corruption the more appropriate term for my purpose.

1.5 OUTLINE: THE ROAD AHEAD

In Chapter 2, I introduce the different forms of money in politics in more detail, and discuss what we know, and don't know, about them. I highlight the lack of understanding of whether (and how) the different types are connected. Chapter 3 puts forward my argument: That the different forms of money have the same underlying motivations; that they should thus be seen as part of a common system; that a country's legal and electoral campaign environments determine how money enters politics; that a change in one form of money has second-order implications for the other forms; and that this has third-order consequences on various aspects of democracy. I derive a set of empirical implications of my argument.

The following four chapters test these implications in a series of empirical analyses. In Chapter 4, I use detailed asset disclosure and campaign spending data from India and Brazil to examine the connection between enrichment by politicians while in office and campaign spending to stay there. Chapter 5 studies the connection between campaign spending and golden parachute jobs by analyzing campaign spending information as well as newly assembled data tracking the movement of US state legislators into the private sector. In Chapter 6, I use a series of qualitative case

---

[20] If former politicians are hired as lobbyists, or if lobbyists make campaign contributions, then money *is* transferred and is covered by this book.

studies to show that my argument also explains cross-national variation in the way money enters politics. Chapter 7 examines the third-order implications for democracy, and shows that how money enters politics shapes voters' approval or disapproval of elected officials and has systematic effects on who wins elections.

Finally, in Chapter 8, I discuss the implications of my book for future research, public debate, and policy design. I call for an evolution in how we think about money in politics: Instead of looking at the various forms in isolation, we should treat them as part of an interconnected *system*.

2

Types of Money in Politics

The cases of Andimuthu Raja, Walt Minnick, and Gerhard Schröder introduced in the previous chapter represent the three most common ways in which money enters politics: for self-enrichment, for campaign spending, and in the form of golden parachute job salaries. Of course, I am not the first to study money in politics. Nor am I the first to examine any of these three types. In this chapter, I lay out what we know about money in politics – and what we don't – to set the stage for my argument.

2.1 HOW MONEY ENTERS POLITICS

The major obstacle for the *empirical* study of money in politics has always been the dearth of reliable data. Early work typically provided thick descriptive accounts of specific countries or parts of countries (see e.g. Banfield, 1958; Bayley, 1966; Waterbury, 1973; Johnston, 1979; Klitgaard, 1988; Heidenheimer, Johnston, and LeVine, 1989). Due to the limited data availability, few studies examined the topic (cf. Rothstein and Varraich, 2017) until indicators such as Transparency International's Corruption Perceptions Index and the World Bank's Control of Corruption Indicator were introduced in the mid-1990s. These measures allowed researchers to study the causes and consequences of money in politics from a comparative perspective for the first time, which led to a steep increase in research on the topic. Using cross-national regressions, these contributions demonstrate that the level of corruption is correlated with a host of factors, including institutional and legal characteristics, economic conditions, and demographics.[1]

---

[1] See, among many others, Ades and Di Tella (1999); La Porta et al. (1999); Treisman (2000, 2007); Dollar, Fisman, and Gatti (2001); Swamy et al. (2001); Montinola

While these studies provide a broad overview of the causes and consequences of money in politics, cross-national, perception-based data has
at least three limitations. First, the gain in breadth that their introduction
achieved came with a loss in depth, as studies no longer looked at the
minutiae of money in politics. Instead, the indicators are somewhat of a
black box: They incorporate corruption among a wide variety of individuals, including public servants as well as elected politicians, and low-level
policemen or village mayors as well as high-level ministerial bureaucrats,
members of parliament, or even government ministers. The indicators
also include a variety of practices such as accepting bribes, patronage
appointments, and campaign spending.[2]

A second limitation is that the cross-national indicators use perceptions
of corruption as a proxy for actual corruption. However, there are systematic gaps between the two. Asking people about how much corruption
they think is happening provides only limited and biased information on
what is actually happening (Olken, 2009; Razafindrakoto and Roubaud,
2010).

Finally, cross-country studies of corruption are plagued by endogeneity concerns and reverse causality problems. For example, low economic
development is one of the strongest predictors of high levels of corruption,
but corruption has also been shown to have negative consequences for
the economy (Mauro, 1995). In general, it is not uncommon to find that
a purported consequence of corruption identified in one study is used as
an explanatory variable in another (see also Lambsdorff, 2006; Treisman,
2007).

Motivated by these problems, recent research on money in politics has returned to studying microlevel data in specific contexts.

and Jackman (2002); Adsera, Boix, and Payne (2003); Persson, Tabellini, and Trebbi
(2003); Kunicova and Rose-Ackerman (2005); Lambsdorff (2006); Uslaner (2008,
2017); Schwindt-Bayer and Tavits (2016); Esarey and Schwindt-Bayer (2018, 2019);
Bauhr, Charron, and Wängnerud (2019).

[2] A corresponding formal theory literature also treats money in politics as a black box
and does not specify how politicians use it: Interest groups spend resources, politicians
value this expenditure in some unspecified way, and react by changing legislation in the
groups' favor. For example, Persson and Tabellini (2000, ch. 7) model a lobby group
that uses money to try to influence policy and a government that maximizes a weighted
sum of social welfare and special interest money. This basic approach has been used to
study, for example, interest groups' influence on taxes and transfers (Dixit, Grossman,
and Helpman, 1997), economic policy (Persson, 1998), the differences between parliamentary and presidential systems (Persson, Roland, and Tabellini, 2000), and the role
of interest groups' budget constraints and legislators' preferences (Dekel, Jackson, and
Wolinsky, 2009).

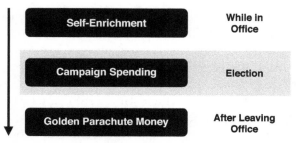

FIGURE 2.1 *Timing of the three types of money in politics*

Because many countries have introduced transparency laws mandating disclosure, scholars now have access to quantitative data of actual money flows. This means that studies emphasize specific ways in which money enters politics. They also increasingly employ research designs that permit credible causal identification, mirroring disciplinary trends (cf. Samii, 2016).[3]

As a consequence, vibrant literatures studying self-enrichment, campaign spending, and golden parachute jobs have developed. Figure 2.1 illustrates how the three types of money differ in terms of when they enter politics. *Self-enrichment* refers to situations in which politicians use their time in office to take money for themselves. At the end of their term, there is an election, at which point money can be used for *campaign spending*. Finally, money can flow to politicians in the form of *golden parachute jobs* after they have left office. In the following sections, I review what we have learned from the separate literatures studying these three forms of money in politics.

2.2 SELF-ENRICHMENT

Probably the most notorious way for money to enter politics is when politicians enrich themselves *while* in office, either directly (cash) or indirectly (material goods). The resources for self-enrichment can come from special interest groups who seek to influence policy (external source) or be taken out of state coffers (internal source).

The setup in formal theories of self-enrichment is a trade-off in which more money comes with the cost of electoral or legal punishment. Based

---

[3] In addition, new research that uses cross-national indicators of corruption places greater emphasis on causal identification, see e.g. Schwindt-Bayer and Tavits (2016); Esarey and Schwindt-Bayer (2018, 2019).

on this framework, studies examine specific questions such as the effect of electoral systems and other political institutions on self-enrichment (Myerson, 1993; Helpman and Persson, 2001; Alt and Lassen, 2003), how enrichment affects politicians' decisions about whether to run for office (Besley and Coate, 2001; Felli and Merlo, 2006), what effects it has on candidate quality (Snyder and Ting, 2008), or its interaction with violent punishment (Dal Bó, Dal Bó, and Di Tella, 2006).

There is very little empirical data available for this form of money. Because self-enrichment is usually illegal and is almost always considered immoral, politicians try to make it as difficult as possible for the public to find out about it. On rare occasions, direct evidence is uncovered. For example, the "Panama Papers" that were leaked to journalists in 2015 revealed secret offshore entities by former and sitting heads of state and government officials. However, such revelations are rarely comprehensive enough for systematic study (for an exception, see McMillan and Zoido, 2004).

The next best option is "forensic" approaches, which examine publicly available data and try to detect patterns that indirectly provide evidence of hidden immoral or illicit behavior (Zitzewitz, 2012). For example, Golden and Picci (2005) compare spending on public infrastructure in Italy's provinces and regions to actual infrastructure. The higher the spending-to-infrastructure ratio, they surmise, the more money is being siphoned off or used for bribes, kickbacks, and the like. Thus, with sufficient creativity, it is possible to use publicly available data to discover and study illicit behavior.

Past studies have used a variety of forensic methods to detect potential enrichment in office. A number of countries require candidates for political office to disclose their assets (Djankov et al., 2010), which makes it possible to infer how the wealth of candidates who contest consecutive elections developed over the course of a legislative period (Di Tella and Weinschelbaum, 2008). For example, prior research has examined such data from India (Bhavnani, 2012; Fisman, Schulz, and Vig, 2014; Asher and Novosad, 2020), Romania (Klašnja, 2015), and South Korea (Jung, 2020). Other studies have used census information (Querubin and Snyder, 2013), stock transaction data (Eggers and Hainmueller, 2013, 2014), public tax returns (Berg, 2020a, 2020b; Cirone, Cox, and Fiva, 2020), and probate records (Eggers and Hainmueller, 2009) to infer the growth of politicians' wealth while in office.

The goal of most of these studies has been to establish whether being in office affects politicians' asset growth.[4] Most of them do so by employing regression discontinuity designs that compare politicians who won close elections to those who ran but narrowly lost. Because who wins and who loses in close contests is as good as random, such research designs provide well-identified estimates of how much being in office is worth.[5]

The overall conclusion of studies in this vein is that in many contexts, there is a premium to being a politician, but that this premium varies depending on at least three factors. First, it is larger for politicians in influential positions. Fisman, Schulz, and Vig (2014) find that personal wealth growth among Indian politicians is greatest for those who serve as ministers. Asher and Novosad (2020) show greater wealth increases for members of Indian state parliaments from areas with valuable mineral deposits. Querubin and Snyder (2013) demonstrate larger gains among members of parliamentary committees that handled large procurements in the nineteenth century US Congress. Second, the wealth premium is also affected by party membership: politicians who belong to pro-business parties enjoy higher asset growth (Eggers and Hainmueller, 2009; Bhavnani, 2012). Third, extralegal wealth grows faster for politicians who receive a low salary (Klašnja, 2015), and for more experienced officeholders (Fisman, Schulz, and Vig, 2014; Klašnja, 2015).

However, there are also contexts in which officeholders do *not* earn significantly more than their nonpolitician peers, or at least not more than we would expect given their official salary. These null findings come from high-income democracies such as Sweden (Berg, 2020*a*, 2020*b*), Norway (Cirone, Cox, and Fiva, 2020), South Korea (Jung, 2020), and the United States (Eggers and Hainmueller, 2013, 2014).

In summary, while the empirical study of politicians' enrichment in office is still in its infancy, it has produced several valuable insights. First, with sufficient creativity, it is possible to measure politicians' enrichment in office. Second, politicians accumulate more resources in office than those who fail to win an election in some contexts, but not in others. Third, personal enrichment tends to be higher among more powerful and more business-friendly politicians. And finally, while studies do not focus on the sources of this money, the fact that asset growth is higher for politicians on committees in charge of large procurements or for those from

---

[4] Given the nature of the data used, such studies are typically unable to identify the source of the money.

[5] Some studies alternatively use a difference-in-differences design.

mining areas suggests that, to the extent that the money comes from outside interest groups, instrumental motivations such as access and influence are prominent.

Democratically elected politicians do not only use money for their personal enrichment. To stay in office, every few years, they must run for reelection, which often requires considerable financial expenditures. In programmatic contexts, campaign spending is mostly allocated to advertisements, rallies, or get-out-the-vote campaigns. In non-programmatic contexts, candidates spend money on many of these aspects but also try to win votes through material handouts such as cash, food, (adult) beverages, or small-scale infrastructure projects (Kitschelt, 2000; Kitschelt and Wilkinson, 2007). To finance all of these, politicians need money.

Most formal–theoretical studies model campaign spending as part of an instrumental exchange relationship. Donors contribute to politicians, who in response "distort" policy. Politicians, in turn, use the campaign contributions to try to persuade people to vote for them. This mechanism is most clearly articulated in the seminal model by Grossman and Helpman (1994, 2001).[6] Formal accounts of campaign contributions have been extensively used to study campaign spending restrictions and public financing (Prat, 2002; Coate, 2004a, 2004b; Ashworth, 2006; Roemer, 2006) as well as other topics such as inequality and redistribution (Campante, 2011).

Empirically, campaign spending is the most well-researched of the three types. It is primarily studied in the context of the United States, both because it plays an important role there and because ample data is available. Two major questions in the literature are: What do politicians get out of campaign spending? And what effect does campaign money have on politicians' behavior and on policy?

First, why do politicians want campaign money? The obvious answer to this question is of course that it helps them win elections. However, in the American context, studies for a long time found that there is no

---

[6] See also Ben-Zion and Eytan (1974); Bental and Ben-Zion (1975); Rose-Ackerman (1978); Denzau and Munger (1986); Austen-Smith (1987); Baron (1994). For a more subtle way for special interests to influence policy without having to rely on any kind of contract, see Fox and Rothenberg (2011).

correlation between campaign spending and vote shares (e.g. Jacobson, 1978, 1985). These non-findings have been used to claim that money does not influence election outcomes.

However, such arguments ignore the fact that spending is strategic and depends on, for example, how close a race is expected to be. A new generation of studies account for this endogeneity and find that more campaign spending leads to increased vote shares. For example, Huber and Arceneaux (2007) exploit the fact that some citizens who live on the border of battleground states watch TV stations from those states and are thus subject to more political advertising than other voters in their state. They find that such ads have a strong persuasive effect. Gerber et al. (2011) partner with a gubernatorial campaign and randomly determine how much advertising money is spent at different times in different parts of the state, and also find strong effects on voting preferences. Hall (2016) examines the effect of corporate campaign spending bans and finds that if a party's share of campaign contributions grows by one percentage point, its share in the legislature increases by half a percentage point. Other studies in the US context have come to similar conclusions (e.g. Gerber, 1998; Erikson and Palfrey, 2000; Jacobson, 2015). In addition, there is accumulating evidence that (costly) efforts to mobilize citizens to turn out on election day are successful (for an overview, see Green and Gerber, 2015).

Outside the United States, research on campaign finance is much more scarce (cf. Fisher and Eisenstadt, 2004; Scarrow, 2007), partly because data is less readily available and forensic methods have to be used to detect it (e.g. Sukhtankar, 2012; Kapur and Vaishnav, 2018). The studies that do exist find that political competition increases the demand for campaign money (e.g. Golden and Chang, 2001; Chang, 2005), and that campaign spending translates into vote shares (e.g. Pattie, Johnston, and Fieldhouse, 1995; Cox and Thies, 2000; Samuels, 2001b; Maddens et al., 2006; Benoit and Marsh, 2010; Fink, 2012).

There have also been long-standing doubts over whether clientelistic vote-buying efforts are successful, given the lack of monitoring implied by secret ballots (Nichter, 2008). While there are indirect ways to ensure that groups of voters do not simply take money or gifts and then vote as they please, it is true that these methods are imperfect and that vote-buying strategies can be inefficient (e.g. Brusco, Nazareno, and Stokes, 2004; Stokes, 2005; Gingerich and Medina, 2013). However, there is evidence that investing in a vote broker is associated with a significant increase in vote shares (Gingerich, 2014a); that candidates often rely on buying turnout rather than votes, which is easier to monitor (Nichter,

2008; Gans-Morse, Mazzuca, and Nichter, 2014); and that voters are key to perpetuating clientelistic exchanges by demanding goods and services from the parties they vote for (Nichter, 2018).

In addition, material spending does not need to involve a reciprocal relationship in which the benefit for voters is contingent on them casting their ballot for a certain party or candidate. Some parties and candidates provide costly social services as an electoral strategy, giving them inroads into communities to gain voters' trust and build long-term relationships, which can reap dividends on election day (Thachil, 2014). And even ad hoc distributions of material goods are often not contingent upon reciprocity. Rather, parties and candidates can be trapped in a prisoner's dilemma, where they spend money because they fear that they will otherwise be out of the running (see e.g. Björkman, 2014; Chauchard, 2018). In summary, there is good evidence that more campaign spending, clientelistic or not, helps politicians win elections.

The second major question in the literature is how campaign spending affects politicians and policy. Or, put the other way around, what do campaign donors receive in return for their money? Grossman and Helpman (2001) distinguish between two motives. The first is the influence motive: a donor wants to induce a politician to move policy toward its unpopular ideal point, and the contribution compensates for the electoral penalty the politician will incur as a result.[7] The second is the electoral motive, where donors find it in their interest to boost the chances of politicians whose policy positions they prefer.

There is empirical evidence supporting both motivations. The electoral motivation is dominant among individual small-scale donors and among issue groups, such as antiabortion or environmental organizations. Almost all individual US donors state that they give to candidates they ideologically agree with and that they hope to affect the election outcome. Issue groups also exhibit donation patterns that are consistent with an electoral motivation (Barber, 2016).

However, this logic does not apply to contributions from more pragmatic entities such as corporations (La Raja and Schaffner, 2015; Barber, 2016).[8] Can their behavior instead be explained by the influence motive? Do they hope, or even expect, that their large donations will influence the candidate or party on issues they care about?

---

[7] See also Baron (1994).
[8] On the interaction between individual small-scale donors and corporate donations, see Li (2018).

Many citizens are convinced that special interests use their financial prowess to "buy" favorable policy. And many politicians believe the same. For example, former US presidential candidate Bob Dole declared: "I've always believed when people give big money, they – maybe silently – expect something in return."[9] Chris Collins, a former member of Congress, explicitly confirmed this when he explained his support for a tax cut bill by stating that "[m]y donors are basically saying, 'Get it done or don't ever call me again'."[10] Walt Minnick described a more subtle relationship with his donors:

I had some meetings I was pretty uncomfortable at with the lender, the payday-loan kind of lender. ... They contributed to my campaign. ... And so that's an example of – there weren't any people who were applying for payday loans that came in to see me. The consumer side of that doesn't contribute a nickel.[11]

For a long time, however, empirical studies found no connection between campaign money and policy outcomes. Ansolabehere, de Figueiredo, and Snyder (2003) review almost forty studies and find that only about a quarter of them have a significant and "correctly" signed coefficient.[12]

More recent studies in the United States, however, have determined that campaign contributions can result in access and influence. Many donations are strategically directed to incumbents, members of important committees, and party leaders, especially by highly regulated business groups (Fouirnaies and Hall, 2014, 2016, 2018; Powell and Grimmer, 2016; Fouirnaies, 2018). Consistent with these strategic donation patterns, campaign donors have an easier time securing meetings with politicians than non-donors (Kalla and Broockman, 2016). Newer research that examines specific industry-relevant legislation, rather than aggregated roll-call votes, also challenges the conclusions of earlier studies that campaign contributions have small or null effects on legislators' voting behavior (e.g. de Figueiredo and Edwards, 2007; Mian, Sufi, and Trebbi, 2010, 2013; McKay, 2018).[13] Finally, companies that make larger contributions, especially to parties in government, have higher stock returns (Jayachandran, 2006; Cooper, Gulen, and Ovtchinnikov, 2010; Gaikwad, 2013; Huber and Kirchler, 2013; Akey, 2015).[14]

---

[9] "Bob Dole Looks Back," *AARP Bulletin*, July/August 2015.
[10] "GOP Lawmaker: Donors are Pushing Me to Get Tax Reform Done," *The Hill*, November 7, 2017.
[11] "461: Take the Money and Run for Office," *This American Life*, March 30, 2012.
[12] See also Stratmann (2005).
[13] For a similar finding on lobbying, see Kim (2017).
[14] See, however, Fowler, Garro, and Spenkuch (2020); Fouirnaies and Fowler (2022).

Other studies have reported evidence that large campaign contributions result in access and influence in other countries as well. For example, Brazilian firms specializing in public works projects that donate to winning candidates of the ruling party experience a considerable boost in contracts allocated to them (Boas, Hidalgo, and Richardson, 2014). More broadly, Brazilian firms that contribute to elected federal deputies enjoy higher stock returns (Claessens, Feijen, and Laeven, 2008). Contributors to Colombian mayoral candidates are more likely to receive a government contract, especially if they donate more money (Ruiz, 2020; Gulzar, Rueda, and Ruiz, 2021); the same dynamic has been found in the Czech Republic (Titl and Geys, 2018). Finally, there is also evidence that contributions in a number of advanced industrial countries are driven by pragmatic considerations (McMenamin, 2012).

In summary, the literature on campaign finance is much more voluminous than the one on personal enrichment. It finds that spending money on election campaigns helps candidates and parties get elected – or, at the very least, that they are not successful if they do not spend money. The evidence is somewhat mixed regarding whether campaign donations affect policy outcomes. While few effects have been observed for legislators' most visible actions, such as roll-call votes, more subtle impacts have been found, such as on specific legislation relevant to an industry. This is confirmed by the behavior of financiers, who donate strategically and benefit financially.

2.4 GOLDEN PARACHUTE JOBS

Many countries have experienced the rise of a new phenomenon in recent decades: politicians who leave office and take a position in the private sector. This is often referred to as "revolving door" employment, but this can lead to confusion, as others use the same term to describe movement in the other direction – from the private to the public sector (e.g. Gromley, 1979; Makkai and Braithwaite, 1992; Adolph, 2013; Lucca, Seru, and Trebbi, 2014). I therefore use the term "golden parachute employment" instead, which makes it clear that the focus is on moving from politics to the private sector. It is related to *pantouflage* ("parachuting out"), the French expression for the phenomenon, and to the Japanese *amakudari* ("descent from heaven").

Golden parachute employment gives politicians the opportunity to improve their personal financial situation *after* leaving office. While a few formal models examine the practice in the context of regulators (Che,

1995; Salant, 1995; Dal Bó, 2006), little theoretical work focuses on politicians. There are models that study politicians' moves into the private sector, but they focus on cases in which the remuneration for the outside job is set exogenously and unrelated to decisions made while in office (Besley, 2004, 2005; Diermeier, Keane, and Merlo, 2005; Mattozzi and Merlo, 2008; Keane and Merlo, 2010). No theoretical model that I am aware of explicitly ties politicians' moves into the private sector to their time and position in office.

As a consequence, the empirical literature has surged ahead. Just like in the case of campaign contributions, studies of golden parachutes focus mostly on the American context, where many ex-legislators are employed as lobbyists. These jobs pay very well (Etzion and Davis, 2008; Blanes i Vidal, Draca, and Fons-Rosen, 2012; Bertrand, Bombardini, and Trebbi, 2014), so it is not surprising that in recent years, more than half of the members of Congress who left office later registered as lobbyists (Lazarus, McKay, and Herbel, 2016). In addition, former representatives also often serve on boards of directors (Hillman, 2005; Lester et al., 2008; Palmer and Schneer, 2016, 2019).

Why do companies hire former politicians? Previous research has focused on their human capital. The central debate in this strand of the literature is whether *what* or *who* they know is more important (Bertrand, Bombardini, and Trebbi, 2014; de Figueiredo and Richter, 2014). Earlier studies found that lobbyists who used to be in politics have more expertise and better knowledge than their career lobbyist counterparts (Salisbury et al., 1989; Heinz et al., 1993; Esterling, 2004; Parker, 2008). However, the empirical basis for most of these studies is surveys of former legislators, which tell us what they think their role is rather than their employers' actual motivation when hiring them.[15]

More recent work instead analyzes what politicians-turned-lobbyists do rather than what they say they do. It finds evidence that they are mostly sought after for their extensive networks of connections within the legislature (Hillman, 2005; Blanes i Vidal, Draca, and Fons-Rosen, 2012; Bertrand, Bombardini, and Trebbi, 2014; LaPira and Thomas, 2014, 2017). In other words, companies hire ex-politicians because they can influence their former colleagues.[16]

---

[15] An exception is Esterling (2004), which presents case studies that focus on the passage of laws in areas where policy expertise is well developed. However, it is not clear that we can generalize findings from research-driven policy areas to the broader universe of laws (see Hill, 2005).

[16] Consistent with these conclusions, there is evidence that golden parachute employment has positive effects for companies. Former politicians are most likely to be found in

However, golden parachutes may also work in another way, which is probably best exemplified by the former lobbyist Jack Abramoff, who admitted that he regularly promised congressional staffers lucrative employment in the future:

Now the moment I said that to them or any of our staff said that to 'em, that was it. We owned them. And what does that mean? Every request from our office, every request of our clients, everything that we want, they're gonna do. And not only that, they're gonna think of things we can't think of to do.[17]

Shepherd and You (2020) provide systematic evidence supporting this logic in the context of the US Congress, showing that staffers who later become lobbyists are, *before they exit*, more likely to grant access to lobbyists and to push more legislation that is beneficial to future employers. This logic likely applies to politicians as well, as expressed by an anonymous member of Congress: "Committee assignments are mainly valuable as part of the interview process for a far more lucrative job as a K Street lobbyist. You are considered naïve if you are not currying favor with wealthy corporations under your jurisdiction."[18]

It is easy to find anecdotes of politicians taking up lucrative positions with companies that benefited from their decisions in office. The Nord Stream consortium, which later employed Gerhard Schröder, would not exist if the latter had not given the go-ahead to build a pipeline through the Baltic Sea while he was the chancellor of Germany. Another example is David Cameron, who during his time as British prime minister allowed the businessman Lex Greensill to work in Downing Street as a senior adviser. After leaving office, Cameron was then employed by Greensill as a paid adviser and lobbied ministers on behalf of the company.[19]

To be clear, it is probably rare that such future jobs are *explicitly* offered in exchange for current access. But the same is true for campaign contributions, which are usually not a blatant quid pro quo, but instead a continuous exchange based on an (implicit) mutual understanding. If

---

industries that are subject to greater government regulation (Hillman, 2005). Having former politicians as lobbyists is associated with greater chances of political success (Baumgartner et al., 2009; Lazarus and McKay, 2012; Makse, 2017) and improves firms' bottom lines (Hillman, Zardkoohi, and Bierman, 1999; Goldman, Rocholl, and So, 2009; Luechinger and Moser, 2014).

[17] "Jack Abramoff: The Lobbyist's Playbook," *60 Minutes*, May 30, 2012.
[18] "Confessions of a Congressman," *Vox*, July 12, 2015.
[19] "The David Cameron Scandal: Just How Sleazy Is British Politics?" *Financial Times*, April 16, 2021.

future jobs affect politicians' current actions in office, the mechanism is likely to be similarly subtle. For example, the simple prospect of such future employment may be enough to affect legislators, as a *New York Times* editorial worries:

[M]ost incumbent members, as they go about their daily routine of casting votes and attending committee meetings, must have in the back of their minds an awareness that they are likely to go into the influence-peddling business in the future. This knowledge inevitably influences – and arguably corrupts – their votes on legislation crucial to the interests most likely to hire them after they leave the halls of Congress.[20]

Egerod (2019) provides systematic evidence that the prospect of landing a golden parachute job indeed influences politicians' behavior while in office. Comparing changes in voting behavior during the last term of US senators who retire vis-à-vis those who go on to take up a position in the private sector, he shows that the latter converge to the ideological position of companies in their future sector of employment. This suggests that there is not only a demand-side effect for ex-politicians' expertise or connections, but that politicians actively seek out these post-politics jobs, and that it influences their behavior *while still in office*.

Research on golden parachute employment outside the United States is more sparse and focuses mostly on demonstrating how common and lucrative it is. The practice is widespread in the United Kingdom (Eggers and Hainmueller, 2009; González-Bailon, Jennings, and Lodge, 2013), Germany (Dörrenbächer, 2016; Würfel, 2018; Claessen, Bailer, and Turner-Zwinkels, 2021), Ireland (Baturo and Arlow, 2018), the Netherlands (Claessen, Bailer, and Turner-Zwinkels, 2021), and among presidents and prime ministers in general (Musella, 2015; Baturo and Mikhaylov, 2016; Baturo, 2017).

In many countries, the United States being an exception, legislators are also allowed to hold a private sector job *while* in office. Given that this entails employment but happens while in office, this kind of money could be characterized as either golden parachute employment or enrichment in office. However, in separate work, I find that these jobs are unrelated to politicians' *current* positions. Instead, the only increase in private sector earnings happens for ministers *after leaving* their government position, but while still being in parliament (Weschle, 2021*b*). Thus, these kinds of jobs are best grouped into the golden parachute category.

[20] "The Trouble with That Revolving Door," *New York Times*, December 18, 2011.

Of the three types of money in politics, the literature on golden parachute employment is the newest. Nevertheless, its findings so far are similar to those on the other types: The practice is lucrative for politicians and helps them achieve their goals. It also has consequences for policy and thus helps employers realize their instrumental interests.

2.5 WHAT'S MISSING IN THE STUDY OF MONEY IN POLITICS

We have learned a lot from the literatures on the three different ways in which money enters politics. Thanks to creative research designs and careful analyses of high-quality data, we can now quantify the extent to which holding political office affects wealth. We also have a better understanding of why people or groups make campaign contributions, how they affect politicians' decisions, and how much they help win over voters. Finally, research has made headway in documenting the existence of golden parachute jobs and identifying the determinants behind it, as well as its consequences.

And yet, a crucial thing is missing: a connection between them. Studies on personal enrichment focus exclusively on politicians' asset gains during their time in office, research on campaign finance looks only at money spent on elections, and the golden parachute literature only tracks politicians moving into the private sector. The different forms of money in politics are treated as separate phenomena and are studied in separate books and articles – usually by different people.

Figure 2.2 illustrates just how few connections the literature draws between them. I examine all twenty-nine articles on the subject of money in politics that appeared in the three top political science general interest journals between 2010 and 2019.[21] I count the number of times each article mentioned word combinations relating to personal enrichment, campaign spending, and golden parachute employment, and then compute the relative share of mentions.[22]

---

[21] American Political Science Review, American Journal of Political Science, Journal of Politics.

[22] Words were chosen by examining word combination frequencies of all articles together, which ensures that I use the terms used by the authors. For personal enrichment, they are: bribe(s), bribery, wealth accumulation, wealth increase, rent seeking. For campaign spending: donation(s), donor(s), contributor(s), contribution limit(s), campaign contribution(s), campaign finance, citizens united, pac contribution(s), pac spending, contribution(s) from, contribution(s) to, campaign spending, challenger spending, incumbent

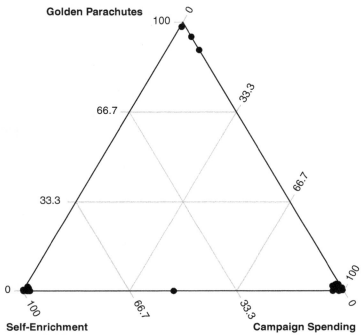

FIGURE 2.2 *Three types of money in politics in political science journal articles.*
Share of words related to personal enrichment, campaign spending, and golden
parachute jobs in twenty-nine articles about money in politics published in three
general interest political science journals between 2010 and 2019. Articles that
only mention one form are located in the corners (points are jittered for better
visual representation). A hypothetical article that mentions each form the same
number of times would be located in the center at the intersection of the gray
lines marked with 33.3

The vast majority of papers (twenty-one out of twenty-nine) are
located in the corners of the ternary plot, meaning they *only* mention one
form and *never* any others (points are jittered for better visual representation). Not only does this mean that articles study a single type in isolation,
it also indicates that they do not draw connections to the other forms or
discuss the literature that studies them. Of the eight papers that mention more than one type, seven focus overwhelmingly on one form and
mention a second one a few times (10 percent or less). Only one article
mentions two forms of money in relatively equal proportions, and none

spending, corporate pac. For golden parachute employment: board service, revolving
door, corporate board(s), boards per year, serve on boards.

mentions all three. Figure 2.2 thus clearly illustrates the siloed nature of the inquiry into money and politics to date.

To be clear, this is not a criticism of these studies or of any others that only focus on one type. They provide important insights, and all articles must omit discussions of many interesting connections. However, this siloed approach creates a number of blind spots. By narrowing the focus of our attention to specific mechanisms, we only get a partial equilibrium understanding and miss out on the bigger, general equilibrium picture.

This leaves us with a number of unanswered questions. How exactly are the different types of money connected? Under what conditions is each form present? What does having less of one form mean for the others? And what are the downstream consequences for democracy if a particular type is more prevalent? Because we do not have an integrated account of all three types, we do not have answers to these questions. In the next chapter, I lay out a theory that provides them.

3

The System of Money in Politics

Why did Andimuthu Raja decide to use his position to enrich himself? Why did Walt Minnick spend several hours every day wooing potential donors to support his reelection campaign? And why did Gerhard Schröder leave electoral politics to take up a well-paid private sector position? Are these three forms of money in politics connected to each other? What does a change in one type imply for the others? And what happens if a particular form is more prevalent in a particular context? In this chapter, I lay out my main argument that addresses these questions, and derive a set of testable hypotheses in three steps.

In the first step, I make sure that self-enrichment, campaign spending, and golden parachute employment can – and should – be studied in a common framework by examining why politicians want money in politics in the first place. Many lawmakers are famously motivated by a desire to win (and stay) in office. But several studies have demonstrated that they also care about their personal financial situation. Since money helps them achieve both of these goals, the different forms are at least partly fungible. I also show that much of the money that enters politics is partially interchangeable from the perspective of its source, whether it is instrumentally motivated financiers or state resources appropriated by a politician. This makes clear that the different forms of money in politics should be treated as part of a *common system*.

In a second step, I describe my *comparative theory* that makes sense of when politicians use their time in office to enrich themselves, when they invest in increasing their chances of staying there, and when they use their position as a stepping stone to a lucrative job with the very special interests they previously regulated. I argue that, depending on their level of motivation to stay in office and their financial motives, they use

35

the different types of money in the way that best suits their needs, given the environment they operate in. I focus on two macro-level factors that influence this optimization – the legal and electoral campaign environments. Treating the different forms of money as part of a common system reveals a crucial insight: A change in one type has *second-order effects* in the opposite direction on the others. For example, a decrease in self-enrichment (say, as the result of stricter regulation) leads to an *increase* in campaign spending and/or golden parachute employment. I derive a set of empirical predictions that I test in subsequent chapters.

In a third step, I explore the broader implications of these second-order effects. The three types of money have different consequences for numerous aspects of democracy. A change in one form, which in turn generates second-order effects on the other types, therefore has important *third-order consequences*. First, I argue that voters' attitudes should not only be affected by the total amount of money in politics, but also by how politicians use it. If one form becomes less common, for whatever reason, and another turns out to be more prevalent as a result, this changes how voters view their representatives. Second, because campaign spending helps candidates win, how money enters politics systematically biases election outcomes in favor of some parties or candidates, and against others. And since campaign spending changes as a second-order response to adjustments in other forms of money, this leads to the prediction that any event that alters any type of money can affect election outcomes. I again derive a set of testable empirical implications.

3.1 WHAT POLITICIANS WANT, AND HOW MONEY HELPS THEM GET IT

To determine whether it makes sense to examine enrichment in office, campaign spending, and golden parachute jobs in a single framework, we first need to ask why politicians want money in politics. This, in turn, requires figuring out what they care about in the first place, and how money helps them achieve it.

What do politicians want? The most well-known answer comes from Mayhew (1974), who studied the motivations of US representatives and famously argued that their main goal is to get reelected. To show this, he assumed that politicians *only* care about being reelected, and then demonstrated that they engage in activities that are consistent with this vision of "single-minded seekers of reelection" (Mayhew, 1974, 5).

The "re-election assumption" underlies much modern political science research and is at the core of many formal as well as nonformal theories. In fact, it has reached "near axiomatic status" (Carey, 1998, 103).[1] A sentence in which an author states that they assume politicians care solely about being reelected typically goes undisputed. For example, the style guide of the *Quarterly Journal of Political Science* instructs authors to "not cite works on points that are uncontroversial, such as, 'Members of Congress are reelection-seekers'" (Mayhew, 1974).[2]

But reelection is not the only goal that politicians have, and very often not even the most important one. Mayhew himself acknowledged this, pointing out examples from other countries where politicians are in office for only a short time and allowing that even some US legislators "try to get rich in office, a quest that may or may not interfere with reelection" (Mayhew, 1974, 16). Similarly, Manin, Przeworski, and Stokes (1999) observe that some politicians "may want to get rich at the expense of citizens, while in office or after leaving it" (Manin, Przeworski, and Stokes, 1999, 40).

The literature provides systematic evidence supporting the idea that politicians not only care about getting reelected, but also about their personal finances. Probably the clearest demonstration of this occurred in 1992 in the US Congress. A 1979 amendment prohibited new legislators from personally pocketing unused campaign funds when they left office; existing legislators were not affected by the rule. A second amendment in 1989 ended this exemption, which came into effect in early 1993. This meant that in the 1992 elections, members who had been in Congress since before 1980 could either retire and keep any unspent campaign money for their personal use, or run for reelection and lose it.

Groseclose and Krehbiel (1994) estimate that of the fifty-three retirements that took place that year, nineteen would not have occurred without this payout. Groseclose and Milyo (1999) go one step further and use variation in leftover campaign money to estimate that the average amount required to buy a congressperson out of their seat is about $3 million ($5.5 million in 2021 dollars), but ranging from $0.3 million to $20 million ($0.5 to $36.7 million in 2021) depending on factors such

---

[1] Caring about reelection is most widespread among members of a country's most attractive legislature. Those who are in positions that are considered less important may also exhibit "progressive" ambition, such as a desire to hold higher office (cf. Schlesinger, 1966; Black, 1972; Rohde, 1979). While seeking higher office is slightly different from trying to stay in office ("static ambition"), both share a desire to hold political office.

[2] "Style Guidelines," *Quarterly Journal of Political Science*.

TABLE 3.1 *Politicians' motivations for money in politics.* Reasons why politicians want to receive money in its different forms

	Office Motivation	Financial Motivation
Self-Enrichment	No	Yes
Campaign Spending	Yes	No
Golden Parachute	No	Yes

as legislators' age and wealth. Similarly, Diermeier, Keane, and Merlo (2005) use data on all House and Senate members from 1947 to 1993 to estimate a dynamic structural model of congressional career decisions. They demonstrate that, on average, a payment of about $600,000 in 1995 dollars makes members of the House of Representatives willing to give up their seat, while it takes $1.7 million to convince a senator ($1.1 and $3.1 million in 2021, respectively).[3] So while legislators *do* value being (and staying) in office to a considerable degree, they, just like everyone else, also care about their material wealth.

Regardless of in what proportion a legislator is driven by each of these motivations, money helps with both, as laid out in the literature review in the previous chapter. Table 3.1 summarizes the underlying motivations that were identified for each type. For the financial motivation, lawmakers can try to "supplement" their official income while in office, like Andimuthu Raja did. They can also decide to leave office and cash in on their political position by securing a golden parachute job, as Gerhard Schröder decided to do. Politicians who seek to remain in office must finance a campaign, which means raising funds, as exemplified by Walt Minnick. Money can thus enter politics in different ways, and they satisfy the two main things politicians care about.

3.2 SOURCES OF MONEY AND THEIR MOTIVATIONS

We have to distinguish between two different sources of money in politics. Most commonly, it comes from external sources such as corporations, special interest groups, and wealthy individuals. In some countries, however, money can also come from politicians appropriating internal (state) resources, for example, by stealing taxpayer money. In this section, I discuss each source in turn.

---

[3] See also Kiewiet and Zeng (1993); Hall and van Houweling (1995); Mattozzi and Merlo (2008); Keane and Merlo (2010).

External Sources of Money

If external financiers give money to serving politicians for their *self-enrichment*, they usually have instrumental motivations. A host of anecdotes as well as the systematic studies discussed in the previous chapter show that such payments often lead to political favors: Financiers are more likely to receive government licenses, benefit from public contracts, and have favorable policies enacted (or unfavorable ones discarded).

The literature stresses two motivations for *campaign donors*. The first is, again, instrumental considerations: Campaign money is strategically spent on politicians in influential positions, and donors often expect that they will get face time with lawmakers so they can make their case, and that this will translate into action at least some of the time. Second, campaign donors also give money due to electoral or expressive motivations. Many contributors simply want to express their support for a certain candidate or party and to boost their chances of winning the election. This is especially true for small-scale donors, who are common in the United States, although less prevalent elsewhere.

Finally, the discussion of *golden parachute employment* has also revealed that those who offer it have two potential motivations. The first is former politicians' human capital. During their time in office, they acquire knowledge of certain subject areas and the legislative process, and make valuable contacts. The second motivation is, again, instrumental. There may not be an explicit agreement that politicians will receive a lucrative job in the future in exchange for access and policy favors now. But companies do not give such jobs to politicians who did not support their positions while in office. It is difficult to imagine a Russian pipeline consortium hiring Gerhard Schröder if his policy had been to make Germany less dependent on Russian oil and gas. Consciously or unconsciously, this can – and does – influence politicians' decisions while in office.

Table 3.2 summarizes what financiers want and how money helps them get it. It illustrates that while some motivations are unique to the specific type of money in politics, the instrumental motivation is common to all three. That is, if moneyed private actors want to obtain access to (and potentially influence over) elected officials, they can enrich politicians, help them get reelected, or hire them after they leave office.

TABLE 3.2 *Financiers' motivations for money in politics*. Reasons why financiers want to spend money, in different forms, on politics

	Instrumental Motivation	Other Motivation
Self-Enrichment	Yes	No
Campaign Spending	Yes	Electoral/Expressive
Golden Parachute	Yes	Human Capital

Internal Sources of Money

Few studies have investigated how politicians acquire internal sources of money, partly because getting reliable data on funds stolen from state coffers is even harder than finding information on external money. However, the evidence that does exist suggests that it can be used for both personal enrichment and to fund campaigns.

Perhaps the best-known studies with hard data on stolen taxpayer money come from Brazil. Since 2003, a set of municipalities has been randomly selected every month for a thorough audit to detect misappropriations of federal transfers. This typically involves the diversion of funds (e.g. through the purchase of goods and services that are never provided, or through money simply disappearing from municipal bank accounts), fraud in procurement practices (e.g. noncompetitive bidding processes), over-invoicing, or fake receipts. As Ferraz and Finan (2011) report, "In some cases, the mayor himself is a direct beneficiary. For example, in Paranhos, Mato Grosso do Sul, $69,838 was paid to implement a rural electrification project. As it turns out, one of the farms benefiting from the project was owned by the mayor" (Ferraz and Finan, 2011, 1281).

Pereira and Melo (2015) provide an example of an electoral motivation behind the corruption: "[T]he mayor of Belém, in the northern state of Pará (Duciomar Costa), was reelected despite being investigated for the use of public funds in his electoral campaign" (Pereira and Melo, 2015, 89).

Thus, politicians can use internal money both to enrich themselves and to finance their reelection campaigns (see Table 3.3). However, money stolen from state coffers can clearly *not* come in the form of a golden parachute job. This makes internal money different from external money in one important aspect: whereas the latter can come in all three forms, the former can only come in two. In this chapter, I first examine the more

TABLE 3.3 *Uses for internal money in politics.*Whether internal money can be used for the different forms

	Internal Money
Self-Enrichment	Yes
Campaign Spending	Yes
Golden Parachute	No

general case of external money, and then discuss how the more limited case of internal money fits into the theoretical argument.

3.3 MAPPING THE SYSTEM OF MONEY IN POLITICS

The preceding discussion has made it clear that the different forms of money in politics are not unrelated to each other. Self-enrichment, campaign spending, and golden parachute employment all help politicians achieve objectives they care about. This leads to the book's central argument: the different types of money in politics are partially fungible and thus form a *common system*. In the second major step of this chapter, I now develop a theoretical framework that provides insights into when each form is more or less prevalent, and what downstream effects an increase or decrease in one type has on the others. To facilitate the discussion, I use a stylized theoretical setup to analyze how money enters politics under different conditions. I focus on an intuitive description of the setup and analysis and use graphs to enhance clarity. In the Appendix, I provide a simple decision-theoretic formalization of my setup and mathematically derive all insights discussed here.

Stylized Theoretical Setup

I focus on a stylized *incumbent politician* with access to money. I first consider the case of external money: there are instrumentally motivated special interests willing to give money to the incumbent. Further in the text, I discuss how the argument translates to the more limited case of internal money, for example, through stealing taxpayer money. For simplicity, I assume here that no actors have electoral or expressive motivations to make campaign contributions, and that no actors are interested in employing the incumbent after they leave office for their human capital.

In the Appendix, I show that these simplifications do not affect the main insights of the argument.

The politician faces a standard trade-off: The money is only available to them if they pursue a policy that is favored by the financier(s) but is unpopular with the electorate, so they pay an electoral penalty (cf. Grossman and Helpman, 2001).[4] Of course, real-world interactions rarely involve such a straightforward quid pro quo; they tend to be more subtle. For example, Lessig (2011) describes a long-term "gift economy," in which campaign contributions or gifts indebt politicians to interest groups and policy favors indebt interest groups to politicians, perpetuating a continuous exchange (see also Fox and Rothenberg, 2011). The mechanism described here should thus be seen as a simplified description in the spirit of well-known models of money in politics (e.g. Grossman and Helpman, 2001; Bombardini and Trebbi, 2020).

Since I am exploring *how* the politician uses money, I focus on a situation in which they have already decided to take it. Thus for now, I assume it is optimal for them to do so. I revisit this topic in Chapter 8, where I discuss the connection between how money enters politics and *whether* it does so.

Figure 3.1 provides a schematic overview of the incumbent's situation and the points at which money in different forms can enter. There are two legislative periods, the current and a future one, with an election in between them. The first opportunity to take money presents itself right away: Like Andimuthu Raja, the incumbent can *enrich themselves* in the current period, so *while holding office*.

Next, at some point during their term, our incumbent must decide whether to run for reelection. Let's say they choose to do so, so we go down the left arm of Figure 3.1. They now fight an election campaign, which means they incur personal costs: traveling around their constituency to give speeches, being subject to heightened scrutiny by the media, being attacked by opponents, and so on. As the example of Walt Minnick demonstrated, the campaign is the incumbent's second opportunity to use money, since *campaign spending* will increase their chances of reelection.

If the incumbent wins the election they remain in office for another period, which they value and derive satisfaction from. Of course, the value

---

[4] For details on what these policy favors can look like, see, for example, Ansolabehere, de Figueiredo, and Snyder (2003); de Figueiredo and Edwards (2007); Mian, Sufi, and Trebbi (2010, 2013); Boas, Hidalgo, and Richardson (2014); Kalla and Broockman (2016); McKay (2018); Egerod (2019); Bombardini and Trebbi (2020).

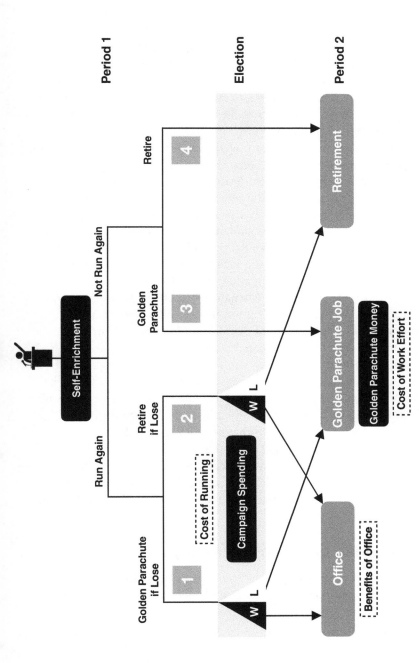

Figure 3.1 *Incumbents' decisions and the three types of money in politics*. Black boxes: Different types of money. Dark gray boxes: What the incumbent does in the second period. Medium gray boxes: Numbering of the incumbent's four possible paths. Light gray box: Election period. Black and white triangles: Election with probabilistic outcome. Dotted boxes: Costs or benefits internal to the incumbent

a politician attaches to being in office vis-à-vis how much money they earn differs between individuals (cf. Groseclose and Milyo, 1999; Diermeier, Keane, and Merlo, 2005). Some politicians care primarily about being rich, while others are mostly driven by a desire to stay in office, perhaps because they are already wealthy or because they have a strong public service motivation. The value a politician associates with holding office may also become less important over the course of their career. I take this diversity into account in the analysis.

Either way, there is no certainty in democratic elections. Campaign spending can increase the chances of staying in office, but does not guarantee it. This means the incumbent must decide what to do if they lose. They can leave electoral politics and retire (the second path in Figure 3.1) or, as shown in the first path, they can make use of the final option in which money can enter politics – *golden parachute employment*, where in the second period they take up a job that is directly or indirectly paid for by a financier.[5] This means that the incumbent benefits from their position *after* leaving office by earning a lucrative salary, in return for which they have to provide a (potentially small) work effort. Many politicians use such a job as an "insurance" option that is only taken up if they lose an election. For example, Gerhard Schröder only became Nord Stream's board chairman after he was defeated by Angela Merkel.

If our incumbent decides not to run for reelection at the end of their term (right arm in Figure 3.1), they again have two options. First, they can go straight into the private sector and take up a golden parachute job (third path in Figure 3.1). For example, in 2009 former British Health Minister Alan Milburn announced that he would not seek reelection and would instead "pursue challenges other than politics."[6] After serving out his term, he worked for several private health companies and in the health industry division of PricewaterhouseCoopers. The incumbent's second option is to not run for reelection and retire, which is the fourth path.

Incumbent Decisions and the Three Types of Money

Figure 3.1 makes clear how the different forms of money are part of a *common system* and how a politician can benefit from them at different

---

[5] A direct way for the interest group to pay the incumbent after leaving office would be to hire them as a board member, strategic adviser, or in-house lobbyist. An indirect way would be if the politician sets up or joins a lobbying or consultancy firm and is then hired to advise or represent the financier.

[6] "Milburn to Stand Down at Election," *BBC News*, June 27, 2009.

points. The question thus is: When is money used for self-enrichment while in office, when does it help politicians win elections to stay in office, and when does it come in the form of a lucrative job after leaving office?

I argue that incumbents, who care about being in office as well as their finances, choose to use the money in the way that benefits them the most, given the environment they operate in. This argument has two elements. First, *politicians* decide how to use the money they have access to. Second, when making that decision, they are essentially solving an *optimization problem* subject to a budget constraint (the amount of money that is available to them). Both of these points require further elaboration.

First, the argument that incumbents have agency over their career, and thus over how they solicit and use money, is a strong one. There is considerable evidence that politicians actively ask for money in specific forms. For example, in 2010 a voicemail left by US Congresswoman Eleanor Holmes Norton on a lobbyist's phone was leaked to the public:

This is Eleanor Norton, Congresswoman Eleanor Holmes Norton. I noticed that you have given to other colleagues on the Transportation and Infrastructure Committee. I am a senior member, a 20-year veteran and I'm handling the largest economic development project in the United States now ... I was, frankly, surprised to see that we don't have a record – so far as I can tell – of your having given to me, despite my long and deep work, essentially in your sector. I'm simply candidly calling to ask for a contribution.

This is not an exception. Many corporations report being approached by politicians, as former US Senator Russ Feingold recalled: "[S]ometimes the corporations that didn't like the system would come to us and say, you know, you guys, it's not legalized bribery, it's legalized extortion. Because it's not like the company CEO calls up to say, gee, I'd love to give you some money. It's usually the other way around."[7]

Given that politicians care about being in office as well as about their personal financial situation, it makes sense that they try to get the money to which they have access in the way that is most useful to them.

By contrast, financiers who are motivated by instrumental interests can achieve them through any of the three forms of money. They therefore have no inherent preference for a particular type, and it would make little sense for them to insist on, say, making a campaign contribution to an incumbent who is not interested in getting reelected. In other words, the

[7] Both quotes appear in: "Take the Money and Run for Office," *This American Life*, March 30, 2012.

most cost-effective way for a financier to achieve their goal is to provide money in the form that the incumbent desires most.[8]

The second element of my argument is that in choosing how to use the money, incumbents implicitly solve a constrained optimization problem. That is, if they ask, for example, for a large campaign contribution, it means that any self-enrichment they engage in, or any chance of getting a lucrative post-politics job, will be lower.

At first glance, it may not seem that politicians trade off between the different forms of money; some appear to be able to have it all. For example, Eric Cantor, a former Republican majority leader of the US House of Representatives, was one of the most prolific campaign fundraisers in Congress while he was in office. He collected more than $7.5 million in donations for his 2012 campaign, and raised more than $26 million over the course of his thirteen years in the lower house.[9] After leaving office in 2014, he took up a job as vice chairman and managing director at the Wall Street investment bank Moelis & Company that earned him around $3.5 million per year.[10] Yet many of his colleagues raise less campaign money and have less lucrative jobs after leaving office, or none at all, which provides the impression that the different forms of money may be complements.

However, the relevant comparison here is *within* – not *between* – individuals. The reason why some politicians have a lot of money in several forms, while others have little of any type, is that the former tend to be more influential, and therefore have access to more money. After all, Eric Cantor was one of the most important politicians in the country. A powerful lawmaker who raises a lot of campaign money and then takes a golden parachute job could have put even more effort into raising campaign funds. If they had done so, and had received even more generous contributions, instrumentally motivated financiers would decide at some point that it does not make sense to spend more money. Therefore,

---

[8] This implies that the assumption that the incumbent decides how to use the money mostly amounts to a rhetorical simplification. If a financier decided how to spend money, and they had knowledge of the politician's preferences, we would expect money to enter politics in the same way as when the politician makes the decision. Of course, financiers may also have an electoral interest, in which case only a campaign contribution makes sense; or they may be interested in the incumbent's human capital, so would offer them a golden parachute job. But if financiers' interests are *instrumental*, they should be happy to provide the money in the ways the politician prefers.

[9] "Rep. Eric Cantor – Virginia District 07," *Center for Responsive Politics*.

[10] "Eric Cantor Lands $3.4 Million Investment Banking Job," *Newsweek*, September 2, 2014.

they will be less inclined to offer the politician a lucrative job down the road. Put a different way, there is only so much a politician can do, and there is only so much a rational, instrumentally motivated financier can pay. Given these constraints, there has to be a trade-off between different forms of money: more of one means less of another.

I develop my theoretical argument that explains how money enters politics by analyzing the optimal course of action for our incumbent in Figure 3.1. To maximize their utility, they "allocate" the money from the different possible forms along the four paths, and choose the path that provides the highest payoff. The outcome of this optimization will differ depending on the macro-level conditions in which they operate, particularly the legal and electoral campaign environments.

Simplifying Assumptions

My theoretical setup simplifies complex processes in numerous ways and neglects many details. However, cutting through the complexities and distilling the process of how money enters politics into its essential components allows me to unify personal enrichment, campaign spending, and golden parachute employment into a single, and tractable, theoretical environment (cf. Healy, 2017). The important thing is that my simple setup captures the core characteristics of money in politics.

First, the allocation of the money between campaign spending, personal enrichment, and golden parachute job is a simplified description of reality. Politicians do not explicitly state that they are foregoing enrichment in office to instead take up a private sector job with a specified salary upon leaving office; nor do they instruct special interests to make a campaign donation worth X and deliver a suitcase containing amount Y in cash. Instead, politicians may make their preferences known by hinting that they might be a valuable addition to a certain company rather than asking for a campaign contribution, or vice versa. Again, in practice these delicate relationships constitute an implicit exchange that depends on mutual understanding and a stock of reputational capital.

Second, the incumbent may not necessarily receive money in different forms from the same source. For example, they may take a campaign contribution from one financier and accept a golden parachute job from another. The trade-off between the different forms is still present: Instead of accepting campaign money from one source and securing a job with another, a politician could have solicited only campaign funds, or could have doubled up on post-employment jobs. The important point is that even the most powerful politician only has a finite amount of special interest money they can draw on, and they have to decide how they want to use it.

Third, each type of money in politics requires a different culture and infrastructure to support it (see Johnston, 2005, 2014). For example, the golden parachute option requires companies to create a job for the politician, such as a board member or lobbyist. In many countries, such roles do not exist, and politicians cannot simply move into the private sector. They might not even be aware that this is a way for them to "cash in" on their position. The results presented in the empirical chapters demonstrate that politicians usually do not consider all three types of money at the same time, and instead only face a subset of options. But the point of the theory is to determine the parameters under which, for example, a golden parachute job is a feasible way for money to enter politics. If it is, entrepreneurial politicians will find out about it sooner or later, and the necessary infrastructure will develop. Similarly, it probably does not cross most US politicians' minds to ask for millions of dollars to enrich themselves, even though they regularly do so to finance their campaigns. However, this has not been true historically (cf. Glaeser and Goldin, 2006; Querubin and Snyder, 2013; Teachout, 2014), and my theory sheds light on the structural conditions that lead away from enrichment in office toward other forms of money in politics.

Fourth, Figure 3.1 simplifies politicians' careers by only focusing on two periods, but most politicians stand in more than one election over the course of their career, so they go through several such cycles. Thus their preferences regarding how much they value being reelected and how much they care about financial gains may change over time. For example, they could care more about obtaining and staying in office early on in their careers, and be more concerned about money later in life. It is also plausible, and indeed likely, that the trade-offs between the different forms of money occur over several electoral cycles. For example, politicians may take a job with a company in an industry whose interests they reliably advocated for during their entire political careers. But again, my simpler theoretical setup captures the relevant features. I discuss the impact of the legal and electoral campaign environments on politicians with different preferences regarding wealth and office, and the basic optimization problem that politicians face is the same regardless of whether that happens over one or several periods.

Finally, I assume that there are no commitment problems. But how is the promise of golden parachute employment credible? Why would someone hire a politician after they leave office? After all, there is no third-party enforcer to invoke. In fact, the commitment problem is much broader than that and applies to the other forms of money as well. Why should someone make a campaign donation after they have already benefited from the incumbent's policies? And as for personal enrichment, why does the incumbent not simply take the money and then implement their own preferred policies? However, such commitment problems primarily arise in single-shot interactions. But, as mentioned earlier, the short-term dynamic described in Figure 3.1 is part of a long-term pattern of interactions. If, for example, a politician provides policy benefits to an industry but never receives any money from it, they will eventually stop listening to the industry's preferences, as will other politicians. Similarly, if a group gives money to politicians and does not perceive any benefits in return, it will not be inclined to continue spending on politics. In technical terms, all actors involved could employ a trigger strategy, and interactions can be sustained if the future is not discounted too highly (cf. Kroszner and Stratmann, 1998). In nontechnical terms, everyone involved has at least some interest in maintaining a reputation of trustworthiness.

Money in Politics in a "State of Nature"

I begin the theoretical discussion of the decisions our incumbent makes with a brief analysis of a "state of nature" – a deliberately simple (and unrealistic) environment in which there are no restrictions or regulations of any form of money. How the incumbent uses money in such a situation will serve as the baseline. I will then layer different macro-environments on top of this baseline to derive a set of empirical implications that I test later in the book.

The first thing to realize is that in a state of nature, taking a golden parachute job *cannot* possibly be the best option for the incumbent. Leaving politics and working in the private sector is an option for lawmakers to become rich after leaving office. But in a state of nature, there are no penalties for personal enrichment *in* office. Thus the benefits of both options are the same. The golden parachute, however, comes with costs: A politician who takes a job in the second period has to put in work effort, however little it may be, and wait for the payout, which thus has a lower present value. In addition, they face opportunity costs, since they cannot hold office and enjoy the associated benefits.

If politicians can accept money for personal enrichment without fear of punishment, they can have their cake and eat it too: They can get monetary compensation in the first period rather than through a golden parachute later on, and they can potentially stay in office in the second period. And even if the incumbent does not run for reelection, taking the money in the first period and without work effort is preferable to receiving the money later and having to work for it. Thus, in the benchmark scenario with no restrictions on money in politics, there is *no golden parachute*.

This eliminates Paths 1 and 3 in Figure 3.1. The remaining options for the incumbent are to (1) use the money in a mixture of personal enrichment and campaign spending, and run for reelection and retire if they lose (Path 2) or (2) use all of the money for personal enrichment and retire straight away (Path 4). Which path the incumbent prefers, and in what proportion they use the money to enrich themselves versus to finance their campaign, depends on a number of incumbent-specific factors.

One is the incumbent's internal motivation – how much they value holding office relative to personal wealth. If they do not value office very much, they will take a "smash-and-grab" approach – get all of the money for their personal enrichment, and not even try to seek reelection (Path 4). If they value being in office to a greater degree, running for reelection and retiring from politics if they lose is the better option (Path 2). In this case, the money is used for both personal enrichment and campaigning. The latter increases when an incumbent values holding office more. At some point, no personal enrichment takes place anymore and all funds raised are allocated to the incumbent's campaign.

Another factor that influences how money enters politics is the cost of running for reelection: higher running costs mean the incumbent is more likely to enrich themselves and retire. Finally, a third factor is how much an incumbent discounts the future. If they value the future to a lower degree, they invest less in their campaign and are less likely to run for reelection in the first place.

These individual-specific factors depend on, for example, candidates' personality and preexisting wealth, and may change over the course of their career. In each context, there will thus be an unobservable distribution of motivations, perceived costs, and valuations of the future among politicians. In the theoretical discussion that follows, I take this into account by examining the impact of changes in the legal and electoral campaign environments given different "starting points" of how money is used and what career path a politician chooses.

3.4 THE EFFECT OF THE LEGAL ENVIRONMENT

Few, if any, democratic countries do not regulate money in politics at all. In this section I explore the impact of various restrictions by focusing on three different forms of regulation in turn: (1) punishing self-enrichment, (2) campaign finance laws, and (3) cooling off periods that impose restrictions on post-politics employment. A large literature has analyzed the direct and immediate impact of such legal restrictions on the form of money they pertain to. However, it has not examined them using a framework that situates the different types in a common system, like in Figure 3.1. The analysis below shows that, in line with the findings in the literature, such restrictions reduce the flow of the particular type of money they target. However, it also shows that such regulations have much less obvious *second-order consequences* on the other forms. By treating the different types of money in isolation, previous studies have largely overlooked these knock-on effects.

Punishing Self-Enrichment

The first target of efforts to get money out of politics is usually politicians who use their position for personal enrichment. Nearly all countries prohibit direct monetary payments to incumbents. Many countries also have restrictions on more hidden ways through which politicians can enrich themselves, such as gifts, sponsored travel, or holding stocks of certain companies (see e.g. Djankov et al., 2010). And while the enforcement of such rules varies, incumbents who use their office to enrich themselves face some risk of being caught and punished in many countries. What is the effect of such regulation on the system of money in politics?

If engaging in self-enrichment may result in being caught and fined, the expected value of doing so declines. Consequently, the incumbent will engage in less of it, as seen in the first row of Figure 3.2. The donuts show how the incumbent uses money, and the lines above indicate which of the four possible career paths they choose. The leftmost column shows a "state of nature" starting point. In the first row, the incumbent runs for reelection and retires if they lose (Path 2 in Figure 3.1). They solicit some money in the form of campaign contributions, and the rest is used for self-enrichment. Moving from left to right, as regulations become stricter and/or better enforced, self-enrichment drops until it eventually disappears completely. This is, of course, not a new insight: several past studies

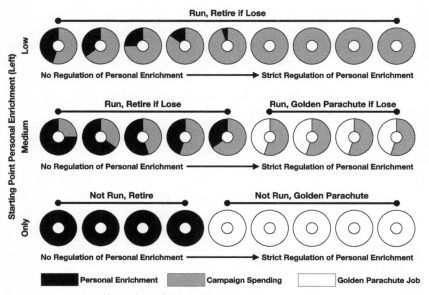

FIGURE 3.2 *Effect of regulation of self-enrichment on how money enters politics*. Effects depending on how much personal enrichment the incumbent engages in during the "state of nature" (left of each row). The donut charts show how money is used, and the lines above indicate the corresponding career path

have demonstrated how tough anti-corruption laws dissuade politicians from enriching themselves (e.g. Glaeser and Goldin, 2006; Teachout, 2014).

What *is* a new insight, however, is that the decrease in self-enrichment leads, as a *second-order effect*, to an *increase* in campaign spending. After a penalty for personal enrichment is introduced, politicians who care about both staying in office and their financial well-being have no easy option to improve the latter anymore. It therefore makes sense to invest more money in campaigning to increase their chances of staying in office. And if the laws against self-enrichment are very stringent, incumbents only use money for their campaign: they become single-minded seekers of reelection. The reelection assumption, so fundamental in political science, is thus endogenous to the legal environment regarding money in politics and holds only under certain circumstances.

The second row in Figure 3.2 shows what happens when an incumbent starts out with more self-enrichment, for example, because they value holding office less. As regulation becomes stricter, they again spend more on campaigning and engage in less self-enrichment. And once the practice becomes risky enough, the incumbent chooses a career path that involves golden parachute employment. Recall that in the "state of nature," it was never optimal for the politician to do so. When politicians expect to be caught and fined if they enrich themselves while in office, this no longer needs to be the case, as both self-enrichment and golden parachute employment come with losses. For the former, it is the expectation of being caught and fined, and for the latter it is the opportunity cost of not being in office in the second period, the discount of being paid later, and the work effort. Thus, the incumbent will choose whichever form comes with the lower costs.

An important implication of this is that politicians will generally *not* engage in enrichment in office *and* take up a golden parachute job.[11] In the second row of Figure 3.2, this means that once self-enrichment becomes risky enough, the incumbent will switch to using money in the form of campaign spending, but also "plan ahead" for a golden parachute job. They run for reelection and only take up the job if they lose: the private sector position is used as an insurance option.

Finally, the last row in Figure 3.2 displays a situation in which the incumbent starts out by *not* running for reelection, and only engaging in self-enrichment. This politician does not value being in office much, or faces prohibitive costs of running again. Stricter regulation does not immediately lead to less self-enrichment, since campaign spending is of little use to them. However, once the restrictions become stringent enough, the expected loss from enrichment in office starts to outweigh the work required to obtain a golden parachute job and having to wait until the next period for the payout. The incumbent now uses their political career as a stepping stone to land a lucrative appointment in the private sector, and all money comes in the form of a golden parachute salary. They do so without seeking reelection. Politicians thus react to stricter and better enforced laws by moving from enrichment *while in office* to enrichment *after leaving office*.

In summary, a crucial insight gleaned from analyzing the different forms of money as part of a common system is that if countries clamp down on enrichment while in office, they can expect *second-order consequences*. Politicians respond by exploiting the arbitrage opportunities due to the fact that the different forms of money are regulated differently. Rather than in suitcases full of cash, money then enters politics in more

---

[11] Note that this only holds when the financier has instrumental motivations and is not interested in hiring former politicians for their human capital, see Appendix.

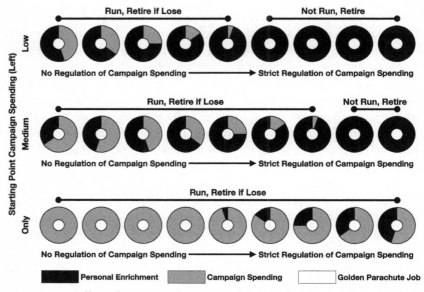

FIGURE 3.3 *Effect of campaign finance regulation on how money enters politics with permissive regulation of self-enrichment.* Effects depending on how much the incumbent spends on their campaign when there is no campaign finance regulation (left of each row). The donut charts show how money is used, and the lines above indicate the corresponding career path

subtle ways. Incumbents who, either because of their personality or their stage in life, care more about being in office use the changed environment to spend more money on their campaigns, thus improving their chances of being reelected. Incumbents who are in politics for the money can still use their position to fulfill this goal, but they now have to wait a bit longer, and have to do at least some work in exchange. Examining only one type of money in politics at a time obscures these knock-on effects on other forms.

Campaign Finance Regulation

Many countries not only have legislation that restricts politicians from enriching themselves in office, but also regulates how much money candidates or parties are allowed to accept and spend on their campaigns (Austin and Tjernström, 2003; Falguera, Jones, and Ohman, 2014; Abel van Es, 2016). This section examines how introducing stricter campaign finance regulation affects how money enters politics.

Figure 3.3 shows the effect of tougher campaign finance laws where the regulation of self-enrichment is permissive. Because enrichment is not very risky, there is no golden parachute employment. The three rows reflect different starting points. In the first row, the incumbent starts out with positive (but low) campaign spending and enriches themselves more than in the other two rows. They run for reelection and will retire if they lose. The same is true in the second row, although here they spend more on their campaign. In the last row, the incumbent is a single-minded reelection seeker and uses all money for campaign spending.

As campaign finance legislation becomes more stringent (moving from left to right in each row), the amount of campaign spending decreases. Again, prior studies have demonstrated how campaign finance regulation leads to cleaner elections (e.g. Eggers and Spirling, 2014; Mutch, 2014; Avis et al., 2021; Fouirnaies, 2021). However, such rules also generate second-order effects, as self-enrichment becomes comparatively more enticing again. Because this means a lower chance of winning reelection, running again and retiring in case of a loss becomes less attractive. Instead, incumbents are more likely to simply retire after their term ends, as seen in the first two rows.

Adding campaign finance laws to the mix can thus lead to a paradoxical situation: Politicians may be more likely to use their office to personally enrich themselves in an environment that penalizes personal enrichment than in one where it is completely unrestricted. If the restrictions are not severe enough to get money out of politics (see Chapter 8), it is the strictness of the prohibitions on self-enrichment and campaign spending *relative to each other* that determines how money enters.

Figure 3.4 illustrates the effect of stricter campaign finance laws when regulation of self-enrichment is stringent, so the dominant ways in which money enters politics are campaign spending and golden parachute employment. As campaign finance regulation becomes stricter, the incumbent again leverages the arbitrage opportunities between the separately regulated forms of money. Campaign spending decreases, but golden parachute jobs become more common as well as more lucrative.

In the first row, the incumbent starts out with relatively low campaign spending. Instead, they can obtain a generous salary if they lose their reelection race and take up a golden parachute job in the second period. As the penalty for campaign spending increases, it is rational for the incumbent to invest even less in their campaign, opening up the possibility of having a more lucrative backup option in the private sector if they lose.

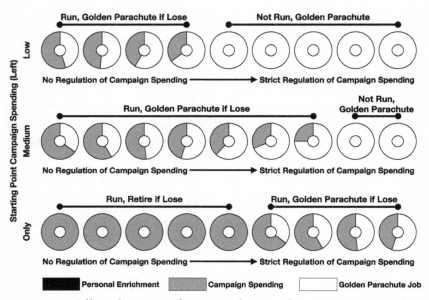

FIGURE 3.4 *Effect of campaign finance regulation on how money enters politics with strict regulation of self-enrichment.* Effects depending on how much the incumbent spends on their campaign when there is no campaign finance regulation (left of each row). The donut charts show how money is used, and the lines above indicate the corresponding career path

At some point, however, the probability of winning becomes so low that it is better to avoid the cost of running again and instead walk straight into a golden parachute job. Note that there is a pronounced drop in campaign spending rather than a gradual tailing off. This is because running for reelection comes with fixed costs. If they are incurred, the incumbent will want to invest enough in campaigning to have a realistic chance of winning. Once campaign spending, and the associated chance of winning, falls below a certain threshold, it becomes preferable to not incur the cost of running and instead go directly into the private sector.

In the second row, the politician also starts out by running for reelection and taking a private sector job if they lose, but solicits more money for their campaign. Their reaction to more stringent campaign finance rules is the same – a decrease in campaign spending, accompanied by a more lucrative golden parachute job. And ultimately, if the penalty becomes very high, the incumbent again ceases to run for reelection and uses their time in office as a stepping stone to a lucrative private sector career.

Finally, the last row depicts a situation in which the incumbent starts out by using only campaign money and retiring if they lose their bid for reelection. Here, an increase in the penalty for campaign spending does not have an immediate effect. However, at some point the incumbent will switch from running and retiring if they lose to running but taking a golden parachute job if their reelection bid is unsuccessful. There is a drop in campaign spending and a jump in the salary to compensate for the fact that a private sector job involves a fixed effort.

In summary, stricter regulation of campaign spending again results in politicians exploiting arbitrage opportunities. While it does decrease the amount of money that incumbents spend on their campaigns, as a second-order consequence it also increases the effort they dedicate to improving their personal financial situation, either while holding office or after leaving it.

Golden Parachute Restrictions

One implication of the preceding discussion is that golden parachute jobs should be most prevalent in countries that have strict rules against enrichment in office as well as restrictive campaign finance laws. I will substantiate this empirically in Chapter 6 in more detail, but a brief look already reveals that this is indeed the case. It is not an accident that prior studies of golden parachute jobs have been conducted exclusively in countries that effectively restrict other forms of money in politics, such as the United States, United Kingdom, Germany, Ireland, or the Netherlands.[12]

Of course, most countries' anti-corruption legislation prohibits offering golden parachute jobs in a *direct* quid pro quo. However, as discussed earlier, these jobs usually come about more subtly. They are more likely to be based on a shared implicit understanding, or on politicians anticipating a lucrative career in the future, which consciously or unconsciously influences their actions in office. Thus, calls for reforms designed to curb golden parachute jobs by restricting or prohibiting former politicians from being employed in the private sector have escalated in many countries.

These regulations typically take the form of "cooling off" laws that prohibit former politicians from holding certain jobs for a limited period of time. For example, more than twenty US states ban former legislators from registering as lobbyists or representing their new employer in interactions with government officials for a set period of time after leaving

---

[12] See González-Bailon, Jennings, and Lodge (2013); Dörrenbächer (2016); Lazarus, McKay, and Herbel (2016); Palmer and Schneer (2016, 2019); Baturo and Arlow (2018); Würfel (2018); Egerod (2019); Claessen, Bailer, and Turner-Zwinkels (2021).

office (see Chapter 5). Thus, existing restrictions narrowly target jobs that directly involve interactions with the government. However, politicians take up many other occupations after leaving office, for example, as advisers or members of boards of directors. As I argue in more detail in Chapter 8, it is very difficult to square restrictions on employing former politicians with common constitutional provisions that guarantee people's freedom of occupation. And indeed, post-politics jobs that do not directly involve lobbying the government are usually unregulated.

Returning to the theoretical setup laid out in Figure 3.1, existing restrictions are best thought of as increasing the cost of the work effort that a politician incurs. Being a lobbyist is probably the private sector job that is best suited to the skill set of someone leaving politics; it is the occupation of choice for most former members of the US House of Representatives (Palmer and Schneer, 2019). If this move is legally prevented, politicians instead need to take up a different job when they leave office – likely one to which they are less suited. This increases their perceived work effort.

The consequences of such golden parachute regulation follow the now familiar pattern. On the one hand, increasing the cost of taking a private sector job makes the incumbent place less emphasis on securing a lucrative post-office salary, and it makes them less prone to pursue such a path at all. On the other hand, there are second-order effects in the other direction again. As they are less likely to leave office for the private sector, the incumbent spends more on campaigning and potentially engages in more self-enrichment while in office.

Empirical Implications

In this section, I have argued that politicians arbitrage differences in how strictly the various types of money in politics are regulated. Changing the law that relates to one form not only has implications for how common that type is; it also affects the *other* forms. While the direct first-order effects have been extensively studied, the second-order effects have received little attention.

Of course, my argument is based on the assumption that a significant amount of money continues to flow after reforms have been implemented, which is borne out in the empirical case studies in Chapters 4 to 6. I discuss how the legal environment affects *how much* money enters politics in more detail in Chapter 8, and show that when there are multiple types of money that can partially substitute for each other, the consequences of reforms are not straightforward. The empirical chapters will test the following implications that can be derived from the discussion in this section:

- Stricter regulation of self-enrichment leads to more campaign spending and more golden parachute employment.
- In environments with permissive regulation of self-enrichment, stricter campaign finance regulation leads to more self-enrichment in office.
- In environments with strict regulation of self-enrichment, stricter campaign finance regulation leads to more golden parachute jobs.
- Golden parachute restrictions lead to more self-enrichment and more campaign spending.

3.5 THE EFFECT OF THE ELECTORAL CAMPAIGN ENVIRONMENT

Democratic politics revolves around elections, and thus campaigns. The circumstances in which these are fought vary dramatically, and I argue that how demanding the *electoral campaign environment* is constitutes a second macro-level variable that shapes the system of money in politics. I focus on two crucial component parts. First, there is considerable variation in the *effectiveness* of the technology used to fight campaigns. Second, electoral campaign environments differ in their *a priori competitiveness*. Both factors can be expected to influence how much a politician spends on campaigning, which in turn has second-order effects on the other forms of money.

Effectiveness of Campaign Technology

Consider some of the options to fight a campaign that a typical US politician has. For example, they can purchase TV ads highlighting their strengths or attacking their opponents, which can bolster their approval ratings and increase their vote share. They can send leaflets or call constituents. And they can set up a canvassing operation that sends campaign workers door to door to persuade citizens to vote for them and motivate voter turnout. All of these techniques are costly, but effective (see e.g. Huber and Arceneaux, 2007; Gerber et al., 2011; Green, McGrath, and Aronow, 2013; Green and Gerber, 2015). They are made even more efficient by the widespread availability of individual-level voter data, which facilitates more precise microtargeting of efforts (Hersh, 2015). And of course, a politician can campaign for many months to increase their chances of being elected.

Contrast this with a politician running for reelection in a European country, where campaign spending tends to be much less effective. For example, door-to-door canvassing has been shown to have considerably smaller effects than in the United States, and often none at all (Bhatti et al., 2019). In many countries, campaigns are only a few weeks long, and only a small number of political ads are broadcast on TV.[13] European campaigns often also lack even basic information about individual voters, as one German campaign manager explains: "A lot of things that are popular in the US are not popular here, like keeping track of who is a Democrat or a Republican. The public would revolt if we did microtargeting."[14]

These differences also exist in contexts where campaigning primarily means vote buying or other targeted goods distribution. For example, Thachil (2014) shows that India's Bharatiya Janata Party (BJP) provides basic social services, such as schools or health clinics, that are cheap and effective at turning out poor voters for the party. In contrast, prior studies have revealed that to make an impact, the value of handouts must increase considerably to be effective among wealthier voters (Calvo and Murillo, 2004; Hicken, 2011; Weitz-Shapiro, 2012, 2016).

How do such differences in the effectiveness of campaign spending affect the system of money in politics? Figure 3.5 illustrates the answer for a situation in which there is little effective regulation of self-enrichment. Baseline campaign spending effectiveness is located in the *middle* of each row. Moving toward the left shows what happens when campaign money becomes less effective; rightward shifts indicate greater efficiency. In the first row, the incumbent starts out with no campaign spending and enriches themselves instead. They do not run for reelection. In the second row, the incumbent runs for reelection but plans to retire if they lose; they thus split the money between self-enrichment and campaign spending. Finally, in the last row they start out with only campaign spending.

When spending is less effective (moving left), its marginal returns are lower. As a consequence, incumbents solicit less money for their campaigns. But again, looking at the different forms of money together

---

[13] These factors are at least partly determined by regulation, so the effectiveness of campaign spending is not independent of legal factors. However, these legal restrictions pertain to campaign *technologies*, whereas those considered in the previous section pertain to campaign *spending*.

[14] "Why Germany's Politics Are Much Saner, Cheaper, and Nicer Than Ours," *The Atlantic*, September 30, 2013.

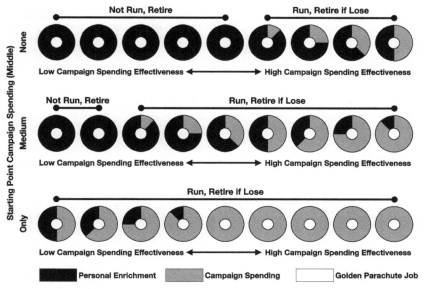

FIGURE 3.5 *Effect of campaign spending effectiveness on how money enters politics with permissive regulation of self-enrichment.* Effects depending on how much campaign money the incumbent uses with baseline campaign spending effectiveness (middle of each row). The donut charts show how money is used, and the lines above indicate the corresponding career path

demonstrates that this opens up the opportunity for them to use their position to enrich themselves. The lower campaign spending and its limited effectiveness also decrease incumbents' chances of winning a second term in office. This can lead them to decide against running for reelection, as happens in the second row.

When spending effectiveness increases (moving right), it leads incumbents to invest more in their campaigns. This comes at the expense of personal enrichment. Because of the higher chances of winning reelection, incumbents who previously would have used the smash-and-grab approach may now decide to run again, as in the first row.

Figure 3.6 illustrates the impact of campaign spending effectiveness if self-enrichment in office is stringently regulated, so the dominant types of money are campaign spending and golden parachute employment. Again, each row displays a situation in which the incumbent starts out (in the middle of each row) with no, medium, or only campaign spending. The basic dynamics are the same as earlier. Lower effectiveness leads to less campaign spending and more golden parachute employment. This can reduce incumbents' desire to run for reelection, as seen in the second row.

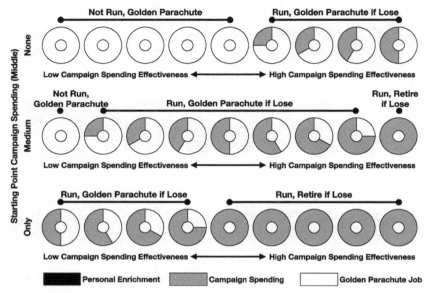

FIGURE 3.6 *Effect of campaign spending effectiveness on how money enters politics with strict regulation of self-enrichment.* Effects depending on how much campaign money the incumbent uses with baseline campaign spending effectiveness (middle of each row). The donut charts show how money is used, and the lines above indicate the corresponding career path

Greater effectiveness leads to more campaign spending and fewer golden parachute jobs. This may lead incumbents who did not run for reelection at baseline to seek another term in office, as exemplified in the first row.

In summary, this section demonstrates that greater campaign spending effectiveness leads to more money being spent on elections – a pattern detected in past research.[15] But again, there are second-order effects, as incumbents enrich themselves less, either while in office or after they leave. And because more, and more effective, campaign spending results in a greater chance of winning reelection, incumbents are more likely to run again. Lower campaign spending effectiveness has, of course, the opposite effect.

Electoral Competitiveness

How demanding elections are also depends on their *a priori competitiveness.* Some incumbents know the outcome is very uncertain. For example, a US campaign strategist recalls the nervousness of many candidates on

---

[15] See, for example, Gingerich (2013).

election day: "There were several I talked to over the years who had been in bed for days with headaches because of stress. There were other candidates who hadn't slept in days."[16]

In contrast, a German member of parliament experienced a different kind of anguish on election day in 2017. When it was announced that he won an eight-candidate election with 48.5 percent of the votes, more than twice as many as the runner-up, local media reported that he appeared visibly shocked when commenting that "the result is a surprise, in the negative sense."[17] Clearly, if he was this upset about a winning margin of almost 25 percentage points, he never had to contemplate that he might actually lose his seat.

Differences in the competitiveness of elections can result from a number of factors. For example, politicians may enjoy a large advantage if they are running on the ticket of a party that has historically performed well in their district. They may also have qualities that make them attractive to voters. For example, they might be perceived as especially charismatic, competent, attractive, or honest.[18] A politician may also have an advantage if they share ethnic or religious attributes with voters, or if they presided over a period of economic growth.[19]

What are the consequences of such differences in a priori competitiveness on how money enters politics? Figure 3.7 shows how it affects the way incumbents use money in a context of permissive regulation of self-enrichment. There are three different starting scenarios (no, medium, and only campaign spending) for the situation in which the incumbent can expect their election to be competitive (on the left of each row).

The first consequence of greater electoral safety is that it affects which career path the incumbent chooses. When the a priori chance of being reelected is higher, independent of any decisions about campaign spending, then the expected benefits of being a legislator in the second period increase as well. The first row shows that this increase may eventually exceed the cost of running, leading an incumbent to seek reelection when they would not have done so in a less electorally safe environment.

---

[16] "How Campaign Staffers Actually Spend Election Day," *MinnPost*, November 7, 2016.
[17] "So hat die Region gewählt," *Mittelbayerische Zeitung*, September 24, 2017. Translated by the author.
[18] Such factors are often referred to as valence terms, see e.g. Adams, Merrill, and Grofman (2005); Schofield and Sened (2006); Adams and Merrill (2009); Stone and Simas (2010).
[19] On ethnicity and voting, see e.g. Chandra (2004); Wilkinson (2004). On religion and voting, see e.g. Lipset and Rokkan (1967); Manza and Brooks (1997); Stegmueller (2013). On economic voting, see e.g. Duch and Stevenson (2008); Weschle (2014).

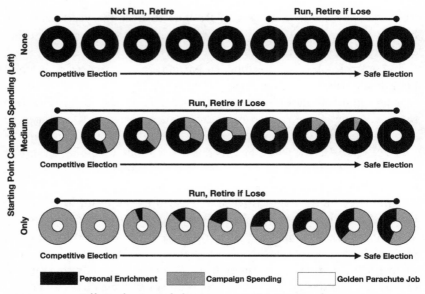

FIGURE 3.7 *Effect of expected election competitiveness on how money enters politics with permissive regulation of self-enrichment.* Effect depending on how much the incumbent spends on their campaign with baseline expected election competitiveness (left of each row). The donut charts show how money is used, and the lines above indicate the corresponding career path

How does greater electoral safety influence how much the incumbent spends on their campaign if they run for reelection? Consider two scenarios. In the competitive one, they have the a priori support of half of the electorate. That means they can potentially still convince the other half of the electorate to vote for them. In the safe scenario, a priori support is, say, 80 percent. Here, campaign advertisements, the distribution of money and gifts, and voter mobilization efforts can only sway a much smaller number of citizens. In other words, campaign spending becomes less effective as elections are a priori safer for the incumbent. Thus, if an incumbent runs for reelection, they will spend less on their campaign. And, in the now-familiar pattern of second-order effects, this opens the door for personal enrichment, as seen in the second and third rows.

Figure 3.8 shows the effect of a less competitive election on how money enters politics when regulation of self-enrichment is stringent. Greater electoral security again affects which of the four paths the incumbent takes. A higher a priori probability of winning reelection makes it more attractive to run again. The first row illustrates that the incumbent will be less likely to move directly into the private sector as a consequence.

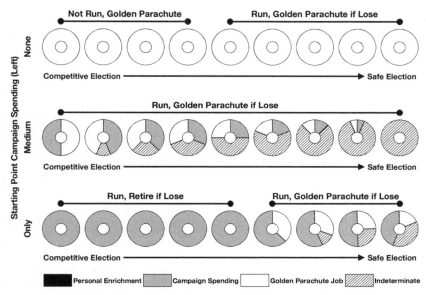

FIGURE 3.8 *Effect of expected election competitiveness on how money enters politics with strict regulation of self-enrichment.* Effect depending on how much the incumbent spends on their campaign with baseline expected election competitiveness (left of each row). The donut charts show how money is used, and the lines above indicate the corresponding career path

Instead, incumbents are more likely to run and take up a golden parachute job if they lose, but the latter becomes increasingly unlikely. The increased electoral security can also influence the behavior of an incumbent who starts out focusing entirely on winning reelection by soliciting money for their campaign, as in the third row. Because they face less risk, they can create an insurance option for themselves in the (unlikely) event that they lose.

If the incumbent runs for reelection and plans to take up a golden parachute job if they lose, the implications of greater electoral security for how much they spend on their campaign, and the salary they are offered for a private sector job, are less clear. This is because there are two opposing forces. On the one hand, a less competitive election makes campaign spending less effective, as discussed earlier. The incumbent therefore has an incentive to use less of it. On the other hand, a greater chance of winning means that the incumbent is increasingly unlikely to need their backup option (golden parachute job), which gives them an incentive to instead invest more in their campaign. Which of these forces wins out depends on factors such as how much the incumbent values holding office, how much they discount the future, and baseline campaign spending effectiveness. The theoretical prediction is therefore ambiguous, as shown by the shaded areas in the second and third rows.[20]

Thus, the straightforward first-order implication of this section is that most of the time, lower electoral competitiveness results in less campaign spending and a higher proportion of incumbents running for reelection, which has been shown in previous research (e.g. Golden and Chang, 2001; Chang, 2005). Yet, this does not mean that money disappears from politics in less competitive electoral races. Instead, there are second-order effects on the other forms of money, since more secure incumbents have greater leeway for self-enrichment in office or after leaving it. This has not been shown in the literature so far.

Empirical Implications

How does the electoral campaign environment influence how money enters politics? Again, the direct first-order impact of campaign spending effectiveness and electoral competitiveness on campaign money is relatively straightforward. Looking at the different forms of money together, however, reveals less intuitive second-order implications on self-enrichment in office or the extent to which politicians get golden parachute jobs. In subsequent chapters, I test the following empirical implications:

- Greater campaign spending effectiveness leads to less self-enrichment and less golden parachute employment.
- Greater electoral security leads to more self-enrichment for incumbents who run for reelection. It also makes it more likely that they run again, and thus less likely that they move directly into a golden parachute job.

3.6 STEALING STATE MONEY

Earlier, I distinguished between *external* money that is given to politicians by instrumentally motivated corporations, interest groups, or individuals and *internal* money, where politicians steal state resources. While the former can come in all three forms, the latter can only be used for self-enrichment or campaign spending. The discussion in this chapter has so

---

[20] This ambiguity is not problematic for the empirics in the later chapters, as data on the salaries of golden parachute jobs is not available.

far focused on external money only. But my basic argument that pertains to the more general case in which all three forms are partially fungible also applies to the narrower case where only two of them are.

If an incumbent appropriates taxpayer money for themselves, they cannot spend that money on public goods such as schools or infrastructure that are popular with voters. They therefore pay an electoral penalty. Once they steal the money, they also face a very clear optimization problem: How much should they keep for themselves, and how much should they spend on their reelection campaign? The legal and electoral campaign environments influence this decision in the ways I outlined earlier.

The major difference between external and internal money is that the latter cannot come in the form of a golden parachute job. However, one of the insights discussed above was that, theoretically, it does not make sense for politicians to engage in self-enrichment while in office *and* take up a golden parachute job after leaving their elected position. In a given empirical context, politicians will thus usually choose between enrichment in office and campaign spending, or between campaign spending and golden parachute employment. For the former, the decision is the same no matter whether the money comes from external sources, state resources, or a mixture of the two. For the latter, the trade-off only exists for external money because internal money can only be spent on campaigning. In practice, however, countries that strictly regulate self-enrichment also tend to have stiff penalties for stealing taxpayer money. Thus, where the dominant forms of money in politics are campaign spending and golden parachute jobs, this money usually comes from external sources only.

3.7 CONSEQUENCES FOR DEMOCRACY

My argument so far has been that when we examine the different forms of money in politics using a common framework, we see that a change in one type has second-order effects on the other types: A decrease in one form leads to an increase in the others, and vice versa. But the implications do not stop there. Even though self-enrichment, campaign spending, and golden parachute employment are all part of a common system, the various forms have different effects on other aspects of politics. As a consequence, if money ceases to go through one channel and instead shows up in another, this has important *third-order effects*.

In the next two subsections I focus on two such effects: voters and winners. First, I argue that if politicians use money in different forms, this affects voters' attitudes toward them. Second, I make the case that how money enters politics affects electoral competition by systematically influencing who is more likely to win. I derive a set of empirical implications for both of these arguments, which I test in Chapter 7.

Voters

Citizens' level of trust in politicians plays an important role in the stability and health of a democracy. Prior studies have found that one of the major factors undermining this trust is the role of money in politics (see e.g. Della Porta, 2000; Anderson and Tverdova, 2003; Chang and Chu, 2006; Chong et al., 2015; Ares and Hernández, 2017; Solé-Ollé and Sorribias-Navarro, 2018).

However, I argue that voters perceive some types of money more negatively than others. An important difference between the three forms is that whereas enrichment in office and golden parachute jobs directly channel money to a politician, campaign spending only has an indirect effect by increasing the probability that they win reelection. Voters likely take a dimmer view of the former. After all, the classic definition of corruption entails using one's office for *personal* gain. By contrast, campaign spending leads to a *political* advantage, which may be seen as less problematic.

Furthermore, campaign spending has positive effects that self-enrichment (in or after leaving office) cannot have. For example, there is evidence that campaign advertisements can improve voters' information about politics (e.g. Zhao and Chaffee, 1995; Valentino, Hutchings, and Williams, 2004). If the money is used for voter mobilization, it can increase turnout (Green, McGrath, and Aronow, 2013; Green and Gerber, 2015). And in contexts with little programmatic competition, election spending in the form of cash handouts, support in times of adversity, or services such as education and health care have direct and tangible benefits for voters (e.g. Thachil, 2014; Chauchard, 2018; Nichter, 2018).[21]

Thus, I argue that when money enters politics, the public views it as more problematic if it personally benefits lawmakers. One implication of this hypothesis is that changes in how money enters politics can affect voters' overall view of politicians. For example, one of the arguments in

---

[21] Relatedly, Fernández-Vázquez, Barberá, and Rivero (2016) show that voters are more tolerant of self-enriching politicians when the policy concessions they make in exchange for a bribe have positive side effects for voters (e.g. construction jobs as a result of illegal building permits).

favor of stricter campaign finance regulation is that it would increase trust in politics. However, if the second-order effect of such a reform is that it leads to more self-enrichment, in office or thereafter, of which voters are more critical, then the third-order effect might be a counter-intuitive *decrease* in public confidence.

Winners

How money enters politics should also matter in relation to its effect on election results. Because campaign spending helps politicians win votes and stay in office, conditions that lead to more campaign expenditures can affect election outcomes. This has important implications for democratic competition, since some candidates and parties have systematically more access to money than others.

This differential access occurs for a variety of reasons. For example, incumbents generally find it easier to get special interest groups to give them money, whether in the form of enrichment in office,[22] golden parachute jobs,[23] or campaign contributions.[24] Politicians with more power or influence, such as ministers or members of important committees, also tend to raise more money.[25] Finally, parties have structural differences in their capacity to raise funds, since some have greater support from wealthy individuals and corporations than others. Politicians who belong to business-friendly parties thus have larger asset growth in office,[26] receive more campaign contributions,[27] and are more likely to take up golden parachute employment.[28]

If conditions are such that money is primarily used for self-enrichment or enters politics in the form of golden parachute jobs, some politicians will be better able to financially benefit from their position than others. But if the legal or electoral campaign environments change in a way

---

[22] Fisman, Schulz, and Vig (2014); Klašnja (2015).

[23] Eggers and Hainmueller (2009); Palmer and Schneer (2016).

[24] Krasno, Green, and Cowden (1994); Hogan (2000); Magee (2012); Fouirnaies and Hall (2014); Jacobson and Carson (2016).

[25] Fisman, Schulz, and Vig (2014); Powell and Grimmer (2016); Weschle (2021*b*).

[26] Bhavnani (2012) demonstrates a high number of "suspicious" rates of asset growth among politicians of the business-friendly BJP in India.

[27] See, for example, Samuels (2001*c*).

[28] Members of Parliament (MPs) from the British Conservative Party are more likely to take up politically linked outside employment than Labour MPs (Eggers and Hainmueller, 2009; Weschle, 2021*b*), and Republican members of the US Congress are more likely to become lobbyists after leaving office than their Democratic colleagues (Lazarus, McKay, and Herbel, 2016).

that increases the amount of money spent on campaigns, these asymmetries translate into *electoral inequality*. And as I have argued earlier, campaign spending can increase as a result of changes in *other* forms of money. This means that regulation which makes personal enrichment or golden parachute employment more difficult, and thus as a second-order effect increases campaign spending, has the third-order consequence of generating a systematic shift in who wins elections.

Empirical Implications

A change to one form of money in politics induces second-order changes to the other forms, which in turn should have third-order effects on certain aspects of democracy. I will test the following empirical implications of the preceding discussion:

- Voters are more likely to disapprove of politicians who enrich themselves in office or take up a golden parachute job compared to incumbents who use money for their reelection campaigns.
- If more money enters politics as campaign spending, parties and candidates who receive more money from financiers are more likely to win elections.

Of course, there are likely other third-order consequences. I focus on voter perceptions of politics and structural inequalities in who wins elections because these are among the most important factors when assessing democratic quality. In Chapter 8, I provide some conjectures about other potential third-order consequences of how money enters politics.

3.8 SUMMARY AND EMPIRICAL STRATEGY

In this chapter, I have laid out my theoretical argument, as summarized in Figure 3.9. I have focused on two factors that influence money in politics – the legal and electoral campaign environments that politicians operate in. A change in either has a first-order effect on the type of money to which it most closely pertains. For example, if stricter campaign finance legislation is implemented, campaign spending will decrease as a consequence. However, because the three types of money all serve important goals that politicians have, they are partially fungible and therefore constitute a common system. This means that the first-order effect is followed by second-order effects on the other types of money: The drop in campaign

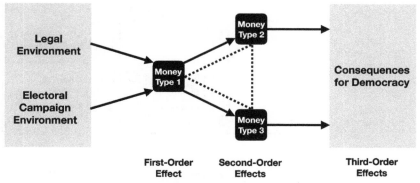

Legal Environment

Electoral Campaign Environment

Money Type 1

Money Type 2

Money Type 3

Consequences for Democracy

First-Order Effect

Second-Order Effects

Third-Order Effects

FIGURE 3.9 *Summary of the argument*

spending as a result of its stricter regulation leads to increases in self-enrichment and/or golden parachute employment. Finally, these first- and second-order effects lead to third-order consequences for democracy, such as how voters evaluate politicians and who wins elections. Most prior studies do not differentiate between different forms of money, or tend to examine them in isolation. This chapter has demonstrated that such a siloed approach can lead to an incomplete, and possibly misleading, understanding of money in politics.

In the next four chapters, I subject my theoretical argument to empirical scrutiny by testing the implications I have derived here. An important challenge is associated with the fact that, as this chapter has made clear, there are good theoretical reasons why it is rare for all three types of money to be present in the same context at the same time. In particular, self-enrichment in office and golden parachute employment should rarely coexist. I therefore cannot study the entire system in one empirical context.

This precludes the kind of case selection that is the norm in most contemporary political science books. I cannot focus on a single country, or on a small number of geographically proximate ones. Instead, I test my general equilibrium theoretical account in a series of partial equilibrium studies, situated in a set of countries that are not usually studied together. Each of them looks at a part of the system, but taken together they paint a larger empirical picture that matches the theoretical one outlined in this chapter. Figure 3.10 provides a schematic view of the empirical strategy used in the remainder of the book.

Chapters 4 and 5 test the second-order effects of the legal and electoral campaign environments using a series of within-country studies. In

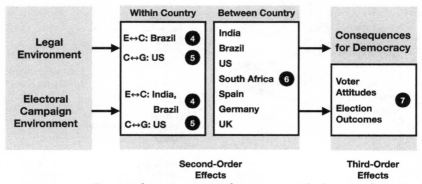

FIGURE 3.10 *Empirical strategy to test the argument.* Black circles denote chapters in which the tests are described. E↔C denotes the connection between enrichment and campaign spending, and C↔G the connection between campaign spending and golden parachute jobs

Chapter 4, I begin by focusing on the connection between self-enrichment in office and campaign spending in two contexts in which both types are common, India and Brazil. For the legal environment, I exploit changes in campaign finance regulation and examine its impact on politicians' self-enrichment. For the electoral campaign environment, I examine the effects of variation in the competitiveness of races on campaign spending and enrichment.

In Chapter 5, I turn to the United States to study the effect of the legal and electoral campaign environments on the link between campaign spending and golden parachute employment. For the legal environment, I examine the consequences of a relaxation of campaign finance laws on golden parachute employment. For the electoral campaign environment, I again exploit differences in competitiveness.

In Chapter 6, I move from within-country studies to between-country comparisons. I present short case studies from countries that vary in their legal and electoral campaign environments and test whether the dominant forms of money in those countries are as expected. In addition to India, Brazil, and the United States, I also study South Africa, Spain, Germany, and the United Kingdom. Note that in accordance with my theoretical focus, Chapters 4, 5, and 6 focus primarily on politicians and how they use the money they have access to. In each case I will briefly discuss where the money typically comes from, but this is not the main empirical focus.

Finally, Chapter 7 tests the empirical predictions related to the third-order consequences. I examine whether voters do indeed react differently to different forms of money using original survey experiments from India and the United States. Then, I explore the effects of how money enters politics on election outcomes, again using data from the United States.

4

The Connection between Self-Enrichment
and Campaign Spending

Holding office is financially lucrative in many democracies around the world. However, politicians' official salaries usually place them nowhere near the highest-paid professions in their country. Instead, lawmakers often enrich themselves by stealing state resources or accepting money from special interests. But staying in office can also be expensive. Every few years, incumbents have to convince a sufficient number of voters that they deserve to stay in the job. Whether they do so through advertising or clientelistic vote buying, this is often costly. So even if their position gives them plenty of access to money, politicians cannot engage in unrestrained personal enrichment. They must also accumulate enough resources for their reelection campaigns.

In the previous chapter, I argued that the different types of money in politics form a common system, and that the legal and electoral campaign environments govern their relative prevalence. In this and the next couple of chapters, I provide empirical evidence that this is indeed the case. Because enrichment in office and golden parachute jobs should not frequently occur in the same environment, I conduct a series of studies that involve two forms of money at a time. I use detailed case knowledge to identify data and research designs that make it possible to study how several types of money in politics are connected to each other, and how the legal and electoral campaign environments determine which is more prevalent in a particular context. Taken together, these studies blend into a coherent macro-level picture that is in line with the theoretical account laid out in Chapter 3.

In this chapter, I begin by examining the connection between campaign spending and personal enrichment while in office. I do so in the contexts of India and Brazil – two countries in which both of these uses for money in politics are well known. In *India*, there are countless examples of politicians whose wealth increased at suspiciously high rates while they held office. In addition to the case of Andimuthu Raja discussed in Chapter 1, other recent scandals include the "Coalgate scam" involving the allocation of coal blocks at throwaway prices, the "Commonwealth Games scam" surrounding the construction of sports venues in Delhi, or the "NRHM scam" related to rural health care delivery. As the former governor of India's central bank and ex-member of the upper house of parliament, Bimal Jalan, admitted: "It is no secret that politics is generally regarded as the most lucrative business in the country" (Jalan, 2007, 60).

But staying in this lucrative business is not cheap. Election campaigns in India have been getting more expensive, and candidates must invest considerable resources to be serious contenders. As a consequence, "recourse to extra-legal sources of political contributions is now widely accepted as being unavoidable" (Jalan, 2007, 26). For example, Gopinath Munde, a former leader of the Bharatiya Janata Party (BJP), acknowledged that his 2009 reelection campaign had cost him Rs80 million (around $1.6 million at the time).[1] An anonymous candidate for the state parliament of Andhra Pradesh followed by Vaishnav (2017) mentioned a similar figure, which exceeds the legal spending limit thirty to forty times over. A large chunk of such expenditures is spent on cash and liquor handouts as well as other clientelistic goods, which are major tools of voter mobilization (Krishna, 2007; Wilkinson, 2007; Chauchard, 2018). Due to the high costs, candidates are expected to self-fund most of their campaigns (Bryan and Baer, 2005; Vaishnav, 2017). Since direct contributions to candidates are against the law in India, incumbents "tend to use their term of office to accumulate war chests for future elections and for nursing their constituencies" (Gowda and Sridharan, 2012, 236).

Money in politics also plays an important role in *Brazil*. The country's largest corruption scandal, "Operação Lava Jato" (Operation Car Wash), erupted in 2014. It became known that for years, the state-owned oil company Petrobras diverted up to 3 percent of the value of its contracts to politicians, which amounted to more than $1.7 billion.[2] The former speaker of the lower house, Eduardo Cunha, was arrested on suspicion of embezzling around $40 million.[3] João Vaccari Neto, the former treasurer

---

[1] "Munde Admits Spending Rs. 8 Crore in 2009 Polls," *The Hindu*, June 28, 2013.

[2] "What is the Petrobras Scandal that is Engulfing Brazil?," *Financial Times*, April 1, 2016.

[3] "Brazilian Lawmaker Who Led Impeachment of President Is Arrested," *New York Times*, October 19, 2016.

of the then-governing Partido dos Trabalhadores, was also arrested in connection to the scandal. But, unlike Cunha, he was not accused of personally benefiting from the kickback scheme. Vaccari Neto was instead charged with accepting "irregular donations" for the party.[4] Thus, both personal enrichment while in office and exorbitant campaign spending are common in Brazil as well.

In this chapter, I use data from these two countries to empirically test the argument that personal enrichment in office and campaign spending are directly, and inversely, linked – and that their relative prevalence is driven by a country's legal and electoral campaign environments. To do so, I build on a growing literature that makes use of new disclosure laws and "forensic" methods to detect potential wrongdoings. Some countries (including India and Brazil) compel candidates for political office to disclose their assets (Djankov et al., 2010), which makes it possible to infer how their wealth has increased if they run in consecutive elections. For both countries it is thus possible to directly or indirectly infer how much emphasis politicians place on spending for their reelection campaigns, and how much they enrich themselves. This allows me to take the study of money in politics a step forward by examining the connection between the two types.

First, I focus on the effect of the electoral campaign environment in India. I show that members of Indian state legislatures who can expect to be in a close reelection race hold larger cash reserves, which are crucial for campaigning. Conversely, those who are electorally more secure tend to enrich themselves, for example, by acquiring land or houses.

In a second step, I repeat the analysis using Brazilian asset and campaign spending data. I again find that vulnerable incumbents spend more on their campaigns, whereas secure ones increase their personal assets. Then, I examine the effect of the legal environment on how money enters politics. I exploit a discontinuity in Brazil's campaign spending limits to show that stricter regulation has the unintended second-order effect of leading to more personal enrichment.

4.1 MONEY AND POLITICS IN INDIA

From 2018 to 2020, India ranked between 78th and 86th out of 180 countries in Transparency International's Corruption Perceptions Index.

---

[4] "Brazil Police Arrest Workers' Party Treasurer Joao Vaccari Neto," *Wall Street Journal*, April 15, 2015.

In the World Bank's Control of Corruption Indicator, it came between 106th and 110th out of 209 between 2017 and 2019. It is widely acknowledged that money has increasingly influenced politics since the country started to liberalize its economy in the early 1990s (Jalan, 2007; Debroy and Bhandari, 2012; Gowda and Sridharan, 2012). Many politicians are presumed to accept illegal payments in return for legislative favors or providing services, and to misappropriate state resources (e.g. Bussell, 2018). As a consequence, corruption scandals have marred national- as well as state-level politics (Bussell, 2012; Gowda and Sridharan, 2012; Vaishnav, 2017).

In 2011 and 2012, the ubiquity of such scandals galvanized Indian voters into action. The India Against Corruption movement drew tens of thousands of protesters demanding measures such as an independent anti-corruption ombudsman. A political party that grew out of the movement, the Aam Aadmi Party, in 2015 won a majority of seats in the legislature of the National Capital Territory of Delhi and its leader, Arvind Kejriwal, became chief minister. Concerns about corruption also played a major role in the 2014 national elections, and helped the BJP gain a parliamentary majority and make Narendra Modi prime minister (Sukhtankar and Vaishnav, 2015).

Money – particularly money obtained in dubious or illicit ways – plays a variety of roles in Indian politics. For one, politicians often substantially increase their wealth while in office. Anecdotes of particularly egregious examples that ended up being prosecuted were mentioned earlier, but the phenomenon is much more widespread. Since candidates for national and state assemblies must submit asset disclosure affidavits, we can systematically study the wealth development of ordinary Indian politicians. Bhavnani (2012) and Fisman, Schulz, and Vig (2014) use a regression discontinuity design to identify the causal effect of holding office on asset development. They compare the change in reported assets of candidates who won their first-past-the-post election by a narrow margin to those of candidates who lost by a narrow margin.

Bhavnani finds that the assets of narrow winners grew by Rs24.2 million (more than $550,000 given exchange rates at the time) over five years – Rs9.6 million *more* than narrow losers. This amounts to a winner's premium of 4–6 percent annually. Members of the Lok Sabha, the national parliament, earn a yearly salary of Rs600,000 (about $9,000), plus Rs2,000 ($30) daily when parliament is in session.[5] Base salaries

---

[5] "Government Spends Rs. 2.7 Lakh a Month per MP," *The Hindu*, September 29, 2015.

for members of state parliaments vary, but ranged between Rs96,000 and Rs840,000 annually for the relevant time period. Even taking into account that legislators receive various other perks such as free housing and travel, the official payments can hardly explain why their assets grew by almost Rs5 million per year. Fisman, Schulz, and Vig use a similar research design and find a winner's premium on net asset development of 3–5 percent per year. The effect is larger for ministers and more pronounced in states that are known for corruption. All in all, it is lucrative to be a politician in India.

Obtaining (and keeping) such a lucrative position requires spending a lot of money. The cost of Indian elections are second only to those in the United States, and candidates finance a large part of their campaigns themselves (Bryan and Baer, 2005; Gowda and Sridharan, 2012; Vaishnav, 2017; Bussell, 2018). A long-time observer of Indian politics notes that "[a]fter watching several Indian general elections, I had come to think they were … designed for the public to fleece aspiring politicians as payback for the previous years when the transaction had gone in the opposite direction" (French, 2011, 85). A news article described Indian general elections as a "quasi-Keynesian boost … rich with multiplier effects from boardroom to tea shop."[6] Voters expect candidates to provide benefits and handouts. A set of PowerPoint slides assembled by the Election Commission of India used to train election monitors mentions no less than forty ways in which candidates try to spend money to secure votes. Examples include "cash in envelopes in morning newspapers pushed beneath the door of the voter," "giving Rs500 note rolled up inside a ball pen/stem of party flag," and "distribution of liquor, drugs, poppy husks among the voters."[7] Candidates and parties also form long-term materialistic relationships, for example, by providing social services (Thachil, 2014). And while these expenses may not automatically convert into votes, candidates who do not provide handouts may not stand a chance of winning (Björkman, 2014; Chauchard, 2018). For example, an article in the *New York Times* describes a hapless candidate who hands out cash to voters, but is overwhelmed by the number of "supporters" who show up. He is forced to hand out less money to each attendee, leading one indignant voter to exclaim: "Does he think we are beggars, giving us only 20 rupees? We will teach him a lesson."[8]

---

[6] "The Economics of India's Election Machine," *Bloomberg View*, May 1, 2014.
[7] "Election Expenditure Monitoring (EEM)-Briefing of Expenditure Observers," *Election Commission of India*, August 16, 2018.
[8] "Financing Indian Elections Turns Costlier and Murkier," *New York Times*, July 5, 2013.

The need to engage in such spending forces candidates to raise money for electoral purposes. There are unrealistically low spending limits once an election is announced – since 2014, Rs5.4–7 million ($80,000–104,000) for parliamentary elections and Rs2–2.8 million ($30,000–42,000) for state assembly elections[9] – so any serious candidate exceeds them (Bryan and Baer, 2005; Gowda and Sridharan, 2012; Sukhtankar and Vaishnav, 2015; Sridharan and Vaishnav, 2016). Although candidates are expected to spend lavishly on their campaigns, Indian law prohibits individuals and companies from contributing directly to candidates. This restriction, combined with the fact that most transactions have to take place off the books to circumvent the unrealistic spending limits, forces candidates to accumulate sufficient cash reserves before an election. Prior studies have documented a number of creative ways in which they do so. Sukhtankar (2012) shows that sugar mills in India pay lower cane prices to farmers in election years if their chairman runs for office. The freed-up funds are presumably siphoned off to help finance the campaign. Kapur and Vaishnav (2018) demonstrate that cement consumption falls during the months in which state assembly elections take place. They argue that this is the result of a liquidity shortage in the construction sector because builders use their cash to support candidates' campaigns.

Taken together, anecdotal as well as systematic evidence thus suggests that money plays an important role in Indian politics, and that it does so in a couple of ways. Politicians use their office to enrich themselves, but accumulating sufficient resources for upcoming election campaigns is a priority as well. So far, these two uses have been looked at separately. In the following section, I describe how mandatory asset disclosure affidavits allow me to study the connection between them.

4.2 MANDATORY ASSET DISCLOSURE AFFIDAVITS IN INDIA

In the early 2000s, the Association for Democratic Reforms (ADR), a Delhi-based non-governmental watchdog organization, filed public interest litigation seeking access to information about the financial, educational, and criminal backgrounds of candidates for political office. In late 2002 and again in early 2003, the Supreme Court agreed and ordered the Election Commission to collect this data. Since November 2003, all

---

[9] "Handbook for Candidate, February 2019," *Election Commission of India*, March 16, 2019.

candidates for national and state elections have been required to submit judicial affidavits disclosing detailed information on the assets held by themselves, their spouse, and any dependents. They are submitted a few weeks before the election as part of the candidate registration paperwork, which ensures complete coverage. Scanned copies of the affidavits are made available on the internet (see Figure 4.1 for an example). ADR digitizes and posts the affidavits on its website to provide easily accessible information to voters.[10]

How to Detect Personal Enrichment and Campaign Spending in the Asset Declarations

So far, the Indian candidate affidavits have been used to analyze the causes and consequences of having politicians with criminal backgrounds as well as the development of the total assets of incumbents who run for reelection (Bhavnani, 2012; Fisman, Schulz, and Vig, 2014; Aidt, Golden, and Tiwari, 2015; Vaishnav, 2017; Asher and Novosad, 2020). But because direct campaign contributions to candidates are prohibited and expenditure limits are unrealistically low, there is no neat separation between personal enrichment and campaign spending. Indian politicians accumulate money over the course of their term in office, and once their reelection contest starts they spend some of it on campaigning. Because the affidavits reflect their assets a few weeks before the election (i.e. in advance of the campaign), they likely contain resources destined for campaign spending that should not be considered personal enrichment.

To determine whether the listed assets are designated for politicians' personal enjoyment or an upcoming reelection campaign, I exploit the level of detail in the affidavits. Candidates have to itemize their assets into a number of categories. For example, they have to declare their cash holdings and bank account balances, list all motor vehicles, and provide information on land and buildings they own. As the second and third pages in Figure 4.1 illustrate, candidates are required to provide specific details such as bank account and insurance policy numbers, make and registration numbers of vehicles, locations and area measurements of land, addresses and sizes of buildings, and so on. Rather than simply looking at total asset development, which conflates resources intended for campaign spending with belongings that reflect personal enrichment, I instead look at changes over time in the different *asset categories*.

---

[10] See www.myneta.info.

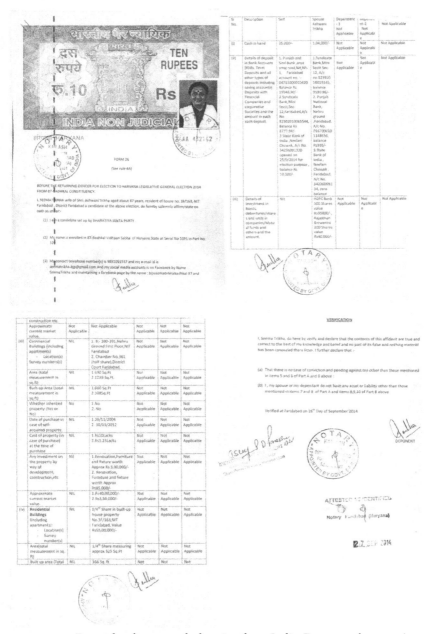

FIGURE 4.1 *Example of an asset declaration from India.* Four sample pages (out of seventeen) of the asset declaration affidavit filed by Seema Trikha, a BJP candidate for the 2014 Haryana Legislative Assembly elections in Badhkal constituency

Some assets are more clearly intended for personal enrichment than others. If a candidate owns more jewelry, increases land holdings, or accumulates houses and buildings, they do so for their personal benefit. In contrast, cash reserves are a very inconvenient way to hold wealth, but are of crucial importance for reelection campaigns.[11] An article by the news portal *NDTV* states that: "[I]llicit cash is the unacknowledged lifeblood for political parties that collect money from candidates and businessmen, and then spend it to stage rallies, hire helicopters and hand out 'gifts' to win votes."[12] The writer Patrick French observes that during elections, "[m]oney that had been stored up in cash for years would be paid out to officials and supporters" (French, 2011, 85). When the Indian government unexpectedly demonetized all 500 and 1,000 rupee notes in November 2016, this was thought to have profound implications for the election campaign in the state of Uttar Pradesh early the following year. A senior leader of the Congress Party explained, "[w]e will have to plan the entire election strategy all over again," and predicted that candidates would hold smaller rallies and distribute fewer "freebies."[13] Indian politicians have therefore devised numerous ways to make sure they have enough cash on hand during campaign season (Sukhtankar, 2012; Kapur and Vaishnav, 2018). One of those ways is accumulating cash reserves in the years prior to an election (Gowda and Sridharan, 2012). Because the affidavits are submitted *before* an election campaign, a large growth in cash holdings thus likely indicates higher planned spending during the campaign.

How Accurate are the Asset Declarations?

While legislators can be disqualified from holding office if they understate their true assets, it is still natural to ask how accurate the affidavits are. It is impossible to say for sure, but there are at least three reasons to believe they reliably reflect politicians' true assets.

First, the declarations exhibit face validity. Reported asset growth is larger for winning candidates than for losers (Bhavnani, 2012; Fisman,

---

[11] While all candidates are required to submit election expense reports to the Election Commission, the unrealistically low spending limits virtually guarantee that the reported spending has little relation to the actual spending.

[12] "How Ban On 500 and 1,000 Rupee Notes Could Hit Uttar Pradesh Election," *NDTV*, November 17, 2016.

[13] "How Ban On 500 and 1,000 Rupee Notes Could Hit Uttar Pradesh Election," *NDTV*, November 17, 2016.

Schulz, and Vig, 2014). This winner's premium is greater for incumbents and more seasoned candidates as well as for ministers, and it is more pronounced in states with a reputation for high levels of corruption (Fisman, Schulz, and Vig, 2014). Incumbents' reported asset growth is also higher if minerals are mined in their district, especially when global prices are high (Asher and Novosad, 2020). Such patterns are unlikely to emerge if the data had no relation to reality. As Cox and Thies (2000) put it in a different context: "Simply put, if these data have been fabricated, they have been fabricated so as to preserve a number of expected correlations and even to fit the theories of political scientists – which does not seem too likely" (Cox and Thies, 2000, 45).

The second reason the affidavits are likely to be truthful is that the accuracy of the data is thought to be higher for state-level members of legislative assemblies (MLAs), the population I study in this chapter. MLAs face intense scrutiny in their comparatively small constituencies. V. B. Singh, a former director of a Delhi-based research institute, states that "[i]t is hard for MLAs to hide details of their assets because of the localised nature of their politics."[14] Consistent with this assessment, Fisman, Schulz, and Vig (2019) show that the introduction of the disclosure requirement led to a 13-percentage-point decrease in incumbents running for reelection when their *second* affidavit was due to be submitted. They provide evidence that those who decided not to run for reelection likely had more to hide rather than more qualms about lying. This means that many politicians preferred not running again to either revealing their (presumably large) asset growth or, more relevant here, to lying about its true magnitude. This suggests that politicians take the disclosure requirement seriously.

Finally, unlike previous studies, I am not interested in the growth of politicians' *overall* assets. Instead, I examine changes in the different asset categories *relative to each other*. Even if some candidates underreport their total wealth, it is unlikely that they would do so selectively in some categories, and that the choice of which categories to underreport depends on their electoral campaign environment.[15] If a consistent picture of different growth rates in different assets emerges, we can be confident that it is not the result of systematic measurement error.

---

[14] "MLAs Getting Richer Faster than MPs," *Business Standard*, November 1, 2014.
[15] Of course, it may be easier to hide wealth in some categories than in others. However, this is constant across MLAs and does not depend on their campaign environment.

Data Characteristics

To analyze the development of the different asset categories during a legislative period, I use pairs of affidavits from re-contesting incumbents for state legislative assemblies.[16] I examine MLAs' disclosure statements at the end of a legislative period, just before they run for reelection, and compare it to the statement they submitted just before the previous election. The first set of affidavits is from 2005 to 2009 and the second is from 2010 to 2014, giving a sample of 2,493 MLAs from 27 states.[17]

The left panel of Figure 4.2 displays basic descriptive statistics of the candidates' assets in the first and second affidavits. The total asset value of the median candidate in the first affidavit is roughly Rs6.4 million (about $155,000 given exchange rates in 2007). In the second affidavit, it is Rs17.6 million. A legislative term is usually five years, so this amounts to an annual increase of about Rs2.25 million. Even taking into account that the average inflation rate between 2005 and 2014 was over 8 percent, this is a large increase in wealth.

As mentioned, the affidavits categorize politicians' assets into detailed categories, which I group as follows: cash; bank deposits, bonds, debentures, and shares in companies; national savings scheme (NSS) and postal savings, as well as Life Insurance Company of India (LIC) and other insurance policies; motor vehicles; jewelry; agricultural and non-agricultural land; commercial and residential buildings.

The right panel of Figure 4.2 plots the mean growth from the first to the second affidavit in the various asset categories. Mean total assets increased by 139 percent. However, this masks considerable heterogeneity across different types of assets. The largest growth was in the

---

[16] Because wealth development can only be inferred for the subset of incumbents who run for reelection, it is not possible to test the effect of the legal and electoral campaign environments on the option to engage in self-enrichment and not run again (Path 4 in Figure 3.1).

[17] The following elections are included: Andhra Pradesh (2009 and 2014), Arunachal Pradesh (2009 and 2014), Assam (2006 and 2011), Bihar (2005 and 2010), Chattisgarh (2008 and 2013), Goa (2007 and 2012), Gujarat (2007 and 2012), Haryana (2009 and 2014), Himachal Pradesh (2007 and 2012), Jharkhand (2009 and 2014), Karnataka (2008 and 2013), Kerala (2006 and 2011), Madhya Pradesh (2008 and 2013), Maharashtra (2009 and 2014), Manipur (2007 and 2012), Meghalaya (2008 and 2013), Mizzoram (2008 and 2013), Nagaland (2008 and 2013), Odisha (2009 and 2014), Punjab (2007 and 2012), Rajasthan (2008 and 2013), Sikkim (2009 and 2014), Tamil Nadu (2006 and 2011), Telangana (2009 as part of Andhra Pradesh and 2014), Uttarakhand (2007 and 2012), Uttar Pradesh (2007 and 2012), and West Bengal (2006 and 2011). I exclude politicians with very low assets (less than Rs100,000 in the first election).

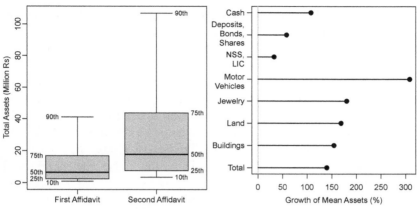

FIGURE 4.2 *Assets of Indian candidates in the first and second affidavits.* Left panel: The black bar denotes total assets of the median legislator. The gray box shows total assets of legislators in the 25th and 75th percentiles, and the whiskers of those in the 10th and 90th percentiles. Right panel: For each category, the line shows the percentage growth from the mean value in the first affidavits to the mean value in the second affidavits. NSS = National Savings Scheme, postal savings; LIC = Life Insurance Corporation of India, other insurance policies

motor vehicles category, with mean assets increasing by 308 percent. This was followed by jewelry (180 percent), agricultural and non-agricultural land (169 percent), and commercial and residential houses and buildings (154 percent). Mean cash holdings increased by 107 percent, assets in deposits and bonds by 58 percent, and money in savings schemes and insurance policies (NSS and LIC) by 33 percent. In the next section, I examine whether MLAs' *electoral campaign environment* influences which categories of assets they increased.

4.3 ELECTORAL SECURITY, SELF-ENRICHMENT, AND CAMPAIGN SPENDING IN INDIA

In Chapter 3, I argued that politicians decide how to best use the money they accumulate during their term in office, and that the electoral campaign environment they operate in plays a major role in such decisions. I hypothesized that incumbents with greater a priori electoral security invest less in their electoral campaigns; and as a second-order effect they have more leeway for self-enrichment. This means that the expected closeness of the upcoming election should influence how incumbents decide to use the money they have accumulated. Candidates who know they are likely to be in a close race in India's first-past-the-post system will want to spend more on their campaign, whereas those who are more secure have more room for personal enrichment.

The key empirical challenge is measuring a priori competitiveness. Ideally, I could analyze preelection district-level polling data. Since such information is not available, I use several alternative strategies in this chapter. I start by using the past as a guide to the future: MLAs who were elected in a landslide are more likely to be electorally secure than those who eked out a narrow win. Thus, the higher the margin with which an incumbent won office, the more they should be able to dedicate themselves to personal enrichment; the smaller their margin of victory, the more they should accumulate cash reserves to finance their reelection campaign.

Empirical Approach

To test this prediction, I examine the effect of the margin of victory on subsequent asset development in the various categories. I estimate the following regression for asset type a of legislator i in state s:

$$\log(\text{Final Assets}_{ais}) = \alpha_s + \beta \, \text{Margin}_{is} + \gamma \log(\text{Initial Assets}_{ais}) + \delta' X_{is} + \varepsilon_{is}$$
$$(4.1)$$

That is, I regress the logged value of all assets in category a (say, the value of all the buildings MLAs own) in the second affidavit on the margin of victory with which they won the first election, the logged value of the assets in the first affidavit, and a set of controls X_{is}.[18] To avoid dropping MLAs who reported zero in any category, I add 1,000 to the initial and final assets before taking the log. Note that I estimate a separate intercept α_s for each state to account for any observed and unobserved differences between them.

However, the margin of victory is obviously not random. Candidates who won by different margins likely also differ in other ways. To address this potential problem, I pre-process the data using a matching approach

---

[18] The controls are i's total initial log assets, a dummy indicating whether the candidate had any criminal convictions or criminal cases pending against them, their gender, age, education level, whether they belonged to a scheduled caste or scheduled tribe, as well as the log number of voters in their constituency, the level of turnout, and the log number of candidates (all in the initial election). I exclude a small number of outliers who won office with a margin larger than 50 percent.

(see Ho et al., 2007). The goal is to weight the observations such that incumbents with different winning margins are similar to each other on other observable characteristics. Of course, we cannot know whether the matching also achieves balance on unobserved variables, so it does not solve the problem entirely.

Because the margin of victory is continuous, I rely on the Covariate Balancing Propensity Score (CBPS) method (Imai and Ratkovic, 2014; Fong, Hazlett, and Imai, 2018). This approach seeks to balance the covariates in order to minimize the weighted correlations between the margin of victory and all observed variables. The weights that achieve this are then used when estimating Equation (4.1). I match on all covariates included in X_{is} as well as log assets in each category from the first affidavit. After re-weighting the observations, all correlations between the outcome of interest and the covariates are close to zero. The CBPS weighting thus effectively breaks the link between the independent variable of interest and the observed covariates.

Electoral Security Leads to Less Campaign Spending and More Personal Enrichment

Table 4.1 shows the effect of the margin of victory on subsequent asset development in each category. Each coefficient comes from a separate regression, where the first column uses the unweighted sample and the second column uses the weights from the CBPS approach. For readability, control variables are not displayed.

The first row reports the effect of the margin of victory on the development of MLAs' *cash* reserves over the following legislative period. Consistent with the argument that less electorally secure incumbents must acquire larger cash reserves to spend on their reelection campaigns, the coefficient is negative and significant. Using the weighted sample, a one-percentage-point increase in an MLA's margin of victory leads to a 0.9 percent *decrease* in his or her subsequent cash holdings, all else equal and controlling for initial cash assets. Note that this does not imply that safer incumbents have less cash in the second affidavit than in the first; most legislators report an increase. The results instead mean that electorally more secure MLAs increase their cash reserves to a lower extent than their less secure counterparts.

This effect is of substantial magnitude. A one-standard-deviation increase in the winning margin (8.7 percentage points) leads to a growth in cash assets that is 8 percent lower, compared to a baseline cash asset

TABLE 4.1 *Effect of margin of victory on asset development in India.*
Coefficients of the margin of victory on log asset values in the second
affidavit, controlling for log asset values in the first affidavit. All
coefficients come from separate regressions. Controls not displayed

Cash	Unweighted	CBPS
Margin of Victory	−0.00679**	−0.00926**
	(0.00302)	(0.00330)

Deposits, Bonds, Shares	Unweighted	CBPS
Margin of Victory	0.00761**	0.00628*
	(0.00358)	(0.00383)

NSS, LIC	Unweighted	CBPS
Margin of Victory	0.00596	−0.00039
	(0.00603)	(0.00651)

Motor Vehicles	Unweighted	CBPS
Margin of Victory	−0.01585**	−0.01924***
	(0.00643)	(0.00706)

Jewelry	Unweighted	CBPS
Margin of Victory	0.00162	−0.00325
	(0.00374)	(0.00435)

Land	Unweighted	CBPS
Margin of Victory	−0.00628	−0.00617
	(0.00569)	(0.00570)

Buildings	Unweighted	CBPS
Margin of Victory	0.01151**	0.01026*
	(0.00551)	(0.00603)

Total	Unweighted	CBPS
Margin of Victory	0.00148	−0.00030
	(0.00175)	(0.00188)

$^*p < 0.1$, $^{**}p < 0.05$, $^{***}p < 0.01$. N = 2,493 for each regression. All regressions
include state fixed effects and control for initial log assets overall and in the
specific category. Additional controls: Criminal conviction dummy, gender, age,
education, log number of electors, turnout, number of contesting candidates (all
in the first election). Robust standard errors in parentheses. NSS = National Savings Scheme, postal savings; LIC = Life Insurance Corporation of India, other
insurance policies.

growth of 107 percent. Going from the lowest winning margin in my sample to the highest corresponds to 45 percent lower cash asset growth.

In contrast, a one-percentage-point increase in the winning margin *increases* the assets held in *bonds, deposits, and shares* by roughly 0.7 percent. Incumbents who are electorally more secure are more likely to prefer accumulating wealth in these long-term assets. A one-standard-deviation increase in the winning margin implies 5.5 percent higher growth in this category, and a move from the sample minimum to the maximum leads to 31 percent higher growth, given a baseline increase of 58 percent. Investment in national savings schemes, postal savings, and insurance policies (NSS and LIC) does not change based on the margin of victory, likely because holdings in these forms change little over time in the sample.

Electoral security affects the value of the *motor vehicles* owned by an MLA and his or her family. A one-percentage-point increase in the victory margin leads to a 1.6–1.9 percent *decrease* of the stated value in the second affidavit. A one-standard-deviation increase in the winning margin thus means asset growth in this category is expected to be about 16.5 percent lower. Based on the assumption that cars are used for personal enjoyment, we would expect asset growth in this category to be higher for MLAs who won by a larger margin, but the opposite is true. There are two ways to interpret this finding. One possibility is that even electorally precarious incumbents engage in some form of self-enrichment. After all, it makes sense to hedge against losing reelection by accumulating at least some personal wealth (see Figure 3.7). It might also be more practical to do so via one-off purchases such as cars rather than taking on long-term commitments like real estate, which are more expensive and harder to hold on to if their income drops due to leaving office.

However, owning a number of cars may also be helpful to candidates fighting for reelection. Vaishnav (2017) relays the following account of a visit by Bihar MLA Anant Singh to a rural village:

Our quiet gossiping was abruptly interrupted by the sound of car engines approaching. Soon a convoy of ten or so high-end SUVs roared into the village, and Singh hopped out of one of the cars, sauntering over to the group accompanied by several burly-looking men and a well-armed bodyguard (Vaishnav, 2017, 182).

A fleet of expensive cars therefore helps candidates to project a certain image to voters. In addition, the distribution of cash and gifts occurs mostly in the forty-eight to seventy-two hours before election day. Owning a number of cars makes it easier to reach as many localities as possible during this crucial time window. Thus, a greater increase in the value of motor vehicles among electorally vulnerable candidates may also reflect an attempt to beef up their campaign operations.

For the next two categories, jewelry and land, electoral security again has no significant effect. It does, however, have a sizable influence on the last asset type – commercial and non-commercial *buildings*. For each additional percentage point in the margin of victory, the value of an MLA's real estate *increases* by 1 to 1.1 percent. This is a sizable effect in accordance with the theoretical argument that more secure incumbents have leeway to grow their personal assets. A one-standard-deviation increase in the winning margin is associated with a roughly 9 percent increase in the reported value of buildings, and moving from the sample minimum to the maximum corresponds to a 50 percent increase, given a baseline growth of 154 percent.

Finally, the last row in Table 4.1 shows that the margin of victory has no effect on *total* asset growth. This addresses a potential objection to the findings, since one might suppose that more electorally secure incumbents accumulate more assets overall. However, incumbents who won by a narrow or wide margin do *not* differ in *how much* their assets increase during a legislative period; they only differ in *how* they increase.

Taken together, the Indian asset disclosure affidavits show that less secure incumbents increase their holdings of cash and motor vehicles. More secure incumbents instead accumulate more deposits and bonds as well as houses and buildings. The results of this first empirical analysis are thus consistent with the argument I made in Chapter 3: An incumbent's electoral campaign environment, particularly how competitive they expect their reelection race to be, influences whether they have the leeway to enrich themselves personally, or whether they invest more into their campaign.

4.4 REDISTRICTING, SELF-ENRICHMENT, AND CAMPAIGN SPENDING IN INDIA

The first analysis has shown that the growth of different asset categories predictably reacts to the margin by which MLAs won office. However, while the CBPS weighting broke the link between the treatment and observable covariates, it is still possible that these results are confounded by unobserved differences related to the margin of victory. I therefore conduct a second analysis, in which I examine how a shock to incumbents' reelection chances affects how they use the money they have access to.

In 2008, MLAs' constituencies were redrawn for the first time in more than forty years, which meant that incumbents competed in different areas than previously. Name recognition and credit for constituency service thus decreased; voters in new areas of the incumbent's district knew little about them and had to be won over. In other words, more redistricting increases electoral competition. As a consequence, affected incumbents should spend more on campaigning. And as a second-order effect, this should give them fewer opportunities to engage in personal enrichment.

The 2008 Delimitation Process

In the early years of the Indian republic, constituencies were regularly redrawn to reflect the country's changing demographics. Delimitation commissions were set up after the censuses of 1951, 1961, and 1971. During the authoritarian "emergency" period between 1975 and 1977, however, Indira Gandhi's government passed a constitutional amendment suspending the process. Due to differential birth and death rates as well as migration, constituency sizes became unequal over time, resulting in significant malapportionment (Delimitation Commission of India, 2008; Bhavnani, 2018). For example, two neighboring parliamentary constituencies in Delhi had populations of 0.35 and 3.1 million, respectively. In 2003 another constitutional amendment was passed to allow redistricting to resume based on the 2001 census.

India's redistricting process is designed to be non-political. The 2003 delimitation commission was headed by Kuldip Singh, a retired Supreme Court judge, and included the chief election commissioner as well as the respective state election commissioners. While political parties were consulted, their influence was limited. There was no political controversy over the redistricting process, and systematic analyses confirm that it was mostly non-partisan (Iyer and Reddy, 2013).

This was partly because the commission operated under strict guidelines and was expected to "remove the gross inequalities in the population size of the Constituencies, on the principle of 'One vote and one value'" (Delimitation Commission of India, 2008, 1). The commission was tasked with creating districts that were of approximately equal size, subject to a number of conditions: They had to be geographically compact and contiguous, all state assembly constituencies had to wholly lie within administrative districts, and the number of constituencies could not be altered. This meant the commission had to draw up constituencies of roughly equal size within districts, which left limited opportunities for political gerrymandering.

Empirical Approach

Of the twenty-seven states in my data, eleven held the election for which the first affidavit was submitted pre-delimitation and the one for which the second affidavit was submitted post-delimitation.[19] This allows me to exploit variation in the degree to which incumbents were affected by redistricting, and to examine the impact it had on their asset development in different categories.

It is difficult to determine the exact extent to which delimitation affected sitting MLAs. To date, there has been no successful effort to link old and new state-level boundaries to census data for the entire country, or even for more than a few states. To proxy for the extent of redistricting, I exploit the fact that constituencies were of different sizes before 2008, and that the primary goal of delimitation was to equalize the population in each district. This means that MLAs in pre-delimitation constituencies that were larger or smaller than the district average were more affected by redistricting (see also Fisman, Schulz, and Vig, 2019). Indeed, population deviation from the district average is highly predictive of the extent of redistricting in the states for which direct data is available (Iyer and Reddy, 2013).

I estimate the following regression for the states in the sample affected by delimitation:

$$\log(\text{Final Assets}_{ais}) = \alpha_s + \beta \, \text{Redistricting}_{is}$$
$$+ \gamma \log(\text{Initial Assets}_{ais}) + \delta' X_{is} + \varepsilon_{is} \qquad (4.2)$$

where I proxy for the extent of redistricting in two ways. First, I take the absolute difference between the pre-delimitation constituency size and the average constituency size in the district (in 100,000). Second, I compute the absolute percentage deviation of the constituency relative to the district average. Figure 4.3 shows a map of the distribution of this second variable for the re-contesting incumbents in the eleven states. I again add 1,000 to the initial and final assets before taking the log, and the controls in X_{is} are the same as above.[20] I estimate separate intercepts for each state to account for any observed and unobserved differences.

---

[19] These states are: Bihar, Goa, Gujarat, Himachal Pradesh, Kerala, Meghalaya, Punjab, Tamil Nadu, Uttar Pradesh, Uttarakhand, and West Bengal.

[20] Because the crucial piece of information for the delimitation propensity is constituency size, I drop that control variable.

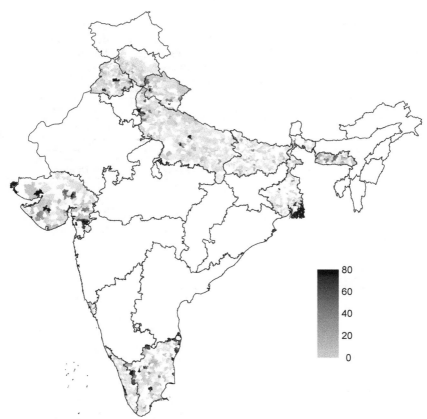

FIGURE 4.3 *Extent of redistricting between elections in eleven Indian states.*
Absolute percentage deviation of the pre-delimitation constituency size relative
to the district average. Black indicates a larger percentage; light gray indicates a
smaller percentage. Entirely white states were not redistricted between the two
elections included in the data. White areas in states that are included in the
sample indicate that the incumbent did not run for reelection and therefore did
not submit a second affidavit

Redistricting Leads to More Campaign Spending
and Less Personal Enrichment

Table 4.2 shows the effects of the two proxies for the extent of redistricting on asset development in the various categories. Higher values
for the redistricting variables indicate greater changes in an incumbent's
constituency. Again, each coefficient comes from a separate regression
and the results for the control variables are not displayed for ease of
readability.

TABLE 4.2 *Effect of redistricting on asset development in India.* Coefficients of the propensity of being affected by delimitation on log asset values in the second affidavit, controlling for log asset values in the first affidavit. All coefficients come from separate regressions. Controls not displayed

Cash	*Population Difference*	*Percentage Difference*
Redistricting	0.11970***	0.00314**
	(0.04641)	(0.00144)

Deposits, Bonds, Shares	*Population Difference*	*Percentage Difference*
Redistricting	0.00848	−0.00110
	(0.05600)	(0.00203)

NSS, LIC	*Population Difference*	*Percentage Difference*
Redistricting	0.05681	0.00093
	(0.11179)	(0.00311)

Motor Vehicles	*Population Difference*	*Percentage Difference*
Redistricting	−0.15086	−0.00533
	(0.13809)	(0.00394)

Jewelry	*Population Difference*	*Percentage Difference*
Redistricting	0.06462*	0.00234*
	(0.03628)	(0.00125)

Land	*Population Difference*	*Percentage Difference*
Redistricting	−0.25760**	−0.00883**
	(0.12992)	(0.00437)

Buildings	*Population Difference*	*Percentage Difference*
Redistricting	0.05902	0.00153
	(0.07462)	(0.00232)

Total	*Population Difference*	*Percentage Difference*
Redistricting	0.02154	0.00062
	(0.03087)	(0.00093)

$^*p < 0.1$, $^{**}p < 0.05$, $^{***}p < 0.01$. N = 1,166 for each regression. All regressions include state fixed effects and control for initial log assets overall and in the specific category. Additional controls: Margin of victory, criminal conviction dummy, gender, age, education, turnout, number of contesting candidates (all in the first election). Robust standard errors in parentheses. NSS = National Savings Scheme, postal savings; LIC = Life Insurance Corporation of India, other insurance policies.

The first row displays the results for *cash* reserves. For both specifications, the effect is positive and significant. The larger the expected changes to an MLA's constituency, the *more* cash reserves they accumulate between the two elections. Based on the second model, for each percentage point that an incumbent's constituency deviates in size from the district average, they increase their cash holdings by 0.3 percent. A one-standard-deviation change in the redistricting variable is associated with a 6.9 percent increase in cash assets. This effect size is roughly comparable to the one of a standard deviation change in the initial margin of victory found in the previous section.

The extent of redistricting does not affect holdings of bank deposits, bonds or shares, NSS and LIC policies, or motor vehicles. However, it has a positive effect on how much *jewelry* an MLA holds: A one-percentage-point deviation in constituency size from the district average leads to a 0.2 percent increase in the value of the incumbent's jewelry. Again, this is possibly the result of an "insurance" mechanism: While electorally precarious incumbents invest more in their campaign to try to keep their seat, they also make some one-off purchases for themselves and their families. However, the result is only significant at the 10 percent level.

Being affected by more redistricting has a large *negative* effect on how much *land* an MLA reports holding in the second affidavit, controlling for its value in the first disclosure. Again, this does not mean they have lost land, but that their assets in this category grew by a smaller amount. For each percentage-point deviation from the district average, land value decreases by around 0.9 percent. This means that a one-standard-deviation shift in the variable amounts to about 19 percent less land holdings in the second affidavit, controlling for holdings in the first affidavit. There is no effect on buildings. Finally, the extent to which a legislator is affected by redistricting has no effect on total asset development.

Thus, the results of this second, independent analysis are again in line with my theoretical predictions. Incumbents who expect more competitive elections accumulate larger cash reserves, which are crucial for campaigning. This in turn has consequences for other uses of money in politics. Specifically, it comes at the expense of growth in long-term assets for personal use, such as land or buildings. Taken together, this first set of analyses thus has shown that self-enrichment in office and campaign spending are directly, and inversely, linked to each other.

4.5 MONEY AND POLITICS IN BRAZIL

In many ways, Brazil is similar to India when it comes to money and politics. Between 2017 and 2020, it ranked between 94th and 106th out of 180 in the Corruption Perceptions Index and 121st to 134th out of 209 in the Control of Corruption Indicator. Corruption scandals have also rocked Brazilian politics, particularly "Operação Lava Jato" (Operation Car Wash). What began in 2014 as a minor investigation into money laundering at a gas station in Brasília became a record-setting inquiry that has implicated dozens of politicians, including multiple presidents.[21] And while this is the most eye-catching case, it is by no means the only one. In 2016, almost 60 percent of the members of the lower and upper houses faced charges or were investigated for corruption and other serious crimes.[22]

Also like in India, this glut of corruption cases led to a significant protest movement. On March 15, 2015, 2.4 to 3 million people took to the streets. A year later, after a new round of corruption allegations against leading politicians, 3.6 to 6.9 million demonstrated against the government.[23] According to surveys, corruption ranked as the most important issue among voters (Jucá, Melo, and Rennó, 2016), and played a significant role in helping the populist Jair Bolsonaro become president in 2019 (Hunter and Power, 2019).

But again, money does not solely enter politics for politicians to enrich themselves. Parties are weak and do not provide voters with strong partisan cues, so campaigns are highly individualized. A strong link has been identified between money spent and votes gained (Samuels, 2001*b*), and the country's elections are among the most expensive in the world (Samuels, 2001*c*). The 2014 elections cost more than $3 billion.[24] As a consequence, "Brazil newspapers report in complete seriousness that elections serve as a strong boost to local economies, principally in the country's poorer regions" (Samuels, 2001*a*, 32).

---

[21] "What is the Petrobras Scandal that is Engulfing Brazil?," *Financial Times*, April 1, 2016.

[22] "The Politicians Voting to Impeach Brazil's President are Accused of More Corruption than She Is," *Los Angeles Times*, March 28, 2016.

[23] "Mapa das Manifestações no Brasil, Domingo, 15/03," *Globo*, March 15, 2015; "Mapa das Manifestações Contra Dilma, 13/03," *Globo*, March 13, 2016.

[24] "Petrobras Corruption Case Overshadows Brazil Presidential Campaign," *Los Angeles Times*, October 24, 2014.

A political operator in one of Rio's favelas reports: "People drive from one candidate to another, shopping around. ... Election time is a time to make money. Everybody around here knows that."[25]

Corporations have traditionally provided most of the campaign money; they in turn receive a good return on their investment. Claessens, Feijen, and Laeven (2008) show that companies that make larger campaign contributions have higher stock returns. Boas, Hidalgo, and Richardson (2014) demonstrate that firms that specialize in public works projects and donate to a federal candidate from the ruling party who wins office can expect to receive contracts worth fourteen times their contribution. Samuels (2002) argues that legislators only spend time and effort to secure "pork" because this helps them raise campaign funds from firms. In addition, politicians often use their own financial resources to fund their campaigns (see e.g. Avis et al., 2021). In response to the corruption scandals engulfing the country, in 2015 the Supreme Court banned all corporate campaign contributions. Starting with the 2016 municipal elections, candidates could only raise money from private persons or self-finance their campaign.

The picture that emerges from these studies is quite similar to the one we saw in India. Money and politics are inexorably intertwined in Brazil, and politicians use it for their personal enrichment as well as to finance their reelection campaigns. Are the two connected, and can the balance between them in this context also be explained by the factors identified in Chapter 3?

4.6 DATA ON ASSETS AND CAMPAIGN SPENDING IN BRAZIL

Major improvements in transparency are often the consequence of major scandals (Rose-Ackerman and Palifka, 2016, ch. 13). In 1992, Brazilian President Fernando Collor de Mello resigned from office after being implicated in a corruption scheme. A few months later, ten members of parliament were dismissed in a separate corruption scandal (Fleischer, 1996; Praça and Taylor, 2014; Jucá, Melo, and Rennó, 2016; Speck, 2016). In response, Congress significantly overhauled the country's campaign finance legislation and transparency requirements. Campaign contributions to candidates had been illegal up to that point, but were

---

[25] "Brazil's Favela Dwellers are Cashing in on Campaign Season," *PRI*, October 3, 2014.

happening anyways, as they still do in India. Such donations were legalized in 1994, and were subject only to generous limitations. The new regulations allowed individuals and candidates to donate up to 10 percent of their yearly gross income to political campaigns. Corporations could give up to 2 percent of their gross annual revenues. In addition, all candidates for office were now required to submit information on all contributions and campaign expenditures. These declarations are made publicly available.[26]

In addition to their campaign contributions and spending, candidates also have to publicly disclose specific details about their personal assets, including their estimated value. For example, candidates have to list the addresses of apartments and houses, the make and license plate numbers of cars, and so on. Figure 4.4 shows an example of a mayoral candidate's campaign finance report (top) and his asset declaration (bottom) from the 2016 election.

The fact that Brazilian candidates for office have to disclose both their personal assets and campaign spending allows for a more direct test of the effect of political competitiveness on the choice between personal enrichment and campaign spending than was possible using the Indian data.

Of course, one may again wonder how accurate the filings are. Just like the affidavits from India, the Brazilian data exhibit the basic pattern one would expect. For example, they show that Brazilian campaigns are extremely expensive, that candidates of right-wing parties report higher contributions and expenditures than those of left-wing parties, and that spending is higher in municipalities located near oil fields (Samuels, 2001c; Bhavnani and Lupu, 2016; Mancuso et al., 2016). There is also a positive correlation between reported contributions and vote shares (Samuels, 2001b), and companies that donate more to winning candidates of the governing party receive more government contracts (Boas, Hidalgo, and Richardson, 2014). Finally, both the reported personal assets and the reported campaign spending are higher for white candidates (Bueno and Dunning, 2017). Taken together, the data again conform to our theoretical expectations, which suggests that they are broadly accurate.

Assets and Campaign Spending of Brazilian Mayors

To examine the effect of the electoral campaign environment, particularly the level of political competitiveness, on the balance between personal

---

[26] For further details, see, e.g., Samuels (2001c); Jucá, Melo, and Rennó (2016); Speck (2016).

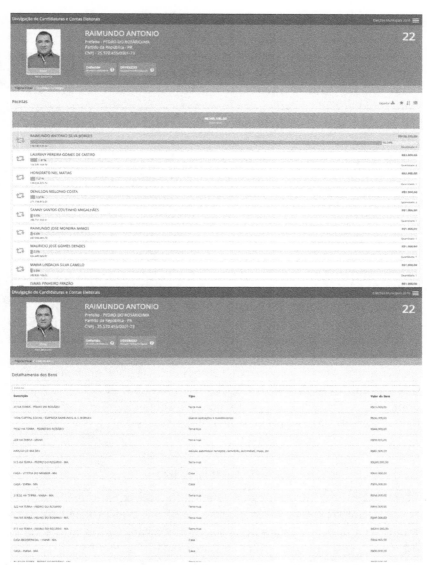

FIGURE 4.4 *Example of campaign finance and asset declaration from Brazil.*
Listing of campaign finance sources (top) and asset declaration (bottom) filed by
Raimundo Antonio, a candidate of the Partido da República for the 2016
mayoral election in Pedro de Rosário municipality in the state of Maranhão

enrichment and campaign spending, I focus my analysis on municipal
mayors. Because Brazil is one of the most decentralized countries in the
world, municipal governments oversee large public budgets and have

significant power. The transfers from the federal government to municipalities amount to $35 billion per year (Ferraz and Finan, 2011). In fact,
the position is so attractive that many members of the national legislature
have the ambition to become mayors. A member of Brazil's lower house
interviewed by Samuels (2003) observed: "In a chamber of 513, a deputy
can't stand out. ... Whereas as a mayor, even of a medium-sized city, he's
the boss. He is the power, he has the power of the pen" (Samuels, 2003,
22).

Focusing on this level of government has a number of advantages.
First, much of the literature on money and politics in Brazil also examines
municipal mayors (Ferraz and Finan, 2008, 2011; Brollo, 2013; Hidalgo,
Canello, and Lima-de-Oliveira, 2016; Avis et al., 2021). Furthermore,
parties at the municipal level are even weaker than at the national level,
so local campaigns are mostly about the candidates themselves (Klašnja
and Titiunik, 2017). This brings the choice between personal and political
money especially into focus. Finally, there are thousands of municipalities
in Brazil, which allows me to assemble a large dataset on the campaign
spending and personal asset development of incumbent politicians.

I focus on two legislative cycles, 2008–2012 and 2012–2016. Since
Brazilian mayors are limited to two consecutive terms in office, I focus
on incumbents who are participating in the one reelection campaign they
are permitted. For each politician, I collect data on how much money they
received and spent on their campaigns.[27] Note that in Brazil, campaign
donations received and campaign money spent correlate almost perfectly.
I also assemble data on politicians' personal assets.

Data Characteristics

There were 1,394 sitting mayors running for reelection in the first cycle.
For this sample, the reported asset value of the median mayor in 2008
was R$203,000 (roughly $125,000 given exchange rates at the time).
After four years in office, this had increased by around 75 percent to
R$358,000. This is less than was the case for Indian MLAs, even after
taking into account that the average annual inflation rate was lower in
Brazil (around 5.5 percent from 2009 to 2012). Campaign spending of
the median mayor was R$42,920 (about $27,000) in 2008 and R$45,240
in 2012. The top row of Figure 4.5 shows other percentiles of declared
assets and campaign money.

[27] This includes candidate self-finance.

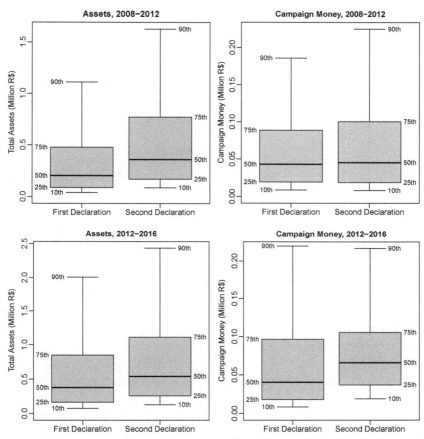

FIGURE 4.5 *Assets and campaign money of Brazilian candidates in the first and second declarations.* The gray box shows total assets or campaign money of legislators in the 25th and 75th percentiles, and the whiskers of those in the 10th and 90th percentiles

For the second cycle, there is data for 1,223 mayors. The median asset value in 2012 was R$377,300, which increased by roughly 45 percent to R$539,000 in 2016. Median campaign spending was R$40,500 in 2012 and R$66,510 in 2016. The bottom row of Figure 4.5 illustrates the other percentiles.

4.7 ELECTORAL SECURITY, SELF-ENRICHMENT, AND CAMPAIGN SPENDING IN BRAZIL

The data on personal assets and campaign contributions for Brazilian mayors allows me to directly test the connection between money used for personal or electoral purposes, and the impact that electoral competitiveness has on it. Mayors who have reason to think they will be re-elected relatively comfortably have leeway to use their position to enrich themselves. By contrast, mayors who expect to be in a competitive race for reelection should prioritize campaign spending. As I did for India, I use a politician's margin of victory in the previous election to proxy for the expected competitiveness of the upcoming race.

Empirical Approach

To analyze the effect of the margin of victory on subsequent asset development, I estimate the following regression for mayor i in state s during cycle c:

$$\log(\text{Final Assets}_{isc}) = \alpha_s + \mu_c + \beta \, \text{Margin}_{isc}$$
$$+ \gamma \log(\text{Initial Assets}_{isc}) + \delta' X_{isc} + \varepsilon_{isc} \qquad (4.3)$$

I regress the logged value of all assets in the second disclosure on the mayor's initial margin of victory and the logged value of the assets in the first disclosure.[28] A set of controls is denoted by X_{isc}.[29] To account for region-specific observed and unobserved differences, I estimate a separate intercept α_s for each state. I also include a cycle-specific fixed effect μ_c to control for differences over time. For political money, the regression is analogous to Equation (4.3), with the log campaign money that was raised and spent as the dependent variable.

To account as much as possible for the fact that politicians with different margins of victory might differ from each other in other ways, I again pre-process the data using CBPS matching. This reduces the correlations between the margin of victory and the observed covariates to nearly zero, so coming close to breaking the link between them.

Electoral Security Leads to Less Campaign Spending and More Personal Enrichment

Table 4.3 shows the effect of the margin of victory in the first election on asset development and campaign money. The first column uses the

---

[28] I add 1,000 before taking the log and exclude a small number of outliers who won with a margin of larger than 50 percent. In addition, municipalities with more than 200,000 registered voters have a runoff election if no candidate receives a majority of the votes. This only affects a small number of politicians in my sample (seventeen). I drop these observations, but the results are robust to including them.

[29] They are age, gender, civil status, education, and the log of campaign contributions received in the first election.

TABLE 4.3 *Effect of the margin of victory on asset development and campaign money in Brazil.* Coefficients of the margin of victory on log asset values and log campaign money in the second election. All coefficients come from separate regressions. Controls not displayed

Assets	Unweighted	CBPS
Margin of Victory	0.00343**	0.00355**
	(0.00155)	(0.00158)

Campaign Money	Unweighted	CBPS
Margin of Victory	−0.00313**	−0.00344**
	(0.00157)	(0.00169)

$^*p < 0.1$, $^{**}p < 0.05$, $^{***}p < 0.01$. N=2,617 for each regression. All regressions include state and election cycle fixed effects and control for initial log assets and donations. Additional controls: Gender, age, education, civil status, log number of electors (all in the first election). Robust standard errors in parentheses.

unweighted sample, and the second one the CBPS-weighted one. Each coefficient comes from a separate regression, and control variables are omitted for brevity.

The first line reveals that more electorally secure incumbents do indeed increase their personal assets to a larger degree. A one-percentage-point increase in a mayor's initial margin of victory is associated with a 0.35 percent *increase* in reported assets. The point estimates are similar for both specifications and reach statistical significance at the 5 percent level.

A one-standard-deviation increase in the winning margin (10.2 percentage points) is associated with a 3.6 percent increase in personal assets. Going from the lowest winning margin in my sample to the highest means personal asset growth is expected to be 17.8 percent higher. These effects are smaller than in the Indian case. However, note that the baseline asset growth in the two cycles I examine was only 75 and 45 percent, respectively. Thus, the effects are again of substantial magnitude.

In contrast, the winning margin has a negative effect on campaign spending. Each percentage-point increase in the winning margin is associated with a 0.34 percent *decrease* in campaign money. A one-standard-deviation increase therefore implies 3.5 percent less campaign spending, and going from the minimum to the maximum means 17.8 percent less. Thus, mayors who won by a relatively comfortable margin see an opportunity to take their foot off the gas, at least relative to their colleagues who won by a smaller margin and expect a tough fight for reelection. This gives them the leeway to instead augment their personal assets.

The analysis of Brazilian mayors thus comes to the same conclusion as the one of Indian state assembly members. There is clear evidence that campaign spending and personal enrichment are directly, and inversely, connected. Incumbents who expect to be in a tight race for reelection place more emphasis on campaign spending, whereas those who have an easier road to reelection have greater freedom to use their position to benefit themselves financially. Taken together, the data from India and Brazil provide support for the argument that campaign spending and personal enrichment in office are directly related to each other, and that the *electoral campaign environment* plays an important role in determining which is more prevalent.

4.8 CAMPAIGN FINANCE REGULATION AND ASSET GROWTH IN BRAZIL

In Chapter 3 I argued that another factor that determines how money enters politics is the *legal environment*, and that politicians arbitrage differences in how tightly the types of money in politics are regulated. If laws forbid one form, politicians will create a second-order effect by seeking to benefit from their position through a *different* channel. In this section I exploit a change in Brazilian campaign finance regulations to test this hypothesis. In response to the fallout from Operation Car Wash, a law passed in 2015 mandated limits on the overall amount that candidates can spend. Did this have the unintended side effect of increasing personal enrichment among politicians?

Campaign Spending Limits in the 2016 Mayoral Elections

Before 2016, there was no cap on the total amount that mayoral candidates could spend. This changed in September 2015, when Brazil's Congress passed a law that imposed a spending limit. The first elections for which the law applied were the municipal elections of October 2016.

Brazil's 5,570 municipalities differ in size and economic development. According to 2014 population estimates, the smallest municipality had just over 800 inhabitants (Serra da Saudade in Minas Gerais). The country's largest city, São Paulo, has almost 12 million inhabitants. The amount that candidates spend on campaigning thus inevitably varies greatly. The law takes this into account by conditioning the

2016 limits on the amount spent on the previous election campaign, in 2012.

To determine the caps, there are two relevant clauses in the law.[30] First, the limit for mayoral candidates in a given municipality was set to R$100,000 or 70 percent of the highest amount spent by a candidate in 2012, whichever is higher. This creates a kink in the limit for 2016. In any municipality in which the highest-spending candidate spent less than R$142,858 (70 percent of 142,858 is around 100,000), the limit was set to R$100,000. Above this number, the cap increases linearly.

Second, a few months after the law was passed, the limits were adjusted to take inflation into account. Two different rates were used for municipalities to the left and right of the kink, which creates a discontinuity. For those that were limited to R$100,000, the adjustment was set to 8.04 percent. For municipalities for which the limit was determined according to the 70 percent of the previous maximum spending criterion, the inflation adjustment was 33.7 percent. This means that a municipality in which the maximum spending in 2012 was just under R$142,858, the 2016 limit was R$108,039. But for a municipality where the 2012 maximum spending was just over R$142,858, the limit was about R$133,700, so around 24 percent higher. The left panel of Figure 4.6 displays these limits.

The right panel of Figure 4.6 plots the reported campaign expenditures in 2016 against the highest amount spent by a candidate in a municipality during the 2012 election. The jump in the limit at the 2012 maximum spending of R$142,858 is clearly visible. Some candidates report greater spending than is allowed. This is possible because exceeding the cap results in heavy penalties, including a 100 percent fee on spending above the limit, but does not result in disqualification (cf. Avis et al., 2021). However, only about 0.6 percent of candidates violate the cap.

Avis et al. (2021) exploit the discontinuity to examine the effect of campaign finance restrictions on various indicators of political competition. They find that such limits increase the number of candidates running for office and decrease incumbents' reelection rates. These findings, as well as Figure 4.6, suggest that the imposed limits were binding for many candidates. Without them, they could (and would) have spent more money on their campaigns. So what happened to the money that was *not* spent because of this imposed ceiling?

---

[30] See "Lei N° 13.165," *Presidência da República, Secretaria-Geral, Subchefia para Assuntos Jurídicos*, September 29, 2015; Avis et al. (2021).

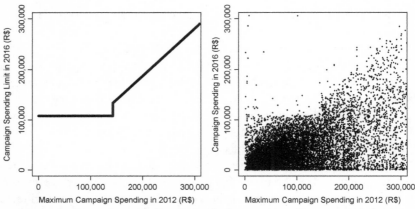

FIGURE 4.6 *Campaign spending limits in the 2016 Brazilian mayoral elections.*
Left panel: Campaign spending by the highest-spending candidate in 2012 and
campaign spending limit in 2016. There is a discontinuous jump at a 2012
maximum spending of R$142,858, where the 2016 limit increases by about 24
percent. Right panel: Campaign spending by the highest-spending candidate in
2012 and campaign spending by candidates in 2016

One of the key empirical implications of Chapter 3 was that where
penalties for self-enrichment are low, as they are in Brazil, stricter campaign finance regulation frees up incumbents to use their position to
enrich themselves while in office. The theoretical expectation is therefore that incumbents who were more restricted in their election spending
(left of the discontinuity) augmented their personal assets more than those
with a more generous expenditure cap (right of the discontinuity).

Campaign Spending Limits Lead to More Personal Enrichment

To assess the effect of spending limits on the growth of personal assets,
I exploit the discontinuous jump of the ceiling at the 2012 maximum
spending of R$142,858 in a regression discontinuity design. The idea
underlying this strategy is that municipalities with maximum spending in
the previous election just above and just below the threshold are very similar on all characteristics that could affect personal asset growth, except
for the fact that the latter have a higher campaign spending limit. For
example, municipalities with higher maximum spending in 2012 are more
likely to be large and wealthy, which may make it easier for incumbents
to enrich themselves. However, municipalities where maximum spending
was around R$142,000 are, on average, very similar to those where it was

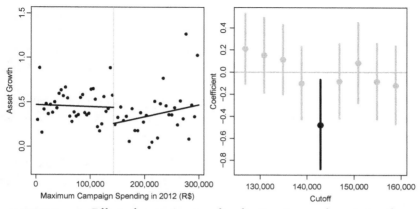

FIGURE 4.7 *Effect of campaign spending limit on personal asset growth, Brazilian mayoral elections 2016.* Left panel: Campaign spending by the highest-spending candidate in 2012 is on the horizontal axis. Binned estimates of personal asset growth from 2012 to 2016, with two separately fitted lines to the left and right of the cutoff at R\$142,858, is on the vertical axis. Right panel: Point estimate and 95 percent confidence interval of the treatment effect of a higher campaign spending limit on personal asset growth is in black (N=1,965, bandwidth=35,896). Gray bars indicate placebo treatment effects where the cutoff is set at lower or higher values (in increments of R\$4,000) than where the discontinuity occurred

R\$143,000. Essentially by chance, candidates in the former can spend less on campaigning than those in the latter. In other words, the assignment of municipalities located near the cutoff to a high or low spending ceiling is as good as random.[31]

The left panel of Figure 4.7 plots binned estimates of asset growth as a function of 2012 maximum spending, with two separately fitted lines to the left and right of the cutoff at R\$142,858. As hypothesized, there is a clear drop in personal asset growth where the campaign spending limit jumps.[32] Incumbents just to the left of the vertical line are subject to stricter campaign finance rules, which gives them scope to grow their personal assets. Those just to the right of the line can spend more on their reelection campaign, which leaves them less room for personal enrichment. Note that since candidates can be self-financed, it is plausible

---

[31] Avis et al. (2021) demonstrate the validity of the regression discontinuity design in this application. They show that there is no evidence of endogenous sorting around the threshold and no discontinuous jumps at the cutoff for other covariates such as economic development, inequality, or population.

[32] The discontinuity is also present when using higher-order polynomials.

that mayors with looser campaign spending caps spent more of their own assets on their campaign, whereas those with stricter limits did not (have to) do so. This is consistent with my theoretical argument, as those to the left of the discontinuity can use the unspent money for themselves, while those on the right cannot.

To assess the impact of campaign spending limits on personal asset growth around the discontinuity in a regression, I estimate the following model for incumbent i in municipality m (where $i = m$):

$$\text{Asset Growth}_i = \alpha + \beta \ \text{Higher Limit}_m + f(\text{Max. 2012 Spending}_m) + \varepsilon_i$$

$$(4.4)$$

The dependent variable is the change in personal asset value from 2012 to 2016.[33] Higher Limit$_m$ is an indicator that takes a value of 1 if the 2012 maximum campaign spending was R\$142,858 or more. The quantity of interest is β, which is expected to be negative. The term $f(\text{Max. 2012 Spending}_m)$ is a function of the running variable that determines the treatment status, fitted separately to the left and right of the discontinuity. I use a first-order local polynomial.[34] To select the optimal bandwidth for the window around the discontinuity, I use the automated procedure implemented by Calonico, Cattaneo, and Titiunik (2014).

The right panel of Figure 4.7 displays the results. In black, it shows the treatment effect β from Equation (4.4) along with the 95 percent confidence interval. Confirming the graphical analysis, there is a significant drop in the growth of personal assets for incumbents subject to higher campaign spending limits.

In gray, I also display the results of a series of placebo tests in which the cutoff is not set at R\$142,858 but at lower or higher values, in increments of R\$4,000. If it is the discontinuous jump of campaign spending limits that caused the drop in the growth of personal assets, we should *not* see significant treatment effects if the cutoffs are set to values at which no such jump occurred. And indeed, the coefficients are not significantly different from zero in any of the placebo regressions. This provides confidence that the lower personal enrichment I observe is indeed caused by the more generous campaign spending limits.

Thus, a country's *legal environment* also strongly influences how money enters politics. Politicians arbitrage differences in how strictly

---

[33] To limit the possibility that outliers are driving the results, I exclude incumbents who had very large (more than threefold) increases in their personal assets.

[34] Results are robust to using higher-order polynomials.

the types are regulated. Therefore the consequences of, say, campaign finance regulations are not straightforward. It is true that they reduce campaign spending. But at the same time, I have shown here that this has second-order consequences on politicians' propensity to use their office for personal enrichment.

4.9 SUMMARY

In this chapter, I have begun the difficult task of testing the theory I put forward in Chapter 3. I focused here on the connection between personal enrichment in office and spending on election campaigns.

The main challenge of empirically examining these two forms of money in politics is, naturally, the lack of available data. Politicians who engage in potentially illegal, or at the very least immoral, acts have little interest in making it easy to detect them. We therefore have to use creative techniques to detect patterns of money in politics. I conducted three separate analyses, exploiting the fact that both India and Brazil require all candidates for office to disclose certain financial details.

First, I used the level of detail in the Indian affidavits to differentiate between assets that signal personal enrichment and cash holdings that are likely meant for campaign spending. Less electorally secure incumbents, identified in two different ways, report higher growth in their cash assets, while their more secure counterparts tend to increase the value of the land and buildings they own.

Second, candidates in Brazil also have to publish the value of their personal assets, as well as their complete campaign finances. This allowed me to directly test the influence of electoral security on whether politicians use their position to accumulate personal or political money. Again, the empirical results are consistent with the theoretical expectations from Chapter 3. The more secure an incumbent is likely to be, the more their personal assets grow while in office. The less secure they are, the higher their reported campaign spending.

Finally, I have shown that legal restrictions on one form of money have second-order effects on other types, which move in the opposite direction. Using a discontinuous jump in campaign spending limits in Brazil's 2016 mayoral elections, I demonstrated that stricter regulation gives incumbents more opportunities for self-enrichment.

Taken together, these analyses provide clear and consistent evidence that campaign money and personal enrichment are directly linked to each other, and that the legal and electoral campaign environments determine which is more prevalent in a given context. I now move from the low-regulation environments of India and Brazil to an environment that more strictly regulates money in politics. In many countries, the penalties for enrichment in office are so severe that it has been all but eradicated. But this does not mean that money no longer enters politics; nor does it remove the choice between personal financial gain and enjoying the benefits of holding office.

5

The Connection between Campaign Spending and Golden Parachute Jobs

At first glance, the situation of money in politics in the United States is very different from that in India or Brazil. It is certainly not the norm that US legislators enrich themselves to the tune of millions of dollars while in office. Of course, it happens on occasion, but the consequences tend to be swift and severe. For example, former Illinois Governor Rob Blagojevich was secretly recorded seeking to extract personal benefits from potential candidates to fill Barack Obama's Senate seat after he was elected president. Within weeks of announcing in graphic language that he would not "give it away for nothing," Blagojevich was arrested, impeached, and barred from ever holding public office in the state again. After two trials, he was convicted on seventeen charges and sentenced to fourteen years in prison.[1] Systematic investigations of US congresspersons have also found no evidence that their financial situation improves in an unusual manner *while* they are in office (e.g. Eggers and Hainmueller, 2013, 2014).[2]

Yet, US politicians *do* have opportunities to benefit financially from their position. The main difference from Brazil or India is that they can usually do so only *after* they leave office. As many as half of all members leaving Congress subsequently register as lobbyists (Lazarus, McKay, and Herbel, 2016). A similar percentage serve on one or more boards of directors (Palmer and Schneer, 2016). In fact, golden parachute jobs are so common that the satirical newspaper *The Onion* responded to the announcement that the devout Christian representative Michele

---

[1] He was pardoned in 2020 by President Trump.
[2] Eggers and Hainmueller (2013, 2014) show that members of Congress' stock portfolios do not grow in an unusual manner.

Bachmann would not seek reelection with an article titled "Michele Bachmann: 'God Wants Me to Earn 7 Figures for a Lobbying Firm'."[3]

Prior studies explain golden parachute jobs as a result of special interest groups' demand for expertise or political connections (cf. de Figueiredo and Richter, 2014). And while this is certainly part of the story, it cannot explain why these jobs exist in the first place. The practice is almost unheard of in many other countries where expertise and connections are just as important as in the United States. What is more, in this chapter I show that there are large differences even *within* the United States in how common such employment is. In Chapter 3, I argued that golden parachute jobs should be seen as part of a larger interconnected system of money in politics. I reasoned that this form of money in politics is directly, and inversely, related to campaign spending, and that the relative importance of the two types is driven by a country's legal and electoral campaign environments.

In this chapter, I test these claims using microlevel data from the United States, the setting of most past studies of both forms of money. In a first step, I examine the effect of the *legal environment* on the prevalence of campaign spending and golden parachute employment. Most prior research has focused on golden parachute jobs at the national level, where there is no variation in regulation.[4] I address this limitation by analyzing state legislatures, the members of which are governed by different rules at different times. Using information from state disclosure agencies, I assemble the first dataset that permits a comparative analysis of golden parachute employment by tracking whether state legislators left office and subsequently took up a lobbying position. I also make use of the detailed campaign finance disclosure data that candidates in the United States must provide.

I exploit the fact that states differ in how stringent their campaign finance laws are, as well as their golden parachute restrictions. According to my argument, these regulations should affect not only the type of money they regulate but also have *second-order* consequences for the *other* form. That is, campaign finance regulation should impact golden parachute employment, and golden parachute restrictions should in turn affect the flow of campaign money into politics.

---

[3] "Michele Bachmann: 'God Wants Me to Earn 7 Figures for a Lobbying Firm'," *The Onion*, May 29, 2013.

[4] For an exception, see Cain and Drutman (2014).

To assess campaign finance laws, I analyze the consequences of a US Supreme Court ruling that introduced an exogenous change to the strictness of campaign finance regulation in some states, but not others. Consistent with the theoretical predictions detailed in Chapter 3, I show that states with more permissive campaign finance laws after the ruling, which resulted in an increase in campaign spending, saw fewer lawmakers taking up golden parachute jobs. Then I study the consequences of golden parachute rules for campaign finance. Many states have introduced "cooling off" laws that restrict how soon politicians can register as lobbyists after leaving office. Exploiting the differential timing of the changes to these laws, I show that such restrictions (1) reduce the probability that legislators will take up a golden parachute job *and* (2) lead to an increase in campaign contributions.

Finally, I analyze the effect of the *electoral campaign environment*. As I argued in Chapter 3, electoral competitiveness (or changes thereof) should influence how attractive staying in office is relative to leaving and taking up a golden parachute job. As I did for India in the previous chapter, I use the extent of redistricting as a shock to competitiveness. Consistent with my argument, I find that more extensive redistricting makes incumbents more likely to accept a golden parachute job.

5.1 MONEY AND POLITICS IN THE UNITED STATES

A 2015 poll revealed the extent to which Americans are fed up with the role that money plays in political campaigns: 84 percent of respondents said money had too much influence; 66 percent were convinced that wealthy people had more influence over elections than other Americans; and 55 percent thought that most of the time, politicians promote the policies of those who donated to their campaigns.[5]

US elections are notoriously expensive. In 2010, candidates for the House of Representatives first broke the billion dollar threshold. Expenditures have increased since then, to more than $1.9 billion in 2020.[6] In 2018, the average winner spent about $2.1 million; the most expensive campaign of that cycle was that of Georgia Democrat Jon Ossoff, which cost just over $30 million. Races for the Senate are even more costly. The average winner in 2018 spent about $15.8 million. Rick Scott of Florida

---

[5] "Americans' Views on Money in Politics," *New York Times*, June 2, 2015.
[6] In the United States, this money typically comes mostly from campaign donors (external sources), or from candidates self-financing their campaigns.

set that year's record by spending $83.5 million. Overall expenditures for Senate races reached a new record in 2020 of more than $2.1 billion.[7]

As staggering as these figures are, they are only the tip of the iceberg. Spending on presidential campaigns easily eclipses the total outlays of races for the House and Senate. The 2020 presidential contest cost more than $6.6 billion.[8] In addition, there are ninety-nine state legislatures with many thousands of candidates, and even local races can involve substantial amounts of money. For example, the candidates in the 2017 mayoral race in Syracuse, New York, a city of less than 150,000 in population, spent more than $1.3 million, a not atypical sum.[9]

On top of this direct spending by candidates, *indirect* election spending must also be taken into account. Private citizens, corporations, and unions can advertise for or against the election of candidates *independently* of politicians or parties. This kind of spending exploded after the Supreme Court ruled in 2010 that restrictions on such activities violated the right to free speech and were therefore unconstitutional (Spencer and Wood, 2014). In 2016, independent campaign spending exceeded $1.5 billion for federal elections alone (Abdul-Razzak, Prato, and Wolton, 2020). Local races have also been affected. For example, outside groups spent almost $15 million on the 2017 elections of the Los Angeles *school board*, translating to more than $110 per vote cast.[10]

But campaign spending is not the only way in which money enters politics in the United States. Many politicians also take up golden parachute employment – often as lobbyists. For example, ex-House Majority Leader Dick Gephardt retired from Congress in 2005. He subsequently joined the lobbying firm DLA Piper before setting up his own practice in 2007. His roster of clients included companies like Goldman Sachs, Boeing, and Visa. In 2010, he billed them more than $6.5 million. The same year, former Republican Representative Billy Tauzin earned more than $11.5 million from his clients, setting a new record for ex-politicians.[11]

While Gephardt and Tauzin are at the higher end of the earnings scale, their career paths are not exceptional. A comprehensive analysis

---

[7] "Elections Overview," *Center for Responsive Politics*; "Election Trends," *Center for Responsive Politics*.

[8] "2020 Election to Cost $14 Billion, Blowing Away Spending Records," *Center for Responsive Politics*, October 28, 2020.

[9] "Crowded Syracuse Mayor's Race Was Most Expensive in History at $1.3M," *syracuse.com*, December 6, 2017.

[10] "How L.A.'s School Board Election Became the Most Expensive in US History," *Los Angeles Times*, May 21, 2017.

[11] "The Trouble With That Revolving Door," *New York Times*, December 18, 2011.

by Lazarus, McKay, and Herbel (2016) shows that around a third of representatives and about half of senators leaving office find employment as lobbyists. Even Walt Minnick, the former congressman we met right at the start of this book who lamented how much time he had to spend raising campaign donations, started his own lobbying firm.[12]

Another lucrative path for former politicians is to join corporate boards of directors. In fact, senators and state governors are more likely to serve as a board member than to be registered as lobbyists (Palmer and Schneer, 2019). These positions are part time and come with a generous salary, on average about $250,000 per year (Palmer and Schneer, 2016). For example, Dick Gephardt not only brought in millions through his lobbying activities, he also served as a director for Ford, Spirit Aerosystems, Dana, Centene, Embarq, and US Steel.[13]

The United States is thus the prime example of money in the form of campaign spending, and its politicians also often benefit financially from their position, although only after leaving it. So far, these two forms of money in politics have been treated separately. In this chapter, I study their connection.

5.2 GOLDEN PARACHUTE JOBS AS A TYPE OF MONEY IN POLITICS

Considering golden parachute jobs in the same framework as campaign contributions and self-enrichment in office is unusual. Indeed, the social science literature on the so-called revolving door has treated such jobs as a separate phenomenon. The main question it investigates is why corporations and interest groups hire former politicians (and their staffers) as lobbyists or in other functions such as members of their board of directors.

One line of studies argues that organizations that hire former politicians gain access to their expertise. People who have spent many years in politics are intimately familiar with the lawmaking process. In addition, many legislators develop subject-matter expertise in policy areas they specialize in. Several studies contend that corporations are more likely to hire legislators who have more knowledge (Salisbury et al., 1989; Heinz et al., 1993; Esterling, 2004; Parker, 2008). An alternative view is that former legislators not only gain expertise during their time in office, they also get to know many important people. Corporations may thus hire

---

[12] "Former Rep. Minnick Blazes His Own Trail," *The Hill*, June 5, 2012.
[13] "Gephardt, Earley Join Ford's Board Of Directors," *Gephardt Group*, March 25, 2009.

ex-politicians because it allows them to tap into their network of connections. A growing body of studies finds support for this motivation (Hillman, 2005; Blanes i Vidal, Draca, and Fons-Rosen, 2012; Bertrand, Bombardini, and Trebbi, 2014; LaPira and Thomas, 2014, 2017).

While this debate has advanced our understanding of golden parachute employment, it has two characteristics that have insulated it from scholarly work on other forms of money in politics. First, it almost exclusively uses data from the United States, and more specifically Congress. Because this is a single institutional environment (or, if we want to be generous, two environments), the only variation available for analysis is *between* subjects: Why are some legislators hired while their colleagues are not? Prior studies have therefore taken it as a given that golden parachute jobs exist, and try to explain who gets one and who does not (and why). A second characteristic is that in trying to explain this variation, the focus has been on the employers' motivation – the *demand side* of golden parachute employment. Previous research has thus implicitly assumed that there is a pool of politicians willing to leave office, and that corporations hire those with the qualities that further their interests the most; the debate is about what exactly those qualities are.

This human capital account does not explain why golden parachute jobs exist in the first place. While it is true that there are plenty of politicians in the contemporary US Congress who are happy to take up private sector employment, this is not the case everywhere and at all times. Whereas Mayhew (1974) described members of Congress in the 1970s as behaving like single-minded seekers of reelection, Tennessee Representative Jim Cooper's view of his colleagues in 2012 was markedly different: "Serving the public used to be considered the highest calling; now, many see it as a stepping stone to lucrative lobbying careers."[14] Demand-side arguments cannot easily explain why this change occurred, as presumably politicians in the past also had expertise and connections that were valuable to the private sector.[15] The same is true for cross-sectional

---

[14] "Cooper First to Sign 'No Lobbying' Pledge," *Jim Cooper Press Release*, September 17, 2012.

[15] LaPira and Thomas (2017) explain the rise of politicians-turned-lobbyists in the United States with the increased demand for such services due to a decline in government capacity to address public problems and the increase in importance and coherence of political parties. However, these trends are unique to the US context. They do not translate to European countries, for example, where parties have become *weaker* over time (e.g. Dalton and Wattenberg, 2002; Van Biezen, Mair, and Poguntke, 2012), while golden parachute jobs have become much more common as well.

differences. In addition to the United States, golden parachute employment has been documented in places such as the United Kingdom, Ireland, and Germany (González-Bailon, Jennings, and Lodge, 2013; Dörrenbächer, 2016; Baturo and Arlow, 2018), but it is notably absent in many other countries (see Chapter 6). And as I show later in the text, there are even large differences between US states. Again, it seems unlikely that special interests need expertise or connections in some countries or states, but not in others.

In other words, while explanations based on politicians' expertise and connections have provided valuable insights into which lawmakers *within* a legislature are most likely to take up golden parachute employment, they have difficulty explaining differences *between* legislatures. Why do many legislators leave behind careers in public service to cash in through a private sector job in some contexts, while in others it rarely or never happens? In Chapter 3, I argued that to answer this question, we need to think about golden parachute jobs as part of the broader system of money in politics, and how it is influenced by the legal and electoral campaign environments. Here, I test this argument.

5.3 DATA ON GOLDEN PARACHUTE EMPLOYMENT IN US STATES

In this section, I introduce the data that for the first time makes it possible to study golden parachute jobs in a *comparative* manner. I do so by shifting from the national level, which has been the setting of almost all prior studies on the topic, to the subnational level. US state legislatures exhibit heterogeneity in both their legal and electoral campaign environments, which allows me to test the theoretical argument laid out in Chapter 3.

Collecting data on golden parachute employment is challenging (cf. Dal Bó and Finan, 2018). Lawmakers who leave politics return to being private citizens, so in many cases there is no public record of when they take up a new job. Some countries require former politicians to register their employment for a certain period of time after leaving office. However, these disclosure requirements usually only apply to a small number of high-level public officials and not to regular members of parliament (MPs) (cf. Weschle, 2021*b*). One can try to reconstruct lawmakers' career paths after leaving office using newspaper articles, internet searches, and the like. This works well for high-level officials who remain in the public spotlight, but is unlikely to be sufficient for analyzing MPs at the national or subnational level. Previous research using such an approach has indeed focused on presidents, prime ministers, or central bankers (e.g. Adolph, 2013; Musella, 2015; Baturo and Mikhaylov, 2016; Dörrenbächer, 2016; Baturo, 2017).

To study golden parachute jobs for ordinary lawmakers, researchers have instead exploited disclosure requirements that apply to some other activity, but that as a byproduct reveal their employment. For example, publicly traded corporations have to publish the names of the members of their board of directors. By matching these names with lists of former lawmakers, one can obtain data on one way in which golden parachute employment manifests itself. This approach has been used for MPs in the United Kingdom (Eggers and Hainmueller, 2009; González-Bailon, Jennings, and Lodge, 2013) as well as for US senators and governors (Palmer and Schneer, 2016, 2019).

Another strategy is to exploit the fact that politicians-turned-lobbyists account for much golden parachute employment, particularly in the United States. Since lobbyists have to register, it is again possible to match their names with those of former legislators. This has been done for both the US Senate and the House of Representatives (Lazarus, McKay, and Herbel, 2016).

I follow the latter approach when looking at golden parachute employment in US states. While this does not capture all jobs, it likely covers the majority of them. Palmer and Schneer (2019) find that high-profile ex-politicians, such as cabinet members, governors, or senators, are more likely to join boards of directors than to become lobbyists. However, lower-profile ex-politicians, such as former members of the US House of Representatives, are much more likely to become lobbyists. It therefore stands to reason that former state representatives, who have an even lower profile, are unlikely to move into board of director positions.

I assemble new data that tracks whether state legislators left office and subsequently took up a lobbying position. Following the convention in the literature, I exclude Nebraska from the sample due to its unusual unicameral, non-partisan legislature. Information on lobbyists comes from the states' lobbyist registries for the years 2006–2013, compiled by the National Institute on Money in State Politics.[16] Many individuals register to lobby at the state level: Their number ranges between 41,134 and 45,151 per year, and totals 112,190 unique individuals during the

---

[16] See www.followthemoney.org.

observation period.[17] The most lobbyists are registered in New York (4,801 lobbyists per year, on average), Arizona (3,559), and Florida (2,351). Wyoming (282), Maine (263), and Alaska (142) have the fewest. Information on state legislators comes from the State Legislative Election Returns dataset (Klarner, 2013; Klarner et al., 2013). Based on the elections to the lower chambers from 2006 to 2012, there were 8,349 state representatives in the 49 states (4,050 Democrats, 4,299 Republicans).

To link the legislator data with the lobbyist information, I use a two-step procedure that minimizes both false positive and false negative matches. First, I employ an algorithm that coarsely matches names between the lists.[18] I allow the name matches to have considerable divergence to ensure that people who appear in the two lists with slightly different names are still linked. For example, it matches a former New Jersey representative who appears as "Kamin, Dick" in the election data, but who is registered as a lobbyist under "Kamin, C Richard." This, of course, leads to a large number of false positives. For example, it matches "Kenny, Bernard F. Jr." and "Flynn, Bernard M." which clearly are not the same person. In a second step, I therefore check all matches manually. If there are doubts about a match, for example if it is a common name, I use supplementary information from internet searches to check whether they are indeed the same person.

This allows me to create a variable that captures how many legislators take up golden parachute jobs as lobbyists. The unit of observation is the legislator-election cycle. Since elections for state lower houses take place every two years, there are four time periods: 2006–2007, 2008–2009, 2010–2011, and 2012–2013. For each cycle, a politician is considered to have taken a golden parachute job if they leave office and register as a lobbyist in their state the same or the following year.[19]

The new data for the first time makes it possible to compare how common golden parachute employment is in each state. Figure 5.1 maps the

---

[17] Definitions of what constitutes a lobbyist differ somewhat between states, as do the registration requirements (de Figueiredo and Richter, 2014). In the analysis, I account for any state-level differences, so they are not a threat to inference.

[18] I use a measure based on the Levenshtein distance, which is a string metric for quantifying the difference between two sequences. Intuitively, it is the minimum number of insertions, deletions, or substitutions required to change one sequence into the other. To make them comparable, I use the following similarity measure: $1 - (d(s1, s2)/max(A, B))$, where d is the Levenshtein distance function, $s1$ and $s2$ are the two strings, and A and B are their lengths.

[19] Lazarus, McKay, and Herbel (2016) show that the overwhelming majority of golden parachute lobbyists at the federal level register within one year of leaving office.

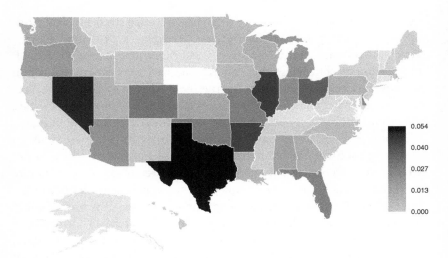

FIGURE 5.1 *Golden parachute employment in US state lower chambers,*
2006–2013. Proportion of representatives who leave office and register as
lobbyists in the same or following year in each election cycle. Darker colors
indicate a greater share. Nebraska (white) is excluded from the sample

proportion of representatives in each election cycle who leave office and
subsequently register as lobbyists in each state. Darker shading indicates
that golden parachute jobs are more common. The map reveals large
differences between states.

The practice is most common in Texas, where on average 5.4 percent of
sitting representatives take up a lobbying job in each election cycle. This
may not sound like much at first. However, since an election cycle is only
two years, it implies that more than a quarter of Texas representatives
leave office and become lobbyists over the course of a decade. Also note
that this is the probability *unconditional* on leaving office. Other studies
and news stories often report the probability of becoming a lobbyist *con-*
ditional on leaving office, which for the US Congress is between 30 and
50 percent. However, the unconditional probability at the federal level is
roughly the same as in the state legislatures in which it is most common.[20]

Other states in which movement from the state house to a lobbying
position is roughly as common as at the federal level are Nevada (5.1

[20] Lazarus, McKay, and Herbel (2016) report that in 2008, roughly 60 of the 435 members
departed the House of Representatives, so about 14 percent. Of these, around 40 percent
subsequently registered as lobbyists. This implies an unconditional probability of 5.5
percent, which is roughly the same as in the Texas state legislature.

percent), Illinois (4.6 percent), and Arkansas (4.5 percent). There are four states in the data (Alaska, Connecticut, Kentucky, and South Dakota) in which no legislators registered as lobbyists in the year of leaving office or the next year during the period of observation.

5.4 CAMPAIGN FINANCE REGULATION AND GOLDEN PARACHUTE EMPLOYMENT

Is golden parachute employment part of the system of money in politics? If it is, I have argued that the *legal environment* should play an important role, since politicians arbitrage variation in how strictly the different forms are regulated. The crucial implication of this is that a change in regulation not only affects the type it applies to, it also has second-order consequences for other types. Here, I show that this is the case for *campaign finance regulation.*

The Impact of *Citizens United* on States' Campaign Finance Laws

The Supreme Court ruling that significantly changed American campaign finance started out as a relatively narrow lawsuit that challenged some provisions of the 2002 Bipartisan Campaign Reform Act (BCRA), also known as the McCain–Feingold Act. This law had imposed a number of restrictions on "electioneering communication," which are TV or radio advertisements that target voters and refer to candidates for federal office, but do not explicitly advocate for or against their election. The BCRA mandated that such ads could not be funded by contributions from corporations or unions. It therefore imposed similar restrictions on electioneering communication as were already in place for "express advocacy" – campaign advertisements that directly advocate for or against the election of a specific candidate.

In 2008, the conservative nonprofit organization *Citizens United* produced a movie critical of Hillary Clinton and wanted to distribute it via TV on demand. Because the movie was classified as electioneering communication and had been financed by corporate donations, this was prohibited by the BCRA. The group thus challenged the ban on corporate and union spending on this type of communication, and the lawsuit made its way to the Supreme Court. After the oral argument, the court surprised litigants and observers by announcing that it would rehear the case. Instead of narrowly focusing on the provisions of the BCRA challenged by *Citizens United*, it would instead revisit "more than twenty years of established campaign finance precedent" (Spencer and Wood, 2014, 327) and *also* review the ban on independent expenditures for express advocacy.

After the second oral argument, the court in early 2010 ruled with a narrow 5–4 majority that not only were the BCRA's restrictions on electioneering communication unconstitutional but that those affecting express advocacy, which had been in place since 1973, were as well. This allowed corporations and unions to henceforth spend unlimited amounts of money on campaign advertisements, as long as this was done *independently* of candidates. In practice, however, the rules regulating the relationship between campaigns and organizations that carry out this independent spending, such as Super PACs or 501(c)(4) groups, are neither strict nor well enforced. For example, candidates can endorse and attend events organized by "their" Super PAC, which tend to be run by former staffers (Spencer and Wood, 2014; Dawood, 2015). There is also at least anecdotal evidence that politicians outsource much of their campaign activity to such groups, and that they explicitly solicit donations on their behalf.[21]

The Supreme Court ruling was met with widespread condemnation. President Obama alleged that it gave a "green light to a new stampede of special interest money in our politics."[22] A *New York Times* article stated that "[t]he Supreme Court has handed lobbyists a new weapon,"[23] and *Newsweek* called the ruling "the most serious threat to American democracy in a generation."[24] The importance of the *Citizens United* decision was magnified three months later, when the US District Court for the District of Columbia additionally decided in *SpeechNow.org vs. FEC* that individuals as well as organizations were allowed to contribute unlimited amounts to groups that make independent expenditures. Taken together, these two rulings meant that lawmakers across the United States were suddenly confronted with dramatically looser campaign finance regulations.

The lawsuit in *Citizens United vs. FEC* only challenged federal law. However, the Supreme Court ruling by extension also applied to any

---

[21] "Scott Walker, the John Doe Files and How Corporate Cash Influences US Politics," *The Guardian*, September 14, 2016.

[22] "Landmark Supreme Court Ruling Allows Corporate Political Cash," *Reuters*, January 21, 2010.

[23] "Lobbyists Get Potent Weapon in Campaign Ruling," *New York Times*, January 22, 2010.

[24] "Alter: The Roberts Court Radicals," *Newsweek*, January 22, 2010.

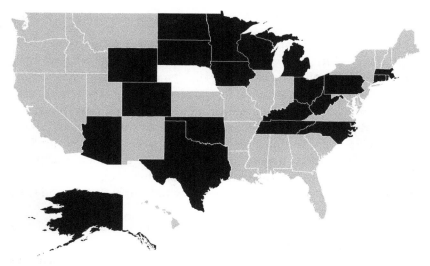

FIGURE 5.2 *Impact of Citizens United on the states.* States affected by the Supreme Court's *Citizens United* ruling in black; unaffected states in gray. Nebraska (white) is excluded from the sample

state laws that limited or prohibited independent expenditures by corporations or unions. In a stroke of good luck for social scientists, some states had laws on their books that were affected, whereas others never had any restrictions on independent campaign spending to begin with. Figure 5.2 shows the twenty-one states that were affected by the Supreme Court ruling. The relevant laws were either directly repealed by the legislatures or invalidated and not enforced by the states' campaign finance bodies. The other twenty-nine states did not have laws affected by the ruling.[25]

This allows me to analyze the consequences of this ruling using a difference-in-differences design. I can examine how the variables of interest changed in states that were "treated" by the Supreme Court ruling compared to the "control group" of those that were not impacted. This makes it possible to isolate the effect of the change in campaign finance laws and separate it from secular trends in campaign expenditure and golden parachute employment.

---

[25] The results are robust to plausible alternative definitions of the set of treated states. For details, see Weschle (2021*a*).

Less Restrictive Campaign Finance Laws Increase Campaign Spending

The *first-order consequence* of the more permissive campaign finance regime after *Citizens United* should be an increase in campaign spending. And indeed, the ruling led to a stampede of money flowing into elections. In the pre-ruling 2008 election campaign, independent expenditures at the federal level totaled $143.7 million. Four years later, post-ruling, they amounted to more than $1 billion, about seven times as much. And in 2016, independent spending increased by a further 37 percent to $1.38 billion.[26] This almost tenfold growth illustrates that there was a willingness to spend money on elections that had been kept in check by the laws the Supreme Court struck down (see also Hansen, Rocca, and Ortiz, 2015; Hansen and Rocca, 2019).

Of course, many other aspects of American politics changed from 2008 to 2016 that could have contributed to this trend. For example, wealthy individuals such as Charles and David Koch increased their political engagement, including through independent campaign spending (see e.g. Hansen, Rocca, and Ortiz, 2015; Mayer, 2016; Skocpol and Hertel-Fernandez, 2016). To address these potential confounding factors, prior studies have turned to state-level analyses, exploiting the fact that *Citizens United* only applied to some of them (see Figure 5.2).

Tracking independent campaign spending is difficult, as disclosure laws vary by state and many of them do not require even basic transparency.[27] Studies therefore have to work with subsets of states for which sufficient information is available. Spencer and Wood (2014) examine independent campaign spending in sixteen states between 2006 and 2010. They find that in 2010, it increased more where *Citizens United* struck down laws than in those where it had no impact. Abdul-Razzak, Prato, and Wolton (2020) compile data from eighteen states and extend the period from 2006 to 2012. They find that in states that were not affected by *Citizens United*, total outside spending increased by 5 percent from before the ruling to afterwards. In states that were affected and had restrictions struck down, outside spending rose by 54 percent. *Citizens United* had

---

[26] "Total Outside Spending by Election Cycle, Excluding Party Committees," *Center for Responsive Politics*.

[27] In an assessment of the laws, the National Institute on Money in State Politics issued twenty-four states a failing grade. See "Scorecard: Essential Disclosure Requirements for Independent Spending, 2014," *National Institute on Money in Politics*, December 3, 2014.

a larger impact on Republicans: independent spending on their behalf increased by 22 percent in unaffected states, and by 95 percent in affected states.

Prior studies have also found that this rise in campaign spending affected incumbents' reelection chances. Consistent with the asymmetric increase in spending for the two parties, the ruling led to an improvement in Republicans' electoral fortunes. In the lower chambers, removing the restrictions increased Republican candidates' chances of being elected by 3–4 percentage points (Klumpp, Mialon, and Williams, 2016; Petrova, Simonov, and Snyder, 2019; Abdul-Razzak, Prato, and Wolton, 2020). Note that this is the aggregate effect across all races, so it does not mean that only Republicans benefited from increased campaign spending on their behalf. As mentioned earlier, outside spending grew more in states affected by the Supreme Court ruling for *both* Democrats and Republicans, only more so for the latter (Abdul-Razzak, Prato, and Wolton, 2020).[28]

Overall, then, loosening campaign finance regulation generated clear *first-order effects*: It increased campaign spending, especially for Republican Party candidates. If my argument is correct, the chain of events set in motion by *Citizens United* does not end here: The increase in campaign spending should be accompanied by a *decrease* in golden parachute employment, especially among Republicans. In the next section, I discuss the empirical approach that allows me to test whether such *second-order effects* indeed occurred.

Empirical Approach

Because *Citizens United* affected some states but not others, its impact on golden parachute employment can be estimated using a difference-in-differences design. The idea is to examine how such employment changed in states that were affected by the Supreme Court ruling (treatment group) compared to those that were not (control group). I compare the difference between the two before and after the intervention by estimating the following regression:

$$y_{ist} = \beta(\text{Ban}_s \times \text{Post-CU}_t) + \mu'Z_{st} + \lambda'X_{ist} + \gamma_s + \delta_t + \xi_s t + \varepsilon_{ist}, \quad (5.1)$$

---

[28] These studies do not find that *Citizens United* had significant first-order effects on upper chambers, so I do not present those results here. Consistent with the previous findings, the ruling did not affect senators' propensity to become lobbyists (see Weschle, 2021a).

where i indicates a legislator, s a state, and t an election cycle. In the main specification, the dependent variable y_{ist} takes a value of one if a legislator leaves office and registers as a lobbyist in the same or the following year. I also estimate models with other dependent variables, which I discuss below. Because the decision of whether to leave politics and become a lobbyist is most relevant for legislators who are up for reelection, I restrict the analyses to incumbents who have reached the end of a legislative term and have to run again to stay in office.[29]

Ban$_s$ is a dummy variable indicating whether state s previously had a ban on independent corporate spending (see Figure 5.2), and Post-CU$_t$ is a dummy that takes the value of one for the post-*Citizens United* election cycles of 2010–2011 and 2012–2013. The quantity of interest is β. State and election cycle fixed effects are denoted by γ_s and δ_t. The former absorb any time-invariant differences between states, such as the size of the legislature or lobbyist registration laws. The latter absorb any common time shocks, such as national trends in partisan support.[30]

There are a number of time-variant differences between states, which are denoted by Z_{st}. They are whether a state has a "cooling off" law that requires ex-politicians to wait for a specified period before they can register as a lobbyist, whether there are term limits, and whether the state has a public campaign finance system.[31] A set of time-variant individual-level covariates is denoted by X_{ist}. They are the number of years a legislator has spent in office, whether his or her party controlled the legislature, and whether he or she held a speaker or party leadership position.

Difference-in-differences regressions require us to make a parallel-trends assumption. That is, we must assume that, absent *Citizens United*, the difference in the dependent variable between states that were affected by it and those that were not would have been the same after 2010 as it was before. To relax this stringent assumption, I include a set of state-specific linear time trends $\xi_s t$ (Angrist and Pischke, 2009).[32] They account

---

[29] This results in a sample of 18,358 legislator-elections. The results are robust to including legislators who have not reached the end of a legislative term (see Weschle, 2021a).

[30] Together, the state and year fixed effects absorb the constituent terms of the interaction effect, Ban$_s$ and Post-CU$_t$.

[31] Sources: "Revolving Door Prohibitions," *National Conference of State Legislatures*; "The Term-Limited States," *National Conference of State Legislatures*; "Public Financing of Campaigns: Overview," *National Conference of State Legislatures*.

[32] There is evidence that the parallel-trends assumption may be violated when studying *Citizens United* (Klumpp, Mialon, and Williams, 2016; Petrova, Simonov, and Snyder, 2019; Abdul-Razzak, Prato, and Wolton, 2020). Therefore, the convention in all studies has been to include state-specific trends.

for secular trends that differ between states and may affect the dependent variable, such as their partisan composition or economic growth. Finally, ε_{ist} is the error term. Following the convention for difference-in-differences estimations with binary dependent variables, I use a linear probability model (see Angrist and Pischke, 2009). Parameter estimates are reported with robust standard errors clustered by state.

Less Restrictive Campaign Finance Laws Decrease Golden Parachute Employment

Table 5.1 displays the *second-order consequences* generated by removing campaign finance restrictions after *Citizens United*. It shows the results from twelve separate models that examine four dependent variables (rows) for three sets of observations (columns). In each case, I only provide the treatment effect and omit all controls for brevity.

First, I focus on the ruling's effect on all legislators combined (first column). In the first model, the dependent variable takes the value of one if a legislator leaves office and registers as a lobbyist in the same or the following calendar year. As predicted, the more permissive campaign finance regime had a clear and significant *negative* effect on politicians' propensity to take up a golden parachute job. Following the court ruling, legislators in the affected states were about 1.9 percentage points *less* likely to leave office and register as a lobbyist than they would have been otherwise. Given the baseline percentages in Figure 5.2, this effect is large in magnitude. Thus, the *first-order increase* in campaign spending after the relaxation of its regulation was accompanied by a *second-order decrease* in golden parachute employment.

The second and third panels in Table 5.1 examine the effect of more permissive campaign finance laws on the two different ways in which legislators can take up golden parachute employment: They can go straight into such a job without running for reelection (voluntary golden parachute), or they can take up a job after an election loss (insurance golden parachute).[33] For voluntary golden parachute employment, the dependent variable takes a value of one if the incumbent did not run for reelection at the end of their term (or resigned in the middle of it) and became a registered lobbyist in the year of leaving office or the next year. The effect of *Citizens United* is again negative, and its magnitude is similar to the one

---

[33] Paths 1 and 3 in Figure 3.1.

TABLE 5.1 *Effect of Citizens United on golden parachute employment.* Coefficients of treatment effect on the probability that a legislator will take up a golden parachute job (overall, voluntary, insurance) or retire without taking on a golden parachute job. Coefficients come from separate regressions. Controls not displayed

Golden Parachute	All	Republicans	Democrats
Citizens United	−0.019***	−0.027**	−0.014**
	(0.007)	(0.013)	(0.007)

Voluntary Golden Parachute	All	Republicans	Democrats
Citizens United	−0.018**	−0.023**	−0.015*
	(0.007)	(0.010)	(0.008)

Insurance Golden Parachute	All	Republicans	Democrats
Citizens United	−0.002	−0.004	0.000
	(0.004)	(0.007)	(0.006)

Non-Golden Parachute Retirement	All	Republicans	Democrats
Citizens United	0.041	−0.026	0.084*
	(0.032)	(0.043)	(0.045)

$^*p < 0.1$, $^{**}p < 0.05$, $^{***}p < 0.01$. N = 18,358 for each model involving all legislators, N = 8,851 for Republican-only models, and N = 9,507 for Democrat-only models. All regressions include state and year fixed effects and state-specific time trends. State-level controls: Cooling off law, term limit law, public campaign finance. Individual-level controls: Years in office, chamber control own party, speaker or leader. Robust standard errors clustered by state in parentheses.

in the first regression, in which the dependent variable combined voluntary and involuntary golden parachute jobs. The Supreme Court ruling thus led to a decrease in the number of politicians who *voluntarily* left office to become lobbyists.

For the insurance path, the dependent variable takes a value of one if the incumbent ran for reelection at the end of their term and became a registered lobbyist the same year or the year after losing their seat. Here, the effect of *Citizens United* is close to zero, so it had no impact on politicians' propensity to become lobbyists after failing to win reelection. This null effect is not too surprising, since insurance golden parachute jobs can only be observed if an incumbent loses, and reelection rates in the

United States are typically over 90 percent. Thus, it is unlikely that the Supreme Court ruling would have much of an effect on the unconditional probability of using a golden parachute job as an insurance option.

Earlier, I cited evidence that the ruling increased independent campaign spending for both Democrats and Republicans, but more so for the latter (Abdul-Razzak, Prato, and Wolton, 2020). I therefore argued that we should see negative effects on golden parachute employment for legislators from both parties, but that the magnitude should be greater for Republicans. The second and third columns of Table 5.1 analyze the effect of *Citizens United* separately for the two major parties.

For overall golden parachute employment, *Citizens United* indeed had a larger effect on Republican representatives: they were 2.7 percentage points less likely to take up a golden parachute job in the states affected by the ruling than they would have been otherwise. For Democrats, the effect was negative and significant at conventional levels as well, but their probability only decreased by 1.4 percentage points. Thus, the impact of *Citizens United* on Democrats was only about half of the magnitude of what it was for Republican legislators.[34] The second panel shows that for both parties, the effect is driven by a drop in the number of incumbents who decided to take up a lobbying position instead of running for reelection. The third panel shows that there was no discernible effect on the share of legislators who resorted to their insurance option after an election loss. Overall then, and consistent with the theoretical predictions, the looser campaign finance laws had more of an effect on golden parachute employment among members of the party that benefited more from additional campaign spending.

Finally, the fourth panel shows the effect of *Citizens United* on retirement from office that is *not* followed by taking up a lobbyist position.[35] The point estimate for the pooled sample is positive and far from statistical significance. Looking at Republican legislators only, the point estimate is negative, but again statistically indistinguishable from zero. For Democrats, the effect is positive and significant at the 10 percent level, which indicates that they were more likely to leave office without getting a golden parachute job.

---

[34] Because each effect is somewhat imprecisely estimated, the difference between them is not statistically significant.

[35] The dependent variable takes a value of one if a legislator voluntarily left office and did not register as a lobbyist in the same or following year, and zero otherwise.

The Supreme Court ruling thus did not make legislators less likely to leave office in general; it only slowed down movement into golden parachute jobs. An interpretation consistent with this pattern is that it reflects heterogeneity in how important legislators are to special interests, and how much money they have access to as a consequence. In Chapter 3, I assumed that politicians can obtain a certain amount of money, and examined the various ways in which they use it. But of course, some politicians have more access to money than others.[36] For those with access to plenty of funding, removing restrictive campaign spending laws should affect whether they take up a golden parachute job. By contrast, legislators who are not on the radar of moneyed special interests benefit less from campaign spending and are unlikely to be offered a lucrative golden parachute job. Since restrictive campaign finance laws do not constrain them very much, making regulation more permissive should be of little consequence to such lawmakers.

And indeed, while we see a clear slowdown of movement into golden parachute jobs in both parties, this was not true for non-golden parachute retirement. Even among Republicans, who overall benefited more from the increased independent campaign spending, many legislators apparently did not expect enough of a shift in their electoral fortunes to warrant a change in their career paths. And a good share of Democratic incumbents seem to have anticipated that the looser campaign finance laws would disadvantage them, likely because they did not expect to benefit from greater spending.[37]

Note that this interpretation contrasts sharply with the implication of the prevailing understanding of the Supreme Court ruling, which is that it opened the floodgates for overall spending on politics. If this were the case, and more campaign money was spent on behalf of everyone, all types of legislators would find the option of trying to stay in office more attractive. Instead, the ruling only resulted in a slowdown of golden parachute jobs, which provides evidence that more permissive campaign finance rules primarily lead to a "reallocation" of money: Incumbents with access to more money forgo a lucrative position as a lobbyist in favor of higher campaign spending on their behalf.[38] In other words, the

---

[36] See e.g. Fisman, Schulz, and Vig (2014); Fouirnaies (2018); Fouirnaies and Hall (2018); Weschle (2021b).

[37] In addition, given the overall partisan imbalance in spending increases, they might also have been more likely to run against a well-financed Republican.

[38] Note that this reallocation does not mean that the money has to come from the same financier in both scenarios.

view that looks at campaign spending in isolation and the system view I put forward in this book provide contrasting empirical predictions, and the evidence supports the latter.

Taken together, these results lend clear support for the argument that money in the forms of campaign spending and golden parachute jobs are part of a common system, and that their relative prevalence is influenced by the *legal environment*. Thus, more permissive campaign finance laws lead to a first-order increase in campaign spending, and trigger a second-order effect in the opposite direction by reducing the frequency with which incumbents leave office to take up employment in the private sector.

5.5 GOLDEN PARACHUTE REGULATION AND CAMPAIGN FINANCE

Given the growing prevalence of golden parachute employment in many countries, there have been increased attempts to rein in this practice by introducing additional legal restrictions. These regulations typically do not take the form of blanket bans on all private sector employment upon leaving office, as this would conflict with constitutionally guaranteed freedom of occupation provisions. Instead, they typically have a narrower target and prohibit former politicians from lobbying the legislature for a certain amount of time.

In this vein, many US states have introduced *cooling off laws* that mandate a waiting period, usually between six months and two years, before former politicians can register as lobbyists. According to the system argument put forward in this book, this should not only slow down golden parachute employment, it should also have second-order effects that increase campaign money. I now test whether this is indeed the case.

Cooling Off Laws in the US States

Figure 5.3 shows the twenty-one states that introduced cooling off laws by 2012.[39] California was the first state to implement such a law in 1991. Once regulation is introduced, it tends to not be reversed. The only exception to this is Ohio, whose law a court struck down in 2010.

---

[39] To determine the relevant dates of these policies, I used information on the laws provided in "Revolving Door Prohibitions," *National Conference of State Legislatures*, and researched their history. Following the convention in the literature, I recorded the starting point as the year they first applied to legislators.

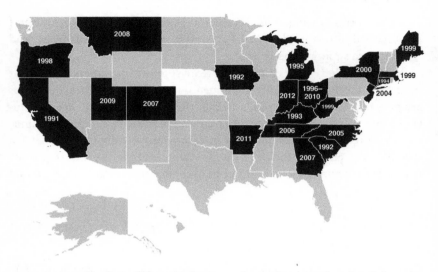

FIGURE 5.3 *Cooling off laws in the states.* States that introduced such laws in black, with year of introduction

I exploit the staggered introduction of the cooling off regulations in a difference-in-differences research design. I compare changes to golden parachute employment and campaign spending patterns in states that introduced or abolished such laws to those that did not. I first show that the laws do indeed have the intended first-order consequence: they reduce golden parachute employment. Then, I demonstrate that as a second-order consequence, they also change the pattern of campaign spending.

Cooling Off Laws Decrease Golden Parachute Employment

A waiting period makes it more difficult for a legislator to move into a lobbying position in the private sector. The straightforward first-order implication of such a regulation is that when states introduce a cooling off law, fewer politicians should accept golden parachute jobs.

My data on golden parachute employment in the states covers the years 2006 to 2013. Thus, I can test the first-order consequences of cooling off laws, exploiting the fact that a subset of states introduced them during that period,[40] and that one state (Ohio) rescinded its law. In the analysis of the consequences of *Citizens United*, one of the controls in Equation (5.1) was whether the state had a cooling off law. Table

---

[40] These states were Arkansas, Colorado, Georgia, Indiana, Montana, and Utah.

TABLE 5.2 *Effect of cooling off laws on golden parachute employment.* Coefficients of the effect of a law requiring a cooling off period on the probability that a legislator will take up a golden parachute job (overall, voluntary, insurance). Coefficients come from separate regressions. Controls not displayed

Golden Parachute	*All*	*Republicans*	*Democrats*
Cooling Off Law	−0.047*	−0.063**	−0.024
	(0.025)	(0.030)	(0.031)

Voluntary Golden Parachute	*All*	*Republicans*	*Democrats*
Cooling Off Law	−0.049***	−0.062**	−0.027
	(0.018)	(0.025)	(0.026)

Insurance Golden Parachute	*All*	*Republicans*	*Democrats*
Cooling Off Law	0.001	−0.001	0.003
	(0.009)	(0.011)	(0.007)

*$p < 0.1$, **$p < 0.05$, ***$p < 0.01$. N = 18,358 for each model involving all legislators, N = 8,851 for Republican-only models, and N = 9,507 for Democrat-only models. All regressions include state and year fixed effects and state-specific time trends. State-level controls: Citizens United, term limit law, public campaign finance. Individual-level controls: Years in office, chamber control own party, speaker or leader. Robust standard errors clustered by state in parentheses.

5.2 displays the coefficients of this variable, which can be interpreted as difference-in-differences estimates.

The first panel shows the first-order impact of cooling off laws on overall golden parachute employment. As expected, these provisions have a negative effect on legislators' propensity to go into the private sector. The share of legislators who become lobbyists drops by almost 5 percentage points. The second and third columns show that this overall effect is mainly driven by Republican legislators, who are more likely to hold golden parachute jobs in the first place. Consequently, after cooling off requirements are introduced, Republican lawmakers are 6.3 percentage points less likely to become a lobbyist. The point estimate for Democrats is also negative, but smaller in size and not statistically significant.[41]

---

[41] Because the cooling off laws changed during the period of observation in only seven states, the effects for Republicans and Democrats are somewhat imprecisely estimated. As a consequence, the difference between the two point estimates is not significant.

The second and third panels distinguish between the impact of cooling off laws on voluntary and insurance golden parachute employment. The overall effect is driven by changes to the former. The point estimates are about the same size as in the first panel. By contrast, the restrictions do not have a discernible impact on movement into the private sector after a lost election. Taken together, Table 5.2 clearly shows that cooling off laws have the expected *first-order consequences*.

Empirical Approach

But what about second-order effects? When restrictions on golden parachute employment are introduced, representatives who would have left office to become lobbyists are instead more likely to run for reelection, so they solicit campaign contributions when they otherwise would not have done so. In particular, because incumbents benefit from instrumental donations in a way that candidates in an open-seat election do not (cf. Fouirnaies and Hall, 2014), we should see an increase in campaign contributions when states introduce cooling off laws. Given that Republicans are more affected by those bans, the impact should be larger for them.

To test whether this is the case, I analyze campaign money in races for state lower houses between 1990 and 2012.[42] I remove all donations from individuals and party organizations, as the underlying motivation for them is electoral or expressive, so my argument does not apply (see Chapter 3).[43] I estimate a difference-in-differences specification that uses the staggered timing of the introduction and abolition of the cooling off laws to identify their impact on donation patterns. The regression compares how donations change when states introduce (or abolish) waiting periods to states that do not alter their regulations. It takes the following form:

$$y_{dst} = \beta \text{ Cooling Off Law}_{st} + \mu' Z_{st} + \gamma_s + \delta_t + \xi_s t + \varepsilon_{st} \qquad (5.2)$$

I look at three dependent variables. The first two are the respective logged total amounts given to Republican and Democratic candidates in district d in state s for election t.[44] Given the larger drop in golden parachute employment for Republicans after cooling off laws are introduced, the effect is expected to be clearly positive for them. Democrats are less

---

[42] Data were compiled by Bonica (2016).
[43] See Hall (2014) for a similar approach.
[44] I add 100 before taking the log.

affected by golden parachute regulation (see Table 5.2), so we would not expect a significant change in their campaign contributions. Finally, the third dependent variable is the *share* of money raised by Republican candidates in a district. This provides an easily interpretable effect of golden parachute regulation on campaign money.

The independent variable of interest is a binary indicator of whether a state had a cooling off law or not, and the coefficient of interest is β. As state-level controls in Z_{st}, I include whether the state had a system of public campaign finance, whether it had term limits, and whether the state bans corporate and union campaign spending (both direct contributions and indirect independent expenditures).[45] A set of state fixed effects is denoted by γ_s, and δ_t is a set of year fixed effects.

The claim for the exogeneity of the introduction of cooling off laws at the state level is certainly weaker than in the case of *Citizens United*. However, it is important to keep in mind that I am interested in the second-order consequences of these policies. Cooling off laws are unlikely to be passed in anticipation of changes in campaign money. Nevertheless, I again include a set of state-specific time trends $\xi_s t$ that can account for some differing trends between the states before such laws are passed. Parameter estimates are reported with robust standard errors clustered by state.

Cooling Off Laws Increase Campaign Spending

Table 5.3 reports the effect of cooling off laws on campaign money. As predicted, the value of donations given to Republicans significantly *increases* after restrictions on golden parachute employment are introduced. Republican candidates receive an average of $32,000 before a cooling off law is introduced. Given the estimated coefficient, this is expected to increase to $42,300 afterwards, which represents an increase of more than 30 percent. At the upper end of the campaign contribution distribution, the coefficient implies very large substantive effects: For a district in the 95th percentile of Republican campaign money, the expected effect is an increase from about $137,750 to $182,079, so almost $45,000 more.

The first-order effect of cooling off laws on Democrats' likelihood of becoming lobbyists was small, so we would also expect a less pronounced impact on their campaign money. And indeed, the second column in

---

[45] Data for spending and contribution bans are taken from La Raja and Schaffner (2014).

TABLE 5.3 *Effect of cooling off laws on campaign money.* Coefficients of the effect of a law requiring a cooling off period on campaign money. Coefficients come from separate regressions. Controls not displayed

Campaign Contributions	*Log Amount Republicans*	*Log Amount Democrats*	*Share Republicans*
Cooling Off Law	0.279***	−0.102	0.045***
	(0.115)	(0.133)	(0.013)

$^*p < 0.1$, $^{**}p < 0.05$, $^{***}p < 0.01$. N = 35,996 for log amount models, N = 35,952 for share model. All regressions include state and year fixed effects and state-specific time trends. State-level controls: term limit law, public campaign finance, ban on union campaign contributions, ban on corporate campaign contributions, ban on union independent spending, ban on corporate independent spending. Robust standard errors clustered by state in parentheses.

Table 5.3 shows an effect that is not significantly different from zero. The point estimate is negative, but small in magnitude: The average amount of contributions to Democrats in a district is about $35,000, which is expected to decrease to $31,600 after the introduction of golden parachute restrictions.[46]

Finally, the third column shows what this implies for the *share* of campaign money going to Republican candidates. A cooling off law leads to a 4.5-percentage-point shift toward them. Given that on average about 48 percent of donations are made to Republicans, the magnitude of this effect is substantial.

Table 5.3 thus yet again provides evidence that legal changes with respect to *any* form of money in politics generate a *second-order effect*: Making it more difficult for politicians to earn money after leaving office has downstream consequences for campaign money. Thus, for both campaign spending and golden parachute employment, the *legal environment* affects the form it regulates as well as the other type, again pointing to the importance of studying them as part of a common system.

5.6 REDISTRICTING AND GOLDEN PARACHUTE EMPLOYMENT

Finally, I investigate the impact of the *electoral campaign environment*. In the previous chapter, I demonstrated that incumbent politicians in India

---

[46] The difference in the effects for Republicans and Democrats is significant at the 1 percent level.

and Brazil make different decisions about whether to allocate resources to campaign spending or to engage in personal enrichment, depending on how competitive their reelection races are likely to be. The same argument should also apply to the choice between campaign spending and golden parachute employment. In particular, in Chapter 3 I hypothesized that lower electoral security makes incumbents more likely to take up a golden parachute job. Here, I test this proposition by using the extent of redistricting an incumbent was subject to following the 2010 census as a shock to their competitiveness.

The 2010 Redistricting Process

Members of the US House of Representatives and the lower state houses are elected in first-past-the-post constituencies. The size of these constituencies changes over time due to migration as well as differential birth and death rates. They are therefore adjusted every ten years following a population census. Within each state, the boundaries of the districts for both the federal and state legislatures are redrawn to be approximately equal in population size.

The more an incumbent's district is changed, the more the relationships and reputation he or she has accumulated over the years disappears. For example, former Illinois Representative Timothy Johnson described his thoughts upon finding out that he would lose many of his constituents due to his district being redrawn: "That is agony, I'll tell you. I thought: All these relationships! All these friendships! All this service!"[47]

In some states, redistricting is performed in a non-partisan manner by commissions or courts, as it is in India. But in other states, legislatures are in charge of the redistricting, which can be conducted in a highly politicized manner. Following the 2010 census, parties in some states used fine-grained geographical data and sophisticated computer programs to create gerrymandered districts to increase their electoral chances (Chen and Rodden, 2015; Chen, 2017). However, this was not the case in many other states, and the overall effect of redistricting on partisan outcomes has been modest (Chen and Cottrell, 2016).

In addition, even if the redistricting procedure is highly politicized in some states, it is largely exogenous to most individual legislators. The idea behind gerrymandering is to advance one party by using "cracking and

---

[47] "Illinois Congressman Johnson May Be Thwarted in Bid to Call His Constituents," *Washington Post*, June 22, 2011.

packing" techniques (cf. Issacharoff and Karlan, 2004). For the former, boundaries are drawn such that supporters of the opposition party are scattered over many districts, and represent a minority in each. In the latter, supporters of the opposition are concentrated in one district where they form an overwhelming majority, leading to wasted votes that are missing in other districts. To the extent that the authors of the 2010 redistricting plans engaged in gerrymandering, they did so to benefit the chances of their party *as a whole*.

I focus here on how district changes affected incumbents' *individual* career decisions. In state-level lower chambers, districts are relatively small and campaigns are based more heavily on personalities and personal contact than in federal races. Losing a large part of one's constituents means losing relationships and goodwill accumulated over a period of years, even if the new district has a favorable demographic makeup. Because the redistricting plans are usually drawn up by a group of legislators with the support of outside expertise, and because the goal of gerrymandering is to benefit a party as a whole, individual legislators are unlikely to be able to influence how much of their district they get to keep.

Data on the Extent of Redistricting

To analyze the impact of redistricting on politicians' career paths – particularly whether they take up a golden parachute job – I again use the data on state representatives and whether they leave office and register as a lobbyist. The one piece of new information needed is the amount of redistricting that each incumbent was exposed to. To create this variable, I adapt a procedure developed by Crespin (2005, 2010) for the state level.

I overlay the old and new district maps with census tract population data from 2010 and estimate how the population that resides in the old districts is distributed into the new ones.[48] To capture how much redistricting an incumbent is subject to, I calculate the minimum share of voters they lose following redistricting. For example, if 60 percent of the voters from an old district are moved to a new district A, 30 percent to a new

---

[48] At the state level, not all census tracts are wholly contained within districts. If they are not, I take the population that is fifteen and older and uniformly distribute it across a census tract, which allows me to approximate how the population of an old district was divided up into new districts. I use the population of fifteen and older rather than eighteen and older since census population data is released in five-year brackets.

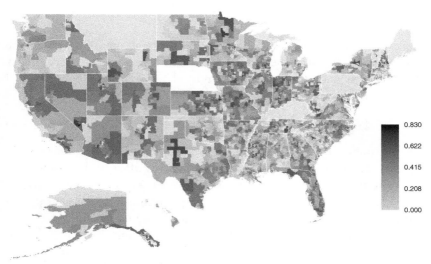

FIGURE 5.4 *Map of redistricting shares after 2010 census.* Darker colors indicate more redistricting. Nebraska (white) is excluded from the sample

district B, and the remaining 10 percent join a new district C, then the incumbent representing the old district can retain at most 60 percent of their constituents. Or, put the other way around, they lose at least 40 percent, resulting in a redistricting share of 0.4. The higher this number, the more an incumbent is affected by redistricting. If there are no changes to their constituency, the number is zero.

Figure 5.4 maps the extent of redistricting for the 2012 elections across 4,904 constituencies in forty-nine state lower houses (again excluding Nebraska). Around 27 percent had a redistricting share of 0.05 or less. The median district has a score of around 0.2, which indicates that half of the incumbents were able to keep up to 80 percent of their constituents. Some states experienced no or very little change, such as Kentucky, Maine, Montana, and Pennsylvania. These states did not implement new boundaries in time, in some cases because courts rejected the original plans, so elections were still held using the old districts. The most extensive redistricting occurred in the fast-growing state of Nevada, where the median state legislator lost about half of their constituents. Florida, Missouri, and Indiana follow at some distance. There is also considerable variation *within* states. For example, there are numerous black regions (indicating a lot of redistricting) right next to light gray regions (indicating little redistricting) in Texas, Minnesota, and West Virginia.

Empirical Approach

To estimate the effect of the extent of redistricting on golden parachute employment, I restrict the sample to the 2012–2013 election cycle. This was the first wave of elections conducted with the new boundaries. I estimate the following regression:

$$logit(Pr(y_{is} = 1)) = \alpha + \beta \text{ Redistricting Share}_{is} + \mu'Z_s + \lambda'X_{is} + \varepsilon_{is}, \quad (5.3)$$

where i indicates a legislator and s a state. The dependent variable y_{is} again takes a value of one if a legislator leaves office and registers as a lobbyist in the same or the following year. Because this is a binary variable and I have a straightforward cross-sectional research design instead of a difference-in-differences approach, I use a logistic regression.

The main independent variable is the redistricting share displayed in Figure 5.4. A value of zero indicates that the district is exactly the same in 2012 as it was in previous elections. The higher the value, the larger the share of constituents an incumbent has lost. The coefficient of interest is β, which is expected to be positive.

State-level control variables, denoted Z_s, are whether the state had cooling off laws, term limits, and a public campaign finance system. Individual-level covariates, denoted X_{is}, are again the number of years a legislator has spent in office, whether his or her party controlled the legislature, and whether he or she held a speaker or party leadership position. Parameter estimates are reported with robust standard errors.

Note that Equation (5.3) does not contain state-level fixed effects. Thus, it estimates the effect of variation in redistricting within as well as between states. I also present results from models with state fixed effects (so α becomes α_s), which only analyze variation within states. Note, however, that this drastically reduces the number of cases, since it drops all legislators from states in which the 2012 districts remained unchanged.

More Redistricting Leads to More Golden Parachute Employment

What is the effect of being subject to more redistricting on legislators' propensity to take up a golden parachute job? Table 5.4 shows the coefficients for the redistricting share, estimated from separate models. The first panel displays the results from regressions without state fixed effects. The first column, which combines legislators from both parties, shows that there is a positive effect, which is significant at the 1 percent level. To ease interpretation of the non-linear logistic regression models, the first row of

TABLE 5.4 *Effect of redistricting on golden parachute employment.*
Logistic regression coefficient of redistricting share on the probability
that a legislator will take up a golden parachute job. Coefficients come
from separate regressions. Controls not displayed

Without State Fixed Effects			
Golden Parachute	*All*	*Republicans*	*Democrats*
Redistricting Share	1.527***	1.351**	1.854*
	(0.623)	(0.623)	(1.051)

With State Fixed Effects			
Golden Parachute	*All*	*Republicans*	*Democrats*
Redistricting Share	1.217	0.889	1.788
	(0.822)	(0.822)	(1.590)

*$p < 0.1$, **$p < 0.05$, ***$p < 0.01$. For models without fixed effects: N = 4,831 (all), 2,640 (Republicans), 2,191 (Democrats). For models with fixed effects: N = 2,793 (all), 1,176 (Republicans), 1,083 (Democrats). State-level controls (for models without state fixed effects): Cooling off law, term limit law, public campaign finance. Individual-level controls: Years in office, chamber control own party, speaker or leader. Robust standard errors in parentheses.

Figure 5.5 shows the predicted probability of golden parachute employment as a function of the redistricting share.[49] The first panel makes clear that the more constituents an incumbent loses, the more likely they are to accept a golden parachute job in the lobbying sector. The (unconditional) predicted probability rises from around 1 percent when a politician's district remains unaltered to around 3 percent at the sample maximum, so the effect of redistricting is substantial.

The second and third columns of the first panel in Table 5.4 analyze the impact on incumbents from the two parties separately. While the point estimate is slightly larger for Democrats than for Republicans, the estimation uncertainty is greater for them as well. The second and third panels of the first row of Figure 5.5 show that the substantial impact is roughly similar for both groups. Given that redistricting affected legislators in both parties at a relatively similar rate, this was to be expected.[50]

The second panel in Table 5.4 displays the results from models with state fixed effects. Because their inclusion means that all legislators from

[49] For the predicted probabilities, control variables are set to the sample median.
[50] The average redistricting share is 0.26 for Republicans and 0.22 for Democrats.

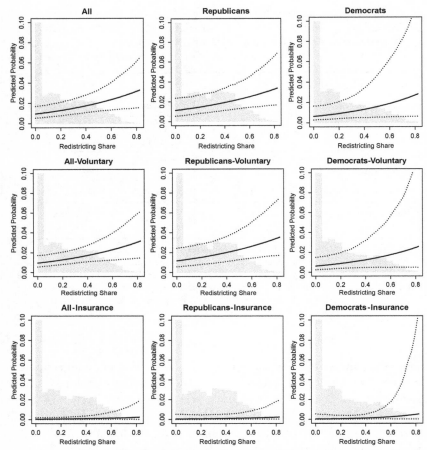

FIGURE 5.5 *Effect of redistricting on golden parachute employment.* Predicted probability of taking up a golden parachute job overall (top row), voluntarily (middle), and after a lost election (bottom) depending on the redistricting share. Point estimate and 95 percent confidence intervals. Density of the redistricting share in the background

states in which there was no redistricting are dropped, estimation uncertainty increases. However, the coefficients are similar to the models without state fixed effects.

Finally, I break down the effect by looking at the two paths of taking up golden parachute employment separately, focusing on a graphical presentation for brevity. The middle row of Figure 5.5 shows the predicted probabilities of leaving office voluntarily and subsequently registering as a lobbyist, using the specification without state fixed effects. Redistricting clearly increases the probability of voluntary golden parachute employment, for all legislators together, as well as when examining Republicans and Democrats separately. The bottom row shows the effect of redistricting on insurance golden parachute employment.[51] In all three models, the slope of the line is nearly flat. Given that we only observe insurance golden parachute employment if an election is lost, and reelection rates are high, this is not surprising. When estimating models for voluntary and insurance golden parachute employment with state fixed effects, the point estimates are similar, but again with larger confidence intervals due to the smaller number of cases.

Thus, politicians' likelihood of leaving office to take up golden parachute employment depends on their *electoral campaign environment* as well. If incumbents suffer a shock to their competitiveness, they are less inclined to run for reelection (and thus use campaign money), and instead are more likely to leverage their position for a lucrative private sector job.

5.7 SUMMARY

In this chapter, I have continued testing the theoretical argument laid out in Chapter 3. The focus was again on the connection between money used by politicians to improve their chances of staying in office and money used to improve their personal financial situation, only this time after leaving office. I have assembled a new dataset that for the first time makes it possible to track golden parachute employment in multiple legislatures, which made a comparative examination possible.

I provided evidence that the relative prevalence of campaign spending and golden parachute jobs is driven by the two key factors I have highlighted, and that a change in one form of money leads to second-order effects on the other. For the *legal environment*, I first used changes in campaign finance legislation to show that this affects how common golden parachute employment is. Second, I demonstrated that stricter regulation of golden parachute lobbying leads to changes in the pattern of campaign contributions.

Legislators' decisions about whether to take up golden parachute employment are also influenced by the *electoral campaign environment*.

---

[51] Due to collinearity issues, I drop the following control variables for the model estimating the effect of redistricting on insurance golden parachute jobs for Democrats: public campaign finance, chamber control own party, speaker or leader. The results are similar when including these variables, although the sample size drops dramatically.

Exploiting variation in the amount of redistricting that incumbents experienced, I have demonstrated that they are more likely to take up golden parachute employment if their reelection chances are lower.

Taken together, these analyses show that campaign spending and golden parachute employment are directly connected to each other. Changes to one form lead to opposing changes in the other. This mirrors the findings from India and Brazil. Thus, these last two chapters have used microlevel data to demonstrate that the three main forms of money in politics are part of a common system, and that the legal and electoral campaign environments affect how politicians use money.

But does the argument also hold at a larger scale? Can it explain cross-national patterns in whether politicians use money primarily for self-enrichment, as campaign spending, or in the form of lucrative jobs? I examine this question in the following chapter.

6

The System of Money in Politics in Comparative Perspective

The previous two chapters investigated the empirical contexts of India, Brazil, and the United States to demonstrate that the different forms of money are directly connected to each other and that the legal and electoral campaign environments in which a politician operates influence which type they choose to use. This approach has many merits. Most importantly, I was able to use microlevel data on the different types of money. It also allowed me to identify situations in which the effect of the legal and electoral campaign environments could be isolated as much as possible. Yet, the findings discussed in the previous chapters naturally raise the question whether the patterns identified *within* these three countries also hold cross-nationally.

In this chapter, I present a series of case studies to test the theoretical argument of the book across space. I examine a range of countries chosen to provide variation along the two explanatory factors I have highlighted. In addition to India, Brazil, and the United States, I also examine South Africa, Spain, Germany, and the United Kingdom. I derive predictions from the argument put forward in Chapter 3 about what forms of money politicians in each country should be more inclined to use based on their location in the two-dimensional space defined by the legal and electoral campaign environments.

I then test these predictions by analyzing the country-specific literature on money in politics, official statistics, as well as reports by watchdog organizations and the media. Of course, a potential concern is that such sources only focus on *revealed* cases of money in politics, which do not necessarily indicate the actual number of incidents. A country with more reported cases could instead indicate that its judiciary is more able and willing to prosecute, or that it has a more active press.[1] However, my focus is not on *how much* money enters politics, but in *what forms*. And looking at revealed cases can help us do this. If many politicians enrich themselves while in office, we would expect journalists to try to document it, anti-corruption activists to bring attention to it, and academic researchers to study it. And if the issue of, say, golden parachute employment does not come up in a particular country even among activists, then this silence suggests that it is not likely to be very common.

The analyses reported in this chapter confirm the theoretical predictions for each country. Politicians base their decisions about whether to use money for self-enrichment, on their reelection campaigns, or to accept golden parachute jobs on their country's legal and electoral campaign environments. Thus, my argument not only applies *within* countries; it also explains variation *between* them. This provides evidence of the external validity of my theoretical account beyond the cases studied in detail in the previous chapters.

6.1 CASE SELECTION AND THEORETICAL EXPECTATIONS

Figure 6.1 illustrates where the cases discussed in this chapter are approximately located in the two-dimensional space defined by the main explanatory variables. This section briefly discusses where each country falls. Of course, their classification is not straightforward, since each dimension consists of several components, and there is no agreed upon way to weigh them. The subsequent individual case studies therefore provide more detailed descriptions of countries' locations along the two axes.

To simplify, I characterize countries' *legal environments* as ranging from permissive to strict. I argued in Chapter 3 that the specific combination of laws pertaining to self-enrichment, campaign spending, and golden parachute employment determines how money is used. However, countries in practice tend to progressively introduce stricter laws, usually starting with regulating enrichment in office and ending with restrictions on golden parachute jobs. Thus, some regulate none of the three types of money very effectively, whereas others have restrictions on several or all of them. This makes it possible to rank them.

As discussed in Chapter 4, both India and Brazil have very permissive legal environments for money in politics, mostly due to a lack of

---

[1] See e.g. Fisman and Golden (2017*a*); Stanig (2018).

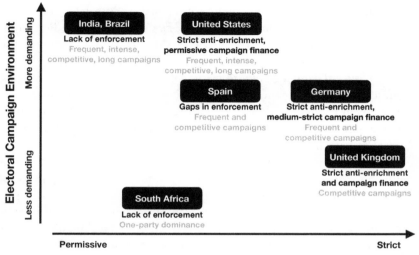

FIGURE 6.1 *Situating the case studies.* Countries discussed in this chapter are selected to provide variation along the two dimensions highlighted as explanatory factors in Chapter 3. The comments below the countries characterize the legal (black) and electoral campaign (gray) environments

enforcement. This is (imperfectly) reflected in aggregate indicators such as the World Bank's Control of Corruption measure, which ranked India 106th–110th and Brazil 121st–134th out of 209 countries from 2017 to 2019.

South Africa also has a relatively permissive legal environment characterized by spotty enforcement, although not quite to the same degree as India and Brazil. It ranks higher than both of these countries in the Control of Corruption indicator, placing between 85th and 91st. Spain has even more stringent and better enforced laws, but still with considerable enforcement gaps, especially for high-ranking politicians. It ranked 56th–67th.

The United States generally does well in aggregate indicators of corruption, ranking between 24th and 33rd from 2017 to 2019. But, as discussed in detail in Chapter 5, this only partially translates to electoral politics. While rules against self-enrichment in office are stringent, the United States is very permissive when it comes to campaign spending. Thus, its legal environment can be described as intermediately strict.

Finally, Germany and the United Kingdom both rigidly regulate money in politics. They place 11th–13th (Germany) and 12th–15th (United

Kingdom) in the Control of Corruption indicator. Both have strict laws against politicians' personal enrichment. For campaign spending rules, both countries are on the stricter side of the spectrum as well, but the United Kingdom stands out due to its imposition of expenditure limits.

The *electoral campaign environment* can be conceptualized as ranging from less to more demanding. Again, this is a simplification, since that environment is comprised of several aspects. One important part, which was the focus of the within-country studies, is electoral competitiveness. Countries with high levels of competitiveness are characterized by close elections and frequent government turnovers, as well as close elections in many individual constituencies. One-party dominance and easy victories indicate low levels of competitiveness.

Another factor that affects the electoral campaign environment is the technology employed in campaigns. If expensive techniques like TV advertisements, get-out-the-vote drives, or widespread clientelistic hand-outs are common and effective, parties and candidates operate in a much more demanding environment compared to a situation in which campaigning primarily entails leaflets and small-scale rallies. At a more systemic level, the electoral campaign environment is also shaped by how many offices in a country are elected, how frequent these elections are, and how long campaigns last.

The countries studied in Chapters 4 and 5, India, Brazil, and the United States, all have highly competitive electoral campaign environments. In the past few decades, each has experienced close elections and multiple government turnovers. Campaigns are fought using clientelistic benefits in India and Brazil, and TV ads and mobilization drives in the United States, all of which are very expensive. Finally, officials in each country are elected at many different levels, and campaigns are long and frequent.

South Africa is located at the other end of the spectrum, since a single party dominates its political landscape. Although it has lost some support over time, the African National Congress (ANC) continues to regularly win national elections with more than 50 percent of the vote, and to date there has not been a government turnover since the country became a democracy in the early 1990s. Thus, its electoral campaign environment is less demanding.

Spain, Germany, and the United Kingdom occupy the middle ground between the two extremes. Each has competitive campaigns and has experienced regular turnovers in government. However, the campaigns are shorter (often only a few weeks) and considerably less demanding. For example, parties cannot purchase TV advertisements, and labor-intensive get-out-the-vote drives are not generally undertaken. This group of countries differs, however, in the frequency of campaigns. Spain and Germany are federal states, so parties contest a large number of subnational elections, while their UK counterparts only compete in a limited number of contests.

If my argument is correct, the location of the countries in Figure 6.1 should translate into systematic differences in how money enters politics. In India and Brazil, with permissive legal and demanding electoral campaign environments, money should primarily be used for enrichment in office and campaign spending; golden parachute employment should be rare. Chapter 4 has already demonstrated the former; in this chapter, I examine the latter.

South Africa's combination of a permissive legal environment and a less demanding campaign environment should make self-enrichment in office the most prevalent form. For the United States, campaign spending and golden parachute jobs should be common, but self-enrichment should be rare. Chapter 5 has already shown that this is indeed what happens, so this chapter does not revisit this case.

Spain occupies an intermediate place on both dimensions. We should therefore observe less campaign spending, which in turn leaves more room for self-enrichment. Because Spain's legal framework for personal enrichment is only medium-strict, this should happen in office, but we can also expect to find a good number of instances in which politicians leave office to take up well-paid positions in the private sector.

Finally, high-regulation Germany and the United Kingdom should have little or no personal enrichment and little campaign spending. Therefore, if my argument is correct, golden parachute employment ought to loom large. It should be most pronounced in the United Kingdom, where campaign finance regulation is especially strict and the electoral campaign environment is somewhat less demanding.

Throughout the chapter, it is important to keep in mind that my argument is about *how* money enters politics rather than *how much* of it there is. The case studies compare very different countries, which have widely varying amounts of money in politics. For example, India's political system has more money overall than that of the United Kingdom, even after adjusting for differences in the size of the two countries. The reasons for this are varied and complex, and I briefly discuss this in the concluding chapter. But since my interest here is to explain how money enters politics, I take the amount of it as given.

Finally, note that the cases analyzed in the previous chapters are located in the upper to center-left of Figure 6.1, which means they have demanding electoral campaign environments and permissive to intermediate legal environments. This allowed me to identify changes in legal conditions as well as within-country variation in competitiveness, which provided evidence with high internal validity. This chapter probes the external validity of these analyses to determine whether the argument extends to between-country differences as well.

6.2 INDIA

In low-regulation environments like India and Brazil, where the flow of money into politics is either loosely regulated or the existing rules are not strictly enforced, I have argued that self-enrichment in office and campaign spending should be the prevailing forms and that golden parachute employment should not be very common. Chapter 4 has demonstrated the prevalence of campaign spending and personal enrichment in India. But what about golden parachute employment?

When I asked academics, journalists, or activists during my fieldwork in India about politicians who go into the private sector, I was usually met either with a blank stare or a puzzled look, followed by an admission that they could not think of any cases where this has happened. They were more likely to express the opposite worry: That it is quite difficult to get politicians to leave politics at all. Indeed, newspaper editorials lament the overrepresentation of the elderly in Indian politics. One writer in 2013 described the cabinet of then-Prime Minister Manmohan Singh, himself eighty-one years old at the time, as "a coterie of septuagenarians and 'youthful' ministers in their 60s."[2] Another columnist observed that: "[a]ll major parties are facing serious problems with senior politicians and do not know how to get rid of them, since they refuse to leave active politics. They keep fighting for [loot] and power ... till the last."[3] A systematic cross-national comparison shows that out of 116 parliaments around the world, the Indian upper house has the sixth-highest average age of MPs, and the lower house ranks 23rd (Power, 2012).

Of course, these anecdotes and the data only look at politicians who *stayed* in elected office. But what about those who lose their position,

[2] "Indian Geronotocracy: Why Are Indian Leaders So Old?," *The Diplomat*, December 24, 2013.
[3] "Younger India, Greying Politicians," *Business Line*, February 6, 2009.

which is relatively common in India (Uppal, 2009)? There are no systematic studies of Indian politicians' career paths that I am aware of. But a little exercise is instructive. When the government coalition led by the Congress Party lost power in 2014, a dozen ministers also lost their seats in parliament. Ministers in general are most likely to move into a lucrative private sector job. So what were the Indian ex-ministers doing in the years after leaving their position?

For example, the former Minister of Mines oversaw an economic area known for deep financial ties between corporations and politicians (Asher and Novosad, 2020). Instead of working as a nonexecutive director or board member of a mining company, he became the head of a museum dedicated to Sardar Patel, one of the founding fathers of the Indian republic. The former Minister of Civil Aviation remained the leader of his party, the Rashtriya Lok Dal, even though it no longer had any seats in parliament. The ex-Minister of Corporate Affairs became head of the Congress Party in the state of Rajasthan, and the former Minister of Health became the opposition leader in the upper house. Media reports refer to the former Minister of Home Affairs as a "senior Congress leader." The former Minster of External Affairs? Also a "senior Congress leader." How about the Minster of Law, the Minster of Housing, or the Minister of Coal? All of them "senior Congress leaders." Not a single one of the dozen ex-ministers, many of whom occupied positions that put them in charge of billion-dollar industries, moved to the private sector.

This pattern is not restricted to government ministers. When Sheila Dikshit was ousted after fifteen years as Chief Minister of Delhi, during which she oversaw the corruption-riddled construction projects for the 2010 Commonwealth Games, she was appointed Chief Minister of the state of Kerala less than three months later. In other words, even if politicians in India lose their office, they stay in politics and try to find another elected or appointed position.

While golden parachute jobs for Indian politicians are uncommon, the practice itself is *not* unheard of. Javid Chowdhury, a veteran civil servant, vividly describes them as a common occurrence in parts of the Indian *bureaucracy*:

Positions in certain areas of governance – commerce, industry, petroleum, power, certain areas of finance – are monopolized by a favoured set of officials. These officials tamely carry out the instructions of the economic tsars .... For some years now, the officials from this cabal are increasingly also found to be suitable for post-retirement sinecures in the private conglomerates. One leading corporate house of Mumbai has cultivated the reputation of very faithfully providing post-retirement financial recompense to those senior officials who looked after them while in government. This has created a favourable reputation for this corporate house in the market as reliable paymasters for favours earlier rendered (Chowdhury, 2012, 67).

One reason why there are golden parachute jobs for bureaucrats but not for politicians is that the former have to retire at age sixty and thus no longer have the chance to profit from their position. Politicians, however, have no such restrictions. Thus, they continue to run for (and win) office, enjoy the associated financial benefits time and time again, and have no need for private sector jobs.

6.3   BRAZIL

What about the second example of a country with a permissive legal but a demanding electoral campaign environment that I analyzed in depth, Brazil? How often do incumbents leave politics for apparently greener pastures in the private sector? Unlike India, there is a literature studying Brazilian politicians' career paths. It provides no evidence that the move from politics into the private sector through golden parachute jobs is common.

Samuels (2003) studies the careers of all members of the lower house between 1945 and 1994. He argues that the reelection assumption does not apply in this context, as legislators do not seek to build a career in the national legislature. Instead, they only spend a short amount of time there before moving on. However, they do not leave politics: "[M]ost Brazilian deputies do continue their political careers, or at least attempt to do so, after serving in the Chamber, and ... most of them do so at the subnational level" (Samuels, 2003, 59). In Brazil, states and municipalities have significant powers, and being a politician at the subnational level is in many ways preferable to being a national politician. Roughly two-thirds of deputies seek to enter state or municipal politics after leaving the national legislature (Samuels, 2003).

But what happens once politicians get to the subnational level? As discussed in Chapter 4, one of the most attractive political positions is to become a municipal mayor. I have shown that, depending on their office security and the stringency of the regulation they are subject to, mayors increase their personal wealth *and* invest in their reelection campaigns. But due to term limits, they can spend at most eight consecutive years in charge of a municipality. What do they do then? Klašnja and Titiunik(2017) analyze the career paths of all mayors who were elected between 1996 and 2008. They show that once they can no longer run again, some do the opposite of what Samuels (2003) documents and run for national office. Most, however, simply wait one election cycle and then run again for mayor.

Politicians in Brazil not only switch between different levels of electoral politics; they also move in and out of other political roles. Some of the most popular positions that federal deputies take up subsequently are state secretary or other state-level positions, as well as jobs in their state party executive (Samuels, 2003). Santos and Pegurier (2011) observe that with respect to career paths, "[i]n Brazil, no clear separation exists ... between the legislative and the executive branches of municipal, state and federal governments" (Santos and Pegurier, 2011, 180).[4] They categorize political careers in Brazil as following an "integrated" model according to a classification by Borchert (2011), which is characterized by a perpetual political career at various levels of government. This type of career provides "[m]ore options for politicians who have passed the zenith of their career. Rather than being forced out of the game altogether, they can still find fall-back positions within the political profession that are acceptable" (Borchert, 2011, 131).

What is notably absent is the notion that politicians might cash in on their position by moving into the private sector. One would expect that if Brazilian politicians were regularly taking up golden parachute employment, this would be mentioned in at least some studies of career paths. Instead, all available evidence suggests that they prefer to stay in politics at whichever level has an opening. This is consistent with my argument that golden parachute employment is a second-best option that only occurs when other forms of money in politics, particularly enrichment while in office, are strictly regulated.

6.4 SOUTH AFRICA

South Africa has somewhat stricter laws regarding money in politics than Brazil and India, and ranks higher on the Control of Corruption indicator (between 85th and 91st from 2017 to 2019). Yet these laws are weakly enforced because anti-corruption bodies lack independence (Robinson and Brummer, 2006; Booysen, 2011; Calland, 2016).

What really distinguishes South Africa from Brazil and India, however, is the electoral campaign environment. It is, in the words of one

---

[4] See also Gingerich (2013) on the interwovenness of bureaucracy and electoral politics in Latin America.

historian, a "one-party democracy" (Thompson, 2014, 368). In the six elections between 1994 and 2019, the ANC received 57.5–69.7 percent of the votes, despite the fact that its record in government is far from perfect; citizens "afford the ANC immense leeway for underperformance and deficits. They have a deep and forgiving bond with *their* ANC" (Booysen, 2011, 86, emphasis in original). And: "The essential repertoire is: first vote ANC, and then in between-election periods protest against the ANC in government to get more attention and better action" (Booysen, 2011, 127). As a consequence, South Africa's campaign environment is significantly less demanding than those of the other cases discussed so far.

The theoretical prediction is therefore that self-enrichment in office should be the dominant way for money to enter politics. Because of the lack of enforcement, politicians who engage in the practice are unlikely to be caught, and even less likely to be convicted. Thus there is little need for golden parachute employment. Since the ANC dominates electorally, its politicians should not need to spend large sums on election campaigns, even though party funding is largely unregulated (cf. Tshitereke, 2002; Lowry, 2008; Calland, 2016).

Self-enrichment in office is indeed common among South African politicians. The wide variety of authors and publications who portray it as rampant is quite impressive:

- "It is accepted that politics brings wealth to the political elites" (Booysen, 2011, 8).
- "It was widely accepted and frequently shown that election into ANC position … was the first step towards financial well-being" (Booysen, 2011, 364).
- "The state is perceived as a source of enrichment" (Thompson, 2014, 390).
- "The [current] ANC is fundamentally a coalition founded on greed and lust for power, and thirst for loot. … They are united by a desire for wealth and position. But there are not enough positions to meet everyone's needs, nor enough wealth to pillage" (Suttner, 2009, 21).
- "Corruption has enriched ANC leaders and their business allies."[5]
- "[T]he ANC has become a machine, not for sensible policymaking but for lavish self-enrichment."[6]

No other politician exemplifies the use of office to gain personal wealth more than former President Jacob Zuma. Allegations against him date back to before he became president. In 1998, when Zuma was deputy president of the ANC, the cabinet approved an arms deal worth around

---

[5] "'They Eat Money': How Mandela's Political Heirs Grow Rich Off Corruption," *New York Times*, April 6, 2018.
[6] "The End May Well Be Nigh for the ANC," *Financial Times*, September 20, 2017.

R30 billion (about $3 billion at the time). Rumors soon emerged that large-scale bribery had occurred during the procurement process. While investigations were impeded at various times, in 2005 Zuma's financial adviser Schabir Shaik was sentenced to fifteen years in prison for soliciting bribes on behalf of Zuma from the French company Thales. This prompted President Thabo Mbeki to fire Zuma. Shaik's conviction led to Zuma being charged with 783 counts of corruption. They were dropped before the 2009 elections, in which Zuma became president. However, the Supreme Court reinstated the charges in 2017.[7]

Zuma also allegedly engaged in self-enrichment during his time as president. South Africans were outraged when it emerged that around $30 million of taxpayer money was used to renovate his sprawling private residence. While the government justified the works as security-related, they reportedly included upgrades to a visitors' center, a swimming pool, and an amphitheater. A court ordered Zuma to repay a share of the cost.[8]

The biggest scandal during Zuma's presidency, however, involved far larger sums of money. It led the Public Protector, an independent oversight institution enshrined in the constitution, to issue a 355-page report called "State of Capture" (Public Protector South Africa, 2016) that investigates Zuma's relationship with the Guptas, three Indian brothers with a large business empire in South Africa. Their close connection to the president allegedly enabled them to get lucrative state contracts, buy a coal mine, and even have a say in the hiring and firing of cabinet ministers. Zuma and other ANC politicians are thought to have been rewarded by receiving a cut of these deals. As a consequence, billions of dollars have been looted from public funds. The accumulation of such scandals finally contributed to Zuma's ouster from the presidency in 2018.[9]

---

[7] See e.g. Hyslop (2005); Robinson and Brummer (2006); Booysen (2011, 51–57); Thompson (2014); "South African Leader Sacks Deputy," *BBC News*, June 14, 2005; "SA Judge Finds Jacob Zuma Should Face Corruption Charges," *BBC News*, April 29, 2016; "South African Supreme Court Upholds Reinstating 783 Corruption Charges against Zuma," *Reuters*, October 13, 2017; "South Africa Arms Deal That Landed Zuma in Court: What You Need to Know," *BBC News*, April 6, 2018.

[8] See e.g. Thompson (2014); "Power Struggle Paralyzes South Africa's Ruling ANC Party," *Los Angeles Times*, December 2, 2012; "Zuma Told to Repay R7.8m Spent on Estate in 'Nkandlagate' Scandal," *Financial Times*, June 27, 2016; "How Jacob Zuma Captured South Africa, and How He Might Lose Control," *The Economist*, December 9, 2017.

[9] See e.g. Booysen (2011, 389–390); "Jacob Zuma Resigns as South Africa's President," *New York Times*, February 14, 2018; "The Guptas and Their Links to South Africa's Jacob Zuma," *BBC News*, February 14, 2018; "In Gupta Brothers' Rise and Fall, the Tale of a Sullied A.N.C.," *New York Times*, December 22, 2018.

There is evidence that South African politicians at all levels of government have engaged in self-enrichment. For instance, Welfare Minister Abe Williams was forced to resign in 1996 after it emerged that he had accepted a bribe from a company contracted to distribute pension funds.[10] Likewise, the Public Protector and the parliament's ethics committee found Dina Pule, Minister for Telecommunications from 2011 to 2013, guilty of funneling contracts to her partner's business.[11] In general:

> [T]he ANC was ensnared with, and probably entrapped in, a new world in which government members across the ranks were becoming rich through business interests that many struggled to declare. Family members and close associates were beneficiaries of deals leveraged through positions of in-state deployment. Syndicates rigged contracts and other procurement processes, whilst anchor persons, including high-level incumbent politicians, were not suspended (Booysen, 2011, 389).

Finally, the abuse of office for self-enrichment also extends to the subnational level. For example, John Block, a cabinet member in the Northern Cape province, was sentenced to fifteen years in prison for receiving kickbacks from a company in exchange for influencing provincial departments in its favor.[12] A commission set up by the ANC in 2011 worried that "ANC membership was now pursued by those with no interest in politics, merely a get-rich-quick attitude" (Johnson, 2015, 145). And in fact, several critics who have spoken out against enrichment in office in recent years have been assassinated.[13]

Because the opportunities for enrichment in office are myriad in South Africa, *golden parachute employment* is rare. This is especially true in recent years. There are several cases of golden parachute jobs among the first generation of post-apartheid politicians. For example, the first Minister of Transport, Mac Maharaj, became a member of the board of directors of FirstRand Bank. His colleague, Minister of Defense Joe

---

[10] Lodge (1998).
[11] "Minister Dina Pule Accused of Nepotism," *Mail & Guardian*, August 3, 2012; "Pule Found Guilty of Breaching Code of Conduct," *Mail & Guardian*, August 7, 2013; "Madonsela Report Finds Pule Guilty of 'Persistently Lying'," *Mail & Guardian*, December 12, 2013.
[12] "John Block Guilty of Corruption, Fraud, Money Laundering," *Mail & Guardian*, October 14, 2015; "John Block Gets 15-Year Jail Term for Money Laundering, Corruption," *Mail & Guardian*, December 6, 2016.
[13] "Hit Men and Power: South Africa's Leaders Are Killing One Another," *New York Times*, September 30, 2018.

Modise, became chair of a company that regularly won government contracts (Hyslop, 2005). However, as personal enrichment in office has become more common, leaving politics and moving into the private sector has become less prevalent.

It is difficult to quantify how widespread golden parachute employment is in South Africa, as to my knowledge there are no systematic studies of politicians' career paths. However, I can conduct a similar exercise as I did above for India. In 2007, there was a power struggle between the incumbent President Thabo Mbeki and Jacob Zuma, his main challenger. During the party conference at the end of the year, Mbeki and most of his cabinet ministers were ousted from the ANC National Executive Committee (NEC). In September 2008, the NEC then asked Mbeki to step down from the presidency. Eleven cabinet ministers resigned, followed by Mbeki himself.[14] After Kgalema Motlanthe's brief interim presidency, Zuma took over in 2009.

What happened to those ministers? In many ways, they were ideal candidates for golden parachute jobs. Not only were they in charge of important portfolios, their continued engagement in politics was also complicated by the depth of the animosity between the Mbeki and Zuma camps. Nevertheless, most ministers who stepped down continued to be engaged in electoral politics, either within the ANC or by founding a new party. Some also took over roles in international organizations or the education sector. Of the eleven, only one could possibly be classified as taking a golden parachute job: The Minister of Public Enterprises, Alec Erwin, became the director of an investment holdings company.

Finally, consistent with the theoretical prediction, *campaign spending* does indeed matter less in South Africa than in Brazil and India. Of course, because the party finance system is almost completely unregulated and even permits foreign contributions (Tshitereke, 2002; Robinson and Brummer, 2006; Lowry, 2008; Calland, 2016), a decent amount of money is spent, especially by the ANC. The South Africa-specific literature stresses that "ANC campaigns are well-resourced and ANC business entrepreneurship and benefactors ensure that its campaign coffers do not run dry" (Booysen, 2011, 220). Campaign money comes from business people, from abroad, from public funding, as well as from the party's investment arm (Tshitereke, 2002; Robinson and Brummer, 2006; Booysen, 2011; Calland, 2016).

---

[14] Booysen (2011, 65–69); "SA Rocked by Resignation of Ministers," *Mail & Guardian*, September 23, 2008.

However, campaigns are nowhere near as expensive in South Africa as elsewhere. For example, cost-intensive clientelistic efforts are comparatively low. An expert survey by the Democratic Accountability and Linkages Project ranks South Africa 33rd out of eighty-eight countries for clientelistic efforts, where higher ranks indicate less clientelism (Kitschelt, 2013). This is roughly on par with Greece and Italy. For comparison, Brazil ranks 59th and India comes in 62nd. The total cost of campaigning in South Africa also lags behind these other countries. During the 1999 elections, the spending of all parties was estimated at R300–500 million, about $50–85 million given exchange rates at the time (Tshitereke, 2002). This is of course not an insignificant amount. However, it certainly is not enough to serve as a short-term economic stimulus, as campaigns do in India or Brazil. It also pales in comparison to the sums involved in the personal enrichment cases discussed earlier.

In addition, there are regular reports of the ANC's financial difficulties. In 2012, its party headquarters could no longer pay its rent and had to partially move into the offices of the trade union federation Cosatu. The same year, it also fell behind paying staff salaries (Johnson, 2015, 124, 153). In 2014, a newspaper reported that "the party has struggled to raise money from private funders over the past few years" and that the secretary general told employees who had not been paid in months to "please bear with us ... the ship is tight."[15] Three years later, the ANC was reported to be "technically insolvent."[16] And in 2018, the party only barely avoided the seizure of Luthuli House, its headquarters, over unpaid fees.[17] Again, this starkly contrasts with the lavish self-enrichment of ANC politicians across the board.

To summarize, the way politicians in South Africa use money is consistent with my theoretical expectations. Given the country's relatively permissive legal environment and the ANC's electoral dominance, enrichment in office is rampant, golden parachute employment is rare, and comparatively little money is spent on elections.

6.5 SPAIN

Spain has more stringent and better enforced rules related to money and politics than the countries discussed earlier, ranking 56th–67th on the Control of Corruption indicator. Its laws against the abuse of office for

---

[15] "The ANC Is Broke," *Mail & Guardian*, October 31, 2014.
[16] "ANC Is Technically Insolvent," *Huffington Post*, December 20, 2017.
[17] "Joburg ANC Saves Luthuli House from Being Seized by City," *Times Live*, June 14, 2018.

personal enrichment are reasonably strict. However, their enforcement can be spotty especially for high-level politicians due to limited judicial independence (Pujas and Rhodes, 2002; Chislett, 2013). The average court case involving corruption lasts for about ten years; and even if it results in a conviction, the perpetrators often get off the hook anyways: Between 2000 and 2012, 132 politicians who were convicted of corruption received a pardon (Jiménez, 2014).

Campaign finance laws are also relatively strict on paper (Pujas and Rhodes, 2002; García Viñuela and Artés, 2008; GRECO, 2009, 2013; Jiménez and Villoria, 2012). There are donation limits in place, and private companies that provide goods and services to a public sector entity are prohibited from making political contributions. However, loopholes make it easy to circumvent these laws. For example, anonymous contributions were allowed for a long time, rendering existing donation limits irrelevant. Unsurprisingly, up to 95 percent of donations came from unnamed sources (GRECO, 2009; Jiménez and Villoria, 2012). Nor do donation restrictions apply to in-kind real estate donations or to loans given to parties (GRECO, 2009; Jiménez and Villoria, 2012). Foundations that are tied to political parties are subject to separate, and less stringent, rules. For example, they are allowed to receive money from corporations that have been awarded public contracts (GRECO, 2009, 2013). Finally, as is the case for personal enrichment, enforcement of campaign finance rules is spotty: The parties are rarely scrutinized, in part because the audit court does not have the necessary resources or the required enforcement and sanctioning powers (GRECO, 2009).

Elections are competitive in Spain: the social-democratic Partido Socialista Obrero Español (PSOE) and the conservative Partido Popular (PP) have regularly alternated in government. The electoral campaign environment is also made more demanding by the fact that there are many elections in Spain's seventeen autonomous communities, each of which has its own government. This, combined with the fact that Spanish parties only emerged post-industrialization and thus never attained mass membership status and the associated reliable stream of membership dues, means that parties have traditionally struggled to keep up with the financial demands associated with this campaign environment (Heywood, 1997; Jiménez and Villoria, 2012).

Spain's intermediate position on both dimensions suggests that we should observe a good amount of money entering politics for electoral purposes, but that there is room for self-enrichment as well. Because the legal framework for personal enrichment is only medium-strict, this should happen in office, but we might also expect to find politicians leaving office to take up well-paid positions in the private sector (although not necessarily the same ones who enrich themselves while in office).

Campaign spending is indeed an important way in which money enters politics in Spain. According to the official statistics, only a relatively small share of parties' budgets come from donations. However, "[d]isclosed donations offer a misleading picture of the role of private money in party financing because they do not include the sums raised from the uncontrolled financing of parties" (García Viñuela and González de Aguilar, 2011, 10).

For example, contributions are often made to foundations that are tied to parties or through real estate donations. And because donation limits do not apply to loans, they have become an important source of party financing. In 2006, political parties had accumulated debts of more than €200 million (GRECO, 2009; Jiménez and Villoria, 2012). What is more, banks were allowed to simply cancel parties' liabilities. By one estimate, debt cancellations between 1997 and 1999 alone were almost €20 million (GRECO, 2013).

The desire to raise and spend money on elections does not stop in the legal gray zone. Examples of illegal activities used to fill candidates' and parties' campaign coffers span the history of modern Spanish democracy. The PSOE was embroiled in a series of scandals in the 1990s that revealed how it received kickbacks from public works projects that were used to finance the party. The most egregious case was the "Filesa affair" in which two elected PSOE representatives ran a front company that charged businesses inflated prices for consultancy work and used the earnings to pay party bills (Heywood, 1997; Pujas and Rhodes, 2002; Chislett, 2013). Other cases of party-serving corruption involved a company receiving a contract for the 1992 Expo in Seville after having paid money to the PSOE, and Siemens doing the same when it won a contract to build a high-speed rail link. The PP has also been implicated in a number of scandals. For example, its treasurer was arrested in 1990 for using local government contracts and property development to raise funds for the party (Heywood, 1997; Pujas and Rhodes, 2002).

But money enters Spanish politics not only to finance elections; politicians also engage in *self-enrichment*. This dual purpose can clearly be seen in the "Bárcenas affair." In January 2013, the newspaper *El País* published a handwritten ledger attributed to Luis Bárcenas, a former treasurer of the PP. It listed hundreds of payments made and received between 1990 and

2008, suggesting the existence of a parallel bookkeeping system. Bárcenas was eventually sentenced to thirty-three years in prison, a verdict that led to the ouster of Prime Minister Mariano Rajoy.[18] During the investigation and trial, Bárcenas "described in detail how donors used to arrive at party headquarters with bags and suitcases full of cash."[19] A total of around €8.3 million was routed through this system. The "contributions" largely came from companies that had public contracts and thus were not legally allowed to make political donations; they often exceeded the annual limit, and were always made in cash (Jiménez, 2014).

PP politicians then used the money *both* for electoral purposes and for personal enrichment. As Bárcenas detailed in testimony, for the former, the black money was sliced up into tranches of less than €60,000 (under the annual campaign contribution limit). These would be donated anonymously, which was legal until 2007, to party accounts. Once the money was laundered in this way, it would be used for campaign spending (Jiménez, 2014). For personal enrichment, part of the money was put into a slush fund, from which quarterly payments to key party leaders were made. Most explosively, the name of Mariano Rajoy appears thirty-five times, and the reported cash payments to him total over €320,000 between 1997 and 2008.[20]

This dual purpose for money can be found all around the country and at different levels of government. In an extensive review of cases, Jiménez and Carbona (2012) conclude: "The main purpose [of corruption] is usually illicit enrichment, but generally, in an instrumental way, there is a second purpose related to it: the financing of electoral campaigns." They provide a first-hand account of conversations, recorded by the authorities, in which politicians discuss both motivations. In one case, a city councilor of a small party in Orihuela, near Murcia, talks with a businessman in the trash collection sector. The latter wants the former to challenge a case where a city contract had been given to one of his competitors:

---

[18] "Governing Popular Party and Its Ex-Treasurer, Sentenced in Massive Corruption Case," *El País*, May 24, 2018; "Spain's Prime Minister, Mariano Rajoy, Is Ousted in No-Confidence Vote," *New York Times*, June 1, 2018.

[19] "PP's Former Treasurer Breaks Silence on Spanish Slush Fund Scandal," *Financial Times*, July 7, 2013.

[20] "PP's Former Treasurer Breaks Silence on Spanish Slush Fund Scandal," *Financial Times*, July 7, 2013.

Businessman: "When the time comes, before the plenary..."
Councilor: "I don't want anything, you pay the campaign."
Businessman: "Yes. You can have 100 percent confidence...an American-style campaign."
Councilor: "No, not American-style, but a campaign so we can win eight or nine council seats."

On the other end of the spectrum, the following conversation between an intermediary and a councilor in Camas, near Seville, could not make the personal enrichment motive any clearer:

Councilor: "What would I receive?"
Intermediary: "Well, you would be set for life, and your children, and twenty generations of yours ... This is a gold mine. This is gold, gold, gold."
Councilor: "I have only seen corruption from afar. I did not think it would come so close."
Intermediary: "For all of us, our time comes one day. For you, it has come now."[21]

Money in Spanish politics is thus used for campaign spending as well as for self-enrichment. But clearly, the legal consequences – especially for the latter – are more severe than in India or Brazil, so enrichment in office is not nearly as pronounced, especially at the highly scrutinized national level. Given the scale and complexity of Bárcenas' shadow accounts, the payments to Rajoy came to less than €30,000 a year, which in truth is rather paltry. Given Spain's intermediate legal position, we should therefore see considerable movement into *golden parachute employment* as well.

And indeed, an investigation by the online newspaper *Público* in 2016 found that at least fifty-eight former politicians were employed by the thirty-five companies listed on Spain's main stock market index. Most of them were former high-ranking government members, but a few also used to be influential figures in regional politics. They collectively earned more than €18 million. Almost half of them worked for companies in the energy sector, followed by the banking and telecommunications sectors. Of the fifty-eight, twenty-two were members of the PP. They earned almost €9 million, so about €400,000 on average. The sixteen PSOE members made about €190,000 on average for a total of €3 million.[22]

---

[21] All quotes appear in Jiménez and Carbona (2012), translated by the author.
[22] "Al menos 58 ex altos cargos políticos trabajan ahora para el Ibex," *Público*, March 17, 2017; "Infografía: 'La trama de los expolíticos en la cúpula del IBEX-35'," *Público*, March 17, 2017.

One prominent example of a politician taking up a golden parachute job is Ángel Acebes, who held a number of positions in the cabinet of José María Aznar. After the PP lost the 2004 election, Acebes returned to being a regular MP until 2011, when he resigned. In April 2012, he became a member of the executive committee of the utility company Iberdrola. The committee met thirty-one times in 2013, for which Acebes received a salary of €317,000.[23] Another representative case involves the PSOE politician Trinidad Jiménez. She was a member of the cabinet of José Luis Zapatero for five years and then became an MP. Roughly three weeks after her resignation in early 2016, it was announced that she would join the telecommunications giant Telefónica in an executive role.[24] Note that neither of those politicians were accused of enrichment while in office, which is consistent with the argument I made in Chapter 3 that the same individuals typically do not engage in enrichment *in* and *after* office.

In summary, Spain falls in the middle of both explanatory dimensions. Consistent with theoretical expectations, we can therefore observe all three forms of money in politics. There is evidence that influential politicians enrich themselves while in office, and they put effort into raising campaign money in both legal and illegal ways. Finally, many of them take up well-paid jobs in private companies after leaving office.

6.6 GERMANY

In the Control of Corruption indicator, Germany ranked between 11th and 13th from 2017 to 2019, higher than any other country discussed so far. It has strict and well-enforced laws regulating high-level enrichment in office. A report by the compliance management company GAN Integrity states that "Germany has strong institutional and legal anti-corruption frameworks" and that it "is among the world's top enforcers of anti-corruption legislation."[25] Germany's campaign finance regulation is somewhat less restrictive. It does not limit how much parties or candidates can spend. However, it has more stringent transparency requirements than most of the countries discussed so far (Scarrow, 2007). In addition, Germany is a pioneer when it comes to generous public

---

[23] "Ángel Acebes ya acaricia el millón de euros de sueldo acumulado en Iberdrola," *eldiario.es*, January 6, 2015.

[24] "Telefónica pone en marcha el fichaje de la ex ministra Trinidad Jiménez," *El Mundo*, February 2, 2016.

[25] "Germany Corruption Report," *GAN Risk and Compliance Portal*, August 2020.

financing, which reduces the need to raise funds from the private sector (Scarrow, 2007; Falguera, Jones, and Ohman, 2014).

Germany's electoral campaign environment is at an intermediate level of demandingness. Elections are competitive: Both the conservative Christliche Demokratische Union/Christlich-Soziale Union (CDU/CSU) and the left-leaning Sozialdemokratische Partei Deutschlands (SPD) have taken turns in government. Since federal- and state-level elections are not synchronized with each other, German parties also must finance campaigns several times a year. However, campaigns are short, get-out-the-vote drives are not effective and thus not common, and parties cannot purchase TV or radio advertisements. Instead, they are allocated limited media slots based on their past performance in elections, membership numbers, and other factors. One of the main modes of campaigning is posters and billboards in public spaces, which are exceedingly cheap.[26]

The stringent and rigorously enforced laws should deter politicians from enriching themselves while in office, unlike what we observe for Spain. Instead, we would expect golden parachute employment to be common among German politicians. The less demanding campaign environment should ensure that the amount of money spent on elections is not overwhelming, but we can still expect it to play an important role. The theoretical expectation is therefore that money should enter politics primarily as campaign spending and through golden parachute jobs.

In the literature on money and politics in Germany, it is widely accepted that the *personal enrichment* of politicians is uncommon: "[P]olitical scandals in post-war German politics show marked similarities. In fact the most serious cases ... all involved violations of party finance laws. Furthermore, apart from some relatively trivial cases, the beneficiaries have usually been party coffers and not individual politicians" (McKay, 2003, 54–55). And: "The politicians who were corrupt or suspected of corruption were above all lured by contributions to their parties" (Seibel, 1997, 87).

These quotes make clear that *campaign spending* plays an important role in German politics. In 2014, the income of the social-democratic SPD was almost €162 million, and that of the conservative CDU was €147 million. A significant portion of this income came from donations. The two parties with the highest percentage of donations in 2014 were

---

[26] "In German Election, Campaign Posters Are More Important Than TV Ads," *NPR*, September 23, 2017.

the CSU (the Bavarian sister party of the CDU) and the liberal Freie Demokratische Partei (FDP), which had 29 percent each. The CDU's share was 18 percent and the SPD's was 9 percent. For the seven major parties, this amounted to €71 million in donations (Korte, 2017).

But not all campaign money always came from legal sources. The two major post-war scandals about money in politics both involve illegal campaign money. The first is known as the "Flick affair." In the 1970s, the Flick industrial consortium was due to pay several billion DM in taxes on profits from selling its share of the car maker Daimler-Benz. Two ministers from the FDP, which had been the beneficiary of lavish donations from Flick that were channeled through a charitable foundation to hide their origins, pushed for an exceptional waiver. Its coalition partner, the SPD, at first objected, but ultimately relented after receiving a generous donation from Flick as well (Seibel, 1997; McKay, 2003).

During the course of the investigations, which led to the conviction of the FDP ministers for tax fraud, it became clear that the Flick consortium had engaged in what its manager Eberhard von Brauchitsch called the "cultivation of the political landscape" (his description of the payments) for decades. The FDP had received a total of DM6.5 million and the SPD got DM4.3 million (around €8.8 million and €5.8 million in today's currency, or $10.4 and $6.9 million, respectively). The biggest beneficiary, however, was the CDU, which had received a total of DM15 million.[27] There are suggestions, however, that these payments are only part of the story. The foundation that was used as a vehicle to channel the money to the parties donated a lot more than these sums. By some estimates, its contributions to just the CDU, CSU, and FDP between 1969 and 1980 amounted to more than DM200 million.[28]

The Flick affair, which came to light in the 1980s, highlights the importance of campaign spending in German politics. But at no point were there suggestions that politicians used the money for their personal enrichment. This pattern also holds for the second major scandal involving money in politics. The "donations scandal" started in 1999 during an investigation of the arms dealer Karlheinz Schreiber for tax evasion. In the process, prosecutors found that he had given campaign money to the CDU that did not show up in the party's annual reports. In a subsequent interrogation, the CDU's former treasurer confirmed that he had accepted cash donations of DM1 million by Schreiber on behalf of the party (Sontheimer,

---

[27] "Ein Mann kaufte die Republik," *Spiegel*, October 6, 2006.
[28] "Die dunklen Seiten von Kohls Vermächtnis," *Spiegel*, December 2, 2017.

2000; Scarrow, 2003). There are suggestions that these payments were linked to various arms deals (McKay, 2003). What followed was revelation upon revelation of dubious campaign financing practices in the CDU (Naßmacher, 2000). For example, the party in the state of Hessen was found to have kept a secret bank account in Switzerland, in which more than DM30 million was stashed. Funds were illegally transferred back into official party accounts disguised as "bequests by Jewish emigrés."

But the most important case involved former Chancellor Helmut Kohl, who admitted to maintaining a campaign slush fund of around DM12 million. In the words of the magazine *Spiegel*: "Especially during campaigns, Kohl's expenses got out of control. He consistently ignored any budgets."[29] Kohl refused to disclose who gave him the money, curtly declaring that he had given the donors his "word of honor" that they would remain anonymous. No amount of shaming, questioning in parliamentary committees, imposition of fines, or threats of imprisonment for contempt of court changed his mind. Regardless, it is clear that Kohl and the CDU supplemented their legal campaign fundraising with illegal efforts. At the same time, "[t]here was no suggestion of personal gain however" (McKay, 2003, 59).

While German politicians do not use their position to get rich while in office, many of them do benefit from *golden parachute employment*. The most famous example was introduced in the first pages of this book. In 2005, Gerhard Schröder took a position as board chairman of Nord Stream, a consortium majority-owned by the Russian energy company Gazprom, less than three weeks after stepping down as chancellor, months after approving a pipeline to be built by the consortium. This was in fact already his second job. Just a day after handing over to Angela Merkel, it was announced that Schröder would serve as an adviser to a Swiss media group.[30] And shortly after taking up the Nord Stream job, Schröder also joined the investment bank Rothschild as an adviser.[31] This flurry of jobs turned the spotlight on golden parachute employment in Germany. When German-born Pope Benedict declared his retirement in 2013, a cartoon titled "Catholics Worried after Pope Announces Retirement" in the newspaper *Frankfurter Allgemeine Zeitung* shows a

---

[29] "Die dunklen Seiten von Kohls Vermächtnis," *Spiegel*, December 2, 2017, translated by the author.
[30] "Schröder wird Berater des Ringier-Verlags," *Spiegel*, November 24, 2005.
[31] "Schröder berät die Investmentbank Rothschild," *Frankfurter Allgemeine Zeitung*, March 24, 2006.

churchgoer worrying "Oh god, in the end the pope will go into the private sector," while another responds: "Hopefully not to Gazprom."[32]

Indeed, Schröder is just the best-known example of a broader pattern in Germany. More than a third of his ministers went into the private sector as well, despite the fact that the SPD continued to be in the governing coalition after 2005. One notable example is former Interior Minister Otto Schily, who advocated for and oversaw the inclusion of biometric data into passport and identity cards, and then joined the boards of directors of two companies that specialize in biometric technology. And Wolfgang Clement, Minister of Economics and Labor under Schröder, joined the boards of directors of no less than seven companies within a year of leaving office (see Klein and Höntzsch, 2007).

Golden parachute jobs are not limited to members of the SPD. One of the harshest critics of Schröder's move was the FDP politician Dirk Niebel, who declared that the arrangements had a "whiff of corruption" (Klein and Höntzsch, 2007, 1). Niebel later became the Minister for Development. In this capacity, he sat on the committee that approves arms sales to foreign countries. After his tenure ended in 2013, he joined the board of defense technology producer Rheinmetall.[33] A systematic study of the post-politics career patterns of cabinet members confirms the importance of golden parachute jobs: Dörrenbächer (2016) shows that since 2000, 30–40 percent of ministers went into the private sector immediately after leaving office.

But golden parachute jobs are not just for high-level politicians. For example, a former MP for the Green Party made headlines when she became the managing director of the interest group of German cigarette producers, and a former SPD member left office to work for the aircraft manufacturer EADS. A systematic study finds that 27 percent of former MPs work in the lobbying sector (Edinger and Schwarz, 2009). This is a large share for at least two reasons. First, it does not count all forms of golden parachute employment. Second, we know that holding a higher political position is associated with a greater probability of being offered an attractive position after leaving office (Würfel, 2018). But a typical German MP has less influence than an average member of, for example, the US Congress, as party discipline is greater and most decisions are

---

[32] "Eine Zeit der Rückschau ist angebrochen," *Frankfurter Allgemeine Zeitung*, February 12, 2013.
[33] "Dirk Niebel to Take Up International Duties at Rheinmetall Starting in 2015," *Rheinmetall Press Release*, July 1, 2014.

made by the leadership. The fact that despite this, more than a quarter of former MPs become lobbyists speaks volumes about the importance of golden parachute employment in Germany.

In summary, Germany is on the stricter end of regulations for personal enrichment, and has an intermediately demanding electoral campaign environment. As a consequence, politicians do not tend to enrich themselves while in office, but many benefit from their position after leaving it. In addition, campaign spending is limited but not negligible. All of this is consistent with theoretical expectations.

6.7 UNITED KINGDOM

Finally, the United Kingdom also has a strict legal environment, ranking directly above Germany in the Control of Corruption measure. GAN Integrity states that "[c]orruption does not represent a constraint to business in the United Kingdom" and that "the UK promotes high ethical standards in public services."[34]

Its campaign finance framework is the most restrictive of all countries discussed in this book. This has a long tradition:

As democratic elections became the norm in Britain, two principles became firmly established in the political and public mind: that individual and party spending on elections should be comparatively small scale, and that the state has a duty to restrict elections spending tightly in the interest of fair competition (Adonis, 1997, 110).

In particular, limits on how much candidates can spend at the constituency level have been in effect since 1883 (Pinto-Duschinsky, 1981; Ewing and Rowbottom, 2012; Johnston and Pattie, 2012; Fouirnaies, 2021). Expenditure control has become even more restrictive since 2000, when *national* expenditure limits were introduced. Parties' campaign spending is restricted to no more than £30,000 per contested constituency in the 365 days before an election (Clift and Fisher, 2004; Ewing and Rowbottom, 2012; Fisher, 2016). This stands in contrast to Germany, which does not place caps on campaign spending. The United Kingdom also places restrictions on donors. Unions must ballot their members once every ten years about whether they should set up a political fund that donates to parties and politicians. Corporations have to poll their shareholders every four years about whether the board of directors has the right to make political donations (Clift and Fisher, 2004; Fisher, 2016).

---

[34] "United Kingdom Corruption Report," *GAN Risk and Compliance Portal*, September 2020.

The UK's electoral campaign environment is somewhat less demanding than Germany's. While campaigns are competitive, they are typically very short. For example, Gordon Brown announced on April 6, 2010 that a general election would take place on May 6 that same year. This means that there are few opportunities to spend on campaigning. In addition, the United Kingdom is characterized by a high degree of centralization, so fewer elections take place (Adonis, 1997).

The theoretical prediction for money in the United Kingdom is thus that enrichment in office should be all but nonexistent, and that campaign spending should be limited as well, even compared to Germany. This only leaves the third option for money to enter politics – golden parachute employment, which is predicted to be even more widespread than in Germany.

There are indeed few instances of post-war British politicians using their offices for *self-enrichment*, and the cases that did occur involve very little money. For example, when an architecture company went bankrupt in 1972, the trustee who took over operations discovered that the firm had made payments to various local and national politicians in the hope of gaining commissions for public buildings. The case received intense public scrutiny, especially as it became clear that three MPs were accused of having accepted money and gifts. While their cases shocked the British public, the sums involved were rather meager. The transaction that received the most attention was a silver coffee pot given to one MP, initially valued at £600 (roughly £9,000 or $11,600 today); its true value was later determined to be only £40. The second MP had received £1,000 (about £15,000 today), and the third went on a paid vacation (Tribe, 2010).

Another case of self-enrichment occurred in 2009, when it emerged that some MPs had made fraudulent expense claims, mostly related to a provision that allowed reimbursement for holding a second home (in London and in their constituency). While this expenses scandal played an important role in public discussion (Pattie and Johnston, 2012; Eggers, 2014), the sums involved were again rather minor, and the legal penalties were swift and severe. For example, Labour MP Jim Devine was sentenced to sixteen months in prison for fraudulent claims of less than £8,500, and Conservative MP John Taylor received twelve months for false expense claims of roughly £11,300.[35] This confirms that enrichment in office in

---

[35] "Former MP Jim Devine Guilty Over Expenses," *BBC News*, February 10, 2011; "Lord Taylor Guilty of Making False Expenses Claims," *BBC News*, January 25, 2011.

the United Kingdom is subject to strict and well-enforced laws. Politicians who engage in it nevertheless do so at a high risk, even if they only take small sums of money.

What about *campaign spending*? Because of the spending restrictions (stringent legal environment) as well as the short election period and the small number of elections (less demanding electoral campaign environment), party expenses are also relatively low. For example, the Labour Party only spent about £11 million on its 2015 general election campaign. Between 2010 and 2016, the total annual expenditure of the central Labour Party has fluctuated between roughly £20 million and £30 million – closer to the former in nonelection years and closer to the latter when general elections were held. Conservative Party expenditures topped £40 million in 2010, but have oscillated between around £20 million and £30 million since. The Liberal Democrats have annual expenses of less than £10 million (Fisher, 2018). While these sums are not insignificant, they are less than what German parties spend. Nor have there been major scandals involving illegal party finance practices.

Given the limited prevalence of campaign money and the almost negligible level of enrichment in office, *golden parachute employment* in Britain should be widespread. And indeed, politicians in the United Kingdom can benefit financially from their position: Eggers and Hainmueller (2009) compare the wealth of MPs who narrowly won elections to that of people who ran for office, but narrowly lost. They find that members of the Conservative Party who, essentially by luck, won a seat in parliament had assets twice as high as their unsuccessful colleagues at the time of their deaths, which amounts to £250,000 on average. This additional wealth is due to corporate directorships, which election winners take up at more than three times the rate of losers (Eggers and Hainmueller, 2009).

One of the most prominent early examples of golden parachute employment was Nigel Lawson, who left Margaret Thatcher's cabinet in October 1989 and took up a directorship with a national bank four months later. He earned a salary of £100,000 per year, about four times the amount he received as an MP (Eggers and Hainmueller, 2009).

A host of politicians (especially cabinet members) have pursued similar career paths. After the 2005 election, Health Minister Alan Milburn took several jobs with private health companies as well as with a private equity firm that received contracts from the National Health Service (Transparency International, 2014). Alan Turnbull stepped down as head of the

Home Civil Service and took up no less than five private sector positions, two as an adviser and three as a nonexecutive director (High Pay Center, 2015).

In the cabinet reshuffle that occurred after Gordon Brown took over from Tony Blair as Prime Minister in 2007, another round of ministers headed into the private sector. For example, Health Secretary Patricia Hewitt became a nonexecutive director for a telecommunications company, earning £128,000 per year, a senior adviser for a private equity firm for £60,000 annually, and a consultant for a pharmacy chain for £55,000 (High Pay Center, 2015).

In 2010, a coalition between the Conservatives and Liberal Democrats under David Cameron took over the government from Labour. Again, outgoing cabinet members headed into golden parachute jobs in droves. For instance, Secretary of State Peter Mandelson became a senior adviser for an investment bank and opened his own consultancy firm to provide advice to corporate clients. Foreign Secretary David Miliband became vice chairman of a soccer club, joined the advisory board of a policy forum organized by the United Arab Emirates, and took up adviser roles at a consulting company as well as at two venture capital investment firms (Advisory Committee on Business Appointments, 2011, 2012).

And finally, when David Cameron resigned as Prime Minister six years later, there was again a rush of cabinet members into the private sector. Cameron himself became an adviser to a US electronic payments firm, a UK–China investment initiative, and a UK supply chain finance company.[36] George Osborne, the former Chancellor of the Exchequer, was given the nickname "six-job George," later upgraded to "nine-job George."[37] Former Secretary for Energy and Climate Change Edward Davey set up his own consultancy firm that accepted commissions from an international law firm and an investment bank. In addition, he became a nonexecutive director at a private equity investment company, a consultant for a public relations firm, and the chairman of an oil and gas company. And Steve Webb, the Minister for Pensions, became a director of a pensions firm with which he had regular meetings during his time in office (Advisory Committee on Business Appointments, 2016, 2017).

---

[36] "What Is David Cameron Doing Now?," *The Guardian*, December 29, 2017; "The David Cameron Scandal: Just How Sleazy Is British Politics?," *Financial Times*, April 16, 2021.

[37] "'Six-Job George' Is Back as Osborne Takes on Another Role," *Sky News*, June 29, 2017; "Nine Jobs George: Osborne Adds New Role at Venture Capital Firm," *The Guardian*, December 14, 2018.

It is possible to quantify the extent of golden parachute employment in the United Kingdom. In the two years after leaving office, all former ministers, junior ministers, and senior civil servants have to seek the permission of the Advisory Committee on Business Appointments before taking up any employment in the private sector. The committee publishes annual reports on all appointments that have been approved. From 2000 to 2017, it decided favorably on a total of 1,275 applications by ministers and senior civil servants.[38]

This allows us to see how widespread the move into the private sector is among senior politicians. I collected the names of all British ministers who appear in the CIA Chiefs of State and Cabinet Members of Foreign Governments directory starting in 2001 and who were not still cabinet members as of early 2018. A total of seventy-one individuals fall into this category. For these politicians, the committee approved a total of 123 appointments, an average of 1.73 per person. Out of the seventy-one, forty had at least one appointment approved, so 56 percent of former ministers took up a private sector job.

This is in line with the theoretical predictions I have laid out earlier. Not only is golden parachute employment widespread in Britain; it plays a more important role than in Germany, where only 30–40 percent of ministers take a similar path. The argument I make in this book suggests that this is not a coincidence, as British politicians and parties are subject to stricter campaign spending regulations and have a less demanding electoral campaign environment.

6.8 SUMMARY

In this chapter, I have tested the book's theoretical argument in a series of qualitative country studies. In addition to India, Brazil, and the United States, I have added the cases of South Africa, Spain, Germany, and the United Kingdom. The overall picture that emerges is that countries' legal and electoral campaign environments can also explain *cross-national differences* in how politicians use money.

Taken together, the last three chapters have provided consistent evidence that the different forms of money in politics are part of a common

---

[38] Based on the compilation in High Pay Center (2015) and supplemented with the numbers reported by the Advisory Committee on Business Appointments for the periods 2014–2015, 2015–2016, and 2016–2017.

system, that they are directly connected to each other, and that a change in one form has countervailing *second-order consequences* for the other types. The final part of my argument was that how money enters politics has *third-order consequences* for various aspects of democratic competition. The next chapter tests this proposition.

7

Consequences for Democracy

The previous chapters were a deep dive into the ways in which politicians use money. They showed that enrichment while in office, campaign spending, and enrichment after leaving office through golden parachute jobs are not simply idiosyncratic ways for money to enter politics. Instead, I have demonstrated that the different types are part of a common system; that they are partially fungible and therefore interdependent; that politicians use them in the ways that optimally serve their goals, subject to the legal and electoral campaign environments they operate in; and that a change in one form has second-order effects on other forms. But the implications of a system view of the types of money in politics do not stop here. I have argued that each form can affect various aspects of *how democracies function*. Thus, if money stops flowing in one way and instead shows up in another, this has important *third-order effects*. In this chapter, I test this final part of my argument.

First, I show that how money enters politics influences *voters' perceptions of politics*. An extensive literature demonstrates that money in politics has a negative effect on citizens' trust in government and democracy (e.g. Della Porta, 2000; Anderson and Tverdova, 2003; Chang and Chu, 2006; Solé-Ollé and Sorribias-Navarro, 2018). However, past studies have mostly examined the impact of corruption writ large, without distinguishing between different forms. I use a pair of survey experiments to show that citizens react differently depending on the type of money. In the first survey experiment, I demonstrate that Indian voters are clearly and consistently more lenient toward politicians who received money for a political favor when they used it to buy votes rather than for personal enrichment. The second survey experiment shows that US voters are significantly less critical of a politician when told that he or she accepted several hundred thousand dollars in campaign contributions than after learning that he or she later earned the same amount working for a special interest group. Thus, a change in one form of money in politics, which in turn leads to changes in the other forms, has the third-order consequence of affecting how voters view politicians. I demonstrate that this helps explain puzzling findings reported in prior research.

In a second step, I show that *how* money enters politics also shapes *who wins elections*. Of the three types, campaign money is unique: rather than having a direct personal benefit, it indirectly helps politicians win votes and stay in office. Conditions that increase the amount of money in the form of campaign spending can thus affect the outcomes of elections, particularly if some candidates and parties systematically have more access to money than others, as is almost always the case. And as we have learned in the previous chapters, an increase in campaign spending can be brought about by changes in *other* forms of money. In Chapter 5, I provided evidence that stricter regulation of golden parachute employment in US states led to more campaign contributions to Republican candidates. Here, I show that the third-order effect of cooling-off laws is that they systematically shift electoral favors toward that party.

These downstream consequences add another layer of implications to my theory. It is not just that a decrease in one form of money leads to an increase in other forms. These shifts in how money enters politics have knock-on effects on how democracies function. This has received little attention to date.

7.1 VOTERS: HOW MONEY ENTERS POLITICS AFFECTS ATTITUDES

Citizens' trust in politicians plays an important role in the stability and health of a democracy. One of the major factors undermining this trust, especially in recent years, has been a widespread conviction that money has too much influence on politics and politicians. But not all types of money are created equally. In Chapter 3, I argued that there are reasons to expect that voters have more of a problem with money in politics when politicians use it to enrich themselves, either in office or after leaving it. In this section, I test whether this is indeed the case. In a given context, only two forms of money are typically present. I therefore first examine how voters view self-enrichment vis-à-vis campaign spending, and then what voters think about golden parachute employment vis-à-vis campaign money.

Self-Enrichment and Campaign Spending

First, I examine how voters view enrichment in office as opposed to using money for campaign spending. Chapter 4 demonstrated that both forms of money in politics are common in India. I therefore embedded an experimental manipulation in a larger face-to-face survey administered in the National Capital Territory of Delhi in 2014. A representative sample of voters was interviewed in Hindi by trained interviewers from a Delhi-based polling company.[1]

To examine whether it makes a difference to voters whether a politician uses money for personal enrichment or to enhance their reelection chances, respondents were randomly assigned to receive one of two questions. The first group was read the following text:

Imagine a politician who received money from a company for a political favor. He used this money to personally enrich himself. What do you think the consequences should be?

The other half of the respondents was given this prompt:

Imagine a politician who received money from a company for a political favor. He used this money to buy votes in an election. What do you think the consequences should be?

The only difference between the two statements is that the politician uses the money for a different purpose. Both texts are formulated in a neutral manner that does not provide too much, and possibly leading, information. For instance, the vote-buying question does not stress who the recipients are or what benefits they receive. Instead, it simply refers to vote buying, which is illegal under Indian law, as is accepting money for self-enrichment in exchange for a political favor. In line with the convention in the literature, I use a fictional rather than a real politician.[2] While this leads respondents to evaluate an abstract situation, it ensures

---

[1] Respondents were selected using the following protocol. First, ten of Delhi's seventy assembly constituencies were chosen randomly. Then, five polling stations from each constituency were sampled by dividing the total number of stations in the constituency by five and then randomly drawing a number smaller than or equal to the result of the division. The first five multiples of the drawn number indicate the sampled polling stations. Finally, for each polling station, twenty voters were selected from the official electoral roll using the same procedure as for the polling stations. A total of 993 interviews were conducted.

[2] I use a hypothetical male politician since the vast majority of Indian politicians are men.

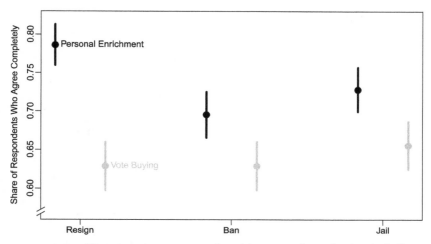

FIGURE 7.1 *Voter reaction to personal enrichment and vote buying in India.*
Share of respondents who agree completely with the punishment statement,
depending on whether they received the personal enrichment treatment (black)
or the vote buying treatment (gray). Point estimates and 95 percent confidence
intervals

that an actual politician's partisanship, religion, or caste do not confound
the results.

Respondents were then asked whether they agreed completely, agreed,
neither agreed nor disagreed, disagreed, or disagreed completely with the
following three possible punishments for the offending lawmaker:

- A politician who took money for political favors to [buy votes/enrich himself]
  should have to resign from his position.
- A politician who took money for political favors to [buy votes/enrich himself]
  should be banned from contesting future elections.
- A politician who took money for political favors to [buy votes/enrich himself]
  should be sentenced to time in jail.

Because the respondents were randomly assigned to receive either the vote
buying or the personal enrichment treatment, all personal characteristics
should, on average, be the same between the two groups. We can thus
analyze whether voters are more or less tolerant depending on what the
money is used for by simply comparing the proportions in the answer
categories.

Figure 7.1 shows the share of respondents who *agree completely*
with the punishment statements for the personal enrichment treatment
(black) and the vote-buying treatment (gray). The figure makes clear that

TABLE 7.1 *Effect of the vote-buying treatment on support for punishment in India.* Coefficient of vote-buying treatment indicator in OLS regressions. Controls not displayed

	Resign	Ban	Jail
Vote-Buying Treatment	0.285***	0.201***	0.178***
	(0.063)	(0.062)	(0.060)

*$p < 0.1$, ** $p < 0.05$, *** $p < 0.01$. N = 926 (Resign), 918 (Ban), 913 (Jail). All regressions include assembly fixed effects. Controls: age, gender, religion, education, scheduled caste or tribe, other caste, number of adults in household, number of children in household, income. Robust standard errors clustered by polling station in parentheses.

tolerance of politicians who accept money for political favors is low, regardless of how it is used. In both conditions and across all statements, a large share of respondents agree completely that a politician who engages in such behavior should be punished.[3]

Despite the high level of overall disapproval of the politicians' behavior, respondents in the vote-buying treatment were consistently more tolerant than those in the personal enrichment treatment: 79 percent completely agreed that the hypothetical lawmaker should have to resign from his position if he used the money for himself, compared to only 63 percent of those who were told the money was used to buy votes. There were also statistically significant differences between the two treatments in support of a ban on contesting future elections (70 vs. 63 percent) and a jail sentence (73 vs. 66 percent).

To make sure that small imbalances between the treatment and control groups for a few covariates are not driving the results, Table 7.1 reports the coefficients of the vote-buying treatment indicator from Ordinary Least Squares (OLS) regressions with a set of controls and constituency fixed effects. The dependent variable takes a value of one if the respondent agrees completely with the proposed punishment, and five if he or she disagrees completely, so higher values indicate greater tolerance of vote buying. The coefficients can be interpreted as the differences in means between the two treatments, controlling for demographic and constituency effects. They are between 0.178 (jail) and 0.285 (resign) on a scale from one to five, and significant at the 1 percent level.[4]

---

[3] One likely reason for this is that the survey took place shortly after the anti-corruption Aam Aadmi Party took over the state government in Delhi, so the topic had high salience among respondents.

[4] For further analyses, see Weschle (2016).

We now have the first piece of evidence that *how* politicians use money affects citizens' attitudes toward them. Voters in India are more critical of legislators who accept money in exchange for political favors if they use it for their personal enrichment. They are less critical when the money is used for campaigning purposes, even though this is done through the less than normatively ideal practice of vote buying.

Campaign Spending and Golden Parachutes

What if, instead of enriching themselves in office, politicians make money after leaving it by taking up a golden parachute job? How do voters react to political and personal money then? As I showed in Chapter 5, campaign spending and post-office jobs are common in the United States, so I conducted a survey experiment on a sample of US adults.

Participants were recruited through the Mechanical Turk platform and received a small amount of money to participate.[5] They were given a short description of a hypothetical member of Congress and then asked to evaluate him.[6] The first part of the description was the same for everyone:

Imagine that you live in a neighborhood similar to your own but in a different state. The member of Congress of that district is called John Davis. During his time in office, he has secured federal funding to improve the district's infrastructure, and he has put efforts into trying to attract companies into the district.

This description establishes a positive first impression of the politician, highlighting his efforts as well as showing that he has delivered results for the district. The second part of the description then introduces a counter-frame (Chong and Druckman, 2013) by informing respondents that he has taken a significant amount of money. Half of the respondents were randomly chosen to receive the following text:

Representative Davis also has accepted several hundred thousand dollars in campaign and PAC contributions from special interests.

---

[5] A total of 984 questionnaires were completed. Around the time I conducted the survey in the fall of 2018, it was reported that a sizable share of respondents recruited through Mechanical Turk were able to circumvent the location filter and pretend to be based in the United States (Kennedy et al., 2020). As a precaution, I therefore checked participants' IP addresses and prevented anyone who was not located in the United States or who used a virtual private server from accessing the questionnaire (see Burleigh, Kennedy, and Clifford, 2018).

[6] I again use a male hypothetical politician since the vast majority of US legislators are men.

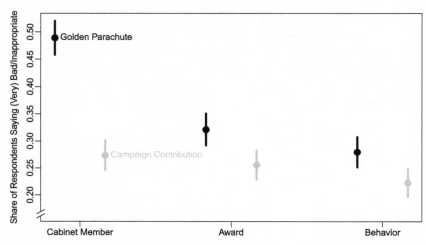

FIGURE 7.2 *Voter reaction to golden parachute jobs and campaign spending in the United States.* Share of respondents that said the politician would be a (very) bad choice or acted (very) inappropriately, depending on whether they received the golden parachute treatment (black) or the campaign spending treatment (gray). Point estimates and 95 percent confidence intervals

The other half was given this information:

Representative Davis has left office and accepted a position as a lobbyist for special interests, earning a salary of several hundred thousand dollars.

Both statements mention the same amount of money and only differ in *how* the congressman benefits from it. The respondents were then asked three questions about the politician, which tap into three dimensions of voter reactions:

- "Representative Davis is being considered for a role as a member of the cabinet. How good of a choice do you think he is?" Possible answers: A very good choice, a good choice, neither a good nor a bad choice, a bad choice, a very bad choice.
- "Representative Davis has been nominated for an award honoring dedicated public servants in his state. How good of a choice do you think he is?" Answers: A very good choice, a good choice, neither a good nor a bad choice, a bad choice, a very bad choice.
- "How appropriate do you think Representative Davis' behavior was?" Answers: Very appropriate, appropriate, neither appropriate nor inappropriate, inappropriate, very inappropriate.

Figure 7.2 displays the share of respondents that think the politician is a bad or very bad choice for the cabinet position and public service award as well as the share that think his behavior was inappropriate or very inappropriate. The results for the golden parachute (campaign contribution) treatment are in black (gray). In all analyses, I use entropy balancing to weigh the observations so that the composition of the convenience sample resembles that of the population (Hainmueller, 2012; Franco et al., 2017).[7]

As I found for Indian voters, disapproval of the politician among Americans is higher if the money was used for personal gain rather than campaigning. Fewer than 30 percent of respondents who were told the congressman received hundreds of thousands in campaign contributions thought he would be a bad or very bad candidate for a cabinet position; this increased to nearly 50 percent among respondents who heard that he became a lobbyist. Respondents were also more likely to think the congressman was not a good choice for a public service award when he took a golden parachute job, and to state that his behavior was inappropriate or very inappropriate.[8]

Table 7.2 shows the results of regressing the respondents' answers on the campaign contribution treatment and a set of controls. The dependent variable takes a value of one if the respondent indicated that the congressman was a very bad choice or behaved very inappropriately, and five if they thought he was a very good choice or behaved very appropriately. All three coefficients are positive and statistically significant, indicating greater tolerance of the politician when the money is used for campaign purposes. Again, the coefficients can be interpreted as the differences in means between the two treatments. They are between 0.369 (award) and 0.540 (cabinet member) on a one to five scale.

This is the second piece of evidence that *how* money enters politics is important to voters. US citizens are more likely to think a politician's behavior was inappropriate and that they are not a good candidate for a future political role or a public service award if they take a golden

---

[7] After reweighing, the sample resembles the population in the marginal distribution of the following variables: gender, race, ethnicity, age, education, income, and marital status.

[8] Note that the disapproval of the politician is surprisingly low throughout. This may reflect that campaign contributions to individual politicians and golden parachute jobs are legal in the United States, whereas both forms of money examined in India are illegal. In addition, and unlike the survey experiment in India discussed earlier, the description of the member of Congress included a number of positive characteristics that suggested he was hard-working and effective.

TABLE 7.2 *Effect of the campaign spending treatment on answering in an unfavorable way in the United States.* Coefficient of campaign spending treatment indicator in OLS regressions

	Cabinet Member	Award	Behavior
Campaign Contribution Treatment	0.540***	0.369***	0.473***
	(0.112)	(0.131)	(0.124)

$^{*}p < 0.1$, $^{**}p < 0.05$, $^{***}p < 0.01$. N = 984. Controls: age, gender, education, civil status, race, hispanic, employment status, partisanship, registered to vote, liberal–conservative scale, income, follow politics. Robust standard errors in parentheses.

parachute job than if they raise money for their campaign. Taken together, both survey experiments show that voters are more critical when money benefits politicians personally.

7.2 WINNERS: HOW MONEY ENTERS POLITICS AFFECTS ELECTION OUTCOMES

The second downstream consequence of how money enters politics that I discussed in Chapter 3 was election outcomes. Some politicians and parties have more access to money than others. If they use this for self-enrichment or if it comes in the form of golden parachute jobs, these asymmetries merely mean that some politicians get richer than others. But if money is mostly spent on campaigning, then these asymmetries can influence who wins elections.

Several prior studies have demonstrated that campaign spending regulations affect election outcomes. For example, since incumbents usually find it easier to raise funds, more permissive campaign finance laws tend to entrench them (see Hogan, 2000; Milligan and Rekkas, 2008; Avis et al., 2021; Fouirnaies, 2021). Similarly, because right-of-center parties benefit from more money, less stringent regulations help them electorally (see Hall, 2016; Klumpp, Mialon, and Williams, 2016; Abdul-Razzak, Prato, and Wolton, 2020). A more equitable distribution of campaign funds generally leads to more electoral competition (Potter and Tavits, 2015). Of course, politicians are aware of this fact and try to shape campaign finance regulation to their benefit (see e.g. Kochanek, 1987; Grzymala-Busse, 2007).

The argument and evidence presented in this book suggests that it is not only the direct regulation of campaign spending that affects election outcomes; instead, *any* change in the regulation of money in politics can shift the balance of power. In Chapter 5, I demonstrated that a change in the legal environment that makes golden parachute employment more difficult has the first-order effect of leading to fewer politicians heading for the private sector, and the second-order consequence of shifting campaign contribution patterns. Here, I examine the third-order effect of cooling off laws on election results.

Cooling Off Laws Affect Who Wins Elections

When a US state introduces a cooling off law, the first-order consequence is that fewer politicians take up a golden parachute job. This is especially true for legislators from the right-of-center Republican Party, who become more than 6 percentage points less likely to move into the private sector. The second-order effect is a 4.5-percentage-point increase in campaign donations to Republican candidates (see Chapter 5). According to my argument, the third-order effect should be that Republicans become more likely to win.

To test this prediction, I estimate the following difference-in-differences model:

$$y_{dst} = \beta \text{ Cooling Off Law}_{st} + \mu Z_{st} + \gamma_s + \delta_t + \xi_s t + \varepsilon_{dst} \qquad (7.1)$$

I use two different dependent variables. In one specification, I use the two-party Republican vote share in district d in state s in year t. In the other, I use a binary indicator that takes a value of one if the Republican candidate wins, and zero if he or she loses.[9] As before, the data cover the period from 1990 to 2012.

The main independent variable is a dummy that equals one if a state had a cooling off law in a given year, and the coefficient of interest is β. As state-level controls in Z_{st}, I include whether the state has a public campaign finance system, whether it had term limits, and whether it had bans on direct as well as indirect corporate and union campaign spending.[10] Again, there is a set of state fixed effects γ_s and a set of year fixed effects δ_t, as well as state-specific time trends $\xi_s t$. Parameter estimates are reported with robust standard errors clustered by state.

Table 7.3 illustrates how cooling off laws affect electoral competition. When a state introduces such restrictions, the two-party vote share

---

[9] Information on election results is taken from the State Legislative Election Returns dataset (Klarner, 2013; Klarner et al., 2013).

[10] I exclude very lopsided races, defined as those with a margin of victory of more than 25 percent.

TABLE 7.3 *Effect of cooling off laws on Republican vote share and win probability.* Coefficient of the effect of a law requiring a cooling off period on the percentage of the Republican two-party vote shares and win probabilities

	Share Republican Votes	Republicans Win
Cooling Off Law	0.010***	0.079***
	(0.003)	(0.020)

*$p < 0.1$, **$p < 0.05$, ***$p < 0.01$. N = 16,343. All regressions include state and year fixed effects and state-specific time trends. State-level controls: term limit law, public campaign finance, ban on union campaign contributions, ban on corporate campaign contributions, ban on union independent spending, ban on corporate independent spending. Robust standard errors clustered by state in parentheses.

for Republican candidates increases by about 1 percentage point. While this may not sound like a large effect, the average two-party vote share for Republicans in the sample is 50.3 percent, and many election races are decided by a few points. Thus, a 1-percentage-point shift could significantly influence who wins a seat.

And indeed, the second column in Table 7.3 reveals that after a cooling off law takes effect, Republican candidates are almost 8 percentage points more likely to win a seat. This is a large effect that has the potential to systemically shift majority control in favor of one party. And given that twenty-one of fifty states introduced cooling off laws during the observation period, they potentially played an important, and so far unrecognized, role in the improvement of Republicans' electoral fortunes since the 1990s.

To be clear, the effects observed in Table 7.3 are unlikely to all run directly through the second-order effect of increased campaign money. It is well known that there is a large (personal) incumbency advantage in the United States, and that seats are much more likely to flip to the other party when the incumbent does not run again (see e.g. Gelman and King, 1990; Gaddie and Bullock, 2000; Ansolabehere and Snyder, 2002; Fowler and Hall, 2014). Thus, if Republican legislators are less inclined to leave office for a golden parachute job, there are fewer open-seat elections, meaning fewer opportunities for Democrats to win them. This likely also contributes to the effects observed in Table 7.3. But of course, a good part of the incumbency advantage is due to the fact that sitting legislators benefit from more campaign money (Fouirnaies and Hall, 2014).

Either way, the findings in this section have broader implications beyond the context of US state elections. In a general sense, they show that changes to one form of money have third-order consequences for who wins elections. If less money flows to politicians for their personal benefit, more will come to them as campaign spending, which is to their political advantage. The overall effect is that less money in politics for personal benefit tilts electoral competition in favor of parties and candidates that have more access to money.

7.3 SUMMARY AND IMPLICATIONS

The results presented in this chapter have far-reaching implications. They suggest that the consequences of changes in the environment that affect how money enters politics are more widespread than previously thought.

First, we already knew that if money plays a large role in politics, it chips away at voters' trust in politicians and the political system. I have shown here that it also matters to voters *how* money enters politics. In two very different contexts, survey respondents who were randomly assigned to hear about a politician who used money for their personal benefit were more critical than those who heard about a politician who used the same amount for campaigning. If money does enter, it is thus especially harmful for the public's confidence in politics if it does so in a way that personally benefits lawmakers.

This finding has important implications. For instance, a central puzzle in the literature is why corrupt incumbents are sometimes voted out of office, but at other times are not.[11] One of the reasons for these inconsistent findings is that prior studies typically examine the effect of generic corruption allegations and do not differentiate between the exact forms of abuse. The fact that voters are more forgiving when money is used for electoral purposes and less tolerant when it involves self-enrichment helps explain why some politicians are punished while others are not.

Second, I showed that it is not only regulation which directly affects campaign spending that influences who wins elections; laws that pertain to *other* forms of money in politics also have an effect. This kind of third-order downstream consequence has not yet featured in public discussions of money in politics. For example, calls for stricter regulation of post-office employment in the United States are especially pronounced among

---

[11] See e.g. Golden (2010); Winters and Weitz-Shapiro (2013, 2017); Golden and Mahdavi (2015); Schwindt-Bayer and Tavits (2016); Chang and Kerr (2017); De Vries and Solaz (2017); Bauhr and Charron (2018); Solaz, De Vries, and de Geus (2019).

Democrats. However, the findings reported in this chapter show that such rules can have the unintended consequence of undermining their own party's electoral standing. If *any* reform of money in politics can affect who wins elections, this should form part of public discussions of the merits and problems before the electoral balance is altered.

Clearly, these two factors do not constitute an exhaustive list of third-order consequences. Yet the empirical results make clear that current debates about money in politics are incomplete at best. In the next chapter, I thus conclude by calling for an *evolution in the conversation about money in politics*.

8

Evolving the Conversation about Money in Politics

This book has demonstrated that enrichment in office, campaign spending, and enrichment after leaving office through golden parachute employment can – and should – be studied together. I have shown that a change in one form of money has second-order consequences on the others, which in turn has third-order effects on numerous aspects of how democracies function.

Prior research has mainly examined the different forms of money in politics in isolation. In this book, I have proposed conceptualizing them as part of a larger *system*. This final chapter concludes by assessing how this approach will advance academic and policy discussions about how money influences the quality of democracy. It discusses the impact on each in turn.

First, I lay out what this implies for *academic research*. My system-level view of money in politics represents one step in a larger research agenda that focuses on the connections between different types of money. The proposed framework outlined in this book can be applied to several avenues of future research, including other determinants of how money enters politics, additional third-order consequences, connecting *how* money enters to the important question of *whether* it does so, and how these forms of money relate to the broader issue of corruption. For each area, I provide a list of open research questions and sketch out some hypotheses to explore. I conclude the discussion of areas for further academic study by recapping the benefits of situating research on money in politics within the system framework.

Second, I discuss the implications of my argument for *public discussion* and *policy design*. Similar to prior academic research, public conversations about money in politics and advocacy work typically focus on one type at a time, and existing regulation tends to treat them in isolation. As this book has made clear, this siloed approach creates alternative avenues through which money can enter politics, which limits the overall effectiveness of reforms. Thus, an obvious policy implication of this book is that reforms should be made more effective by addressing the multiple types of money in politics in a coordinated fashion. However, it is often difficult to marshal the broad support required for such wide-ranging reforms, and freedom of occupation provisions place a natural limit on restrictions regarding politicians' employment after leaving office. Thus, piecemeal reforms continue to be the most realistic option. Therefore, the book's main policy implication is that it is important to have an *ex ante debate* about trade-offs: We need to anticipate the likely second- and third-order consequences of a change to one form of money, and then weigh the positive and negative consequences of reforms once its knock-on effects have played out. This would result in more effective policies with fewer unintended consequences.

8.1 EVOLVING THE RESEARCH ON MONEY IN POLITICS

Figure 8.1 again displays the share of mentions of the different forms of money in twenty-nine articles published in the three top general interest political science journals between 2010 and 2019, first shown in Chapter 2. This time, I add the location of this book as well. It is much closer to the center of the figure than any of the prior studies, which indicates that the book has forged a new path in the study of money in politics. Throughout, I have contrasted my focus on the connection between several forms with the current modus operandi in political science, which is to examine self-enrichment, campaign spending, and golden parachute employment separately. But Figure 8.1 also illustrates that there is still a lot of empty space outside of the three corners. In the following sections, I focus on this white area: This book has started to fill it in, but there is nevertheless considerable room for exploration. With this in mind, in this section I discuss several avenues for future research.

Other Determinants of How Money Enters Politics

This book has focused on how a country's legal and electoral campaign environments determine how money enters politics. The empirical chapters have demonstrated that these two factors explain much of the

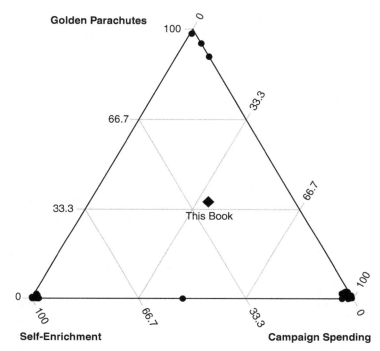

FIGURE 8.1 *Three types of money in politics in this book.* Share of words related to personal enrichment, campaign spending, and golden parachute jobs in this book (square) as well as twenty-nine articles about money in politics published in three general interest political science journals between 2010 and 2019 (round)

variation. But of course, they do not explain all of it. Future research should thus examine other determinants of how money enters politics.

One factor that has indirectly played some role in this book, but is likely important in other ways as well, is *political parties*. For example, in some contexts campaigns are run centrally by the party and individual politicians have little influence over how many resources are spent on their behalf, whereas in other contexts campaigns are decentralized and candidates are expected to raise and spend their own funds. In the latter case, a politician gets to keep the fruits of their fundraising labor, whereas in the former they can only keep a small portion and the rest goes to other candidates. But when a politician instead uses their connections to enrich themselves, or to secure a cushy job after leaving office, all the benefits accrue to them. This implies that when parties have centralized campaigns there should be, all else equal, fewer campaign resources than when each legislator is responsible for their own election finances. We should therefore see more personal enrichment and golden parachute jobs in such contexts. Thus, the system view of money in politics suggests that party-led campaign financing introduces a collective action problem, which has received little theoretical or empirical attention in the literature so far.

Of course, parties that are able to reward or punish members can counteract this incentive to free ride. For example, they can reward top fundraisers by placing them high on the party list or sending the prime minister to campaign in their constituency. Those who do not pull their weight bringing in funds can be punished by denying them a top spot or by sending the assistant secretary of agriculture to give a speech on their behalf. And again, this should not only have implications for campaign money but also for personal enrichment and golden parachute employment.

How campaigns are run and financed, as well as parties' ability to use carrots and sticks, is determined by a country's *electoral system*. For example, politicians running in first-past-the-post single-member districts are much more likely to run their own campaigns, whereas proportional representation encourages centralized, party-run campaigns. Parties' most powerful tool for reward and punishment is control over the rank ordering of their candidates, which they only have in closed-list systems. Parties in countries with primaries or open-list systems have much less sway over their members, who therefore have very different incentives when deciding how to use the money they have access to.[1] Going forward, it will be important to examine these and other consequences of a country's electoral system on how money enters politics.

More broadly, other differences in *institutional environments* should impact whether money is used for self-enrichment, as campaign spending, or in the form of golden parachute jobs. One obvious example is term limits, which activists and think tanks often advocate as a way to limit the influence of money on politics. Almost by definition, they do indeed cause last-term incumbents to fundraise less (cf. Carey, Niemi, and Powell, 1998). However, incumbents still have the option to enrich themselves while in office or to use their position to secure a lucrative golden parachute job. And if campaign spending is no longer necessary, career paths

---

[1] Consistent with this logic, Gingerich (2013) demonstrates that aspiring politicians in closed-list systems are more likely to raise money for their party than those in open-list systems. The other side of the coin, which has not yet been analyzed empirically, is that politicians in open-list systems have more incentives to personally enrich themselves.

involving these options become more attractive. Thus, imposing term limits on legislators should lead to a shift from using money for electoral toward personal purposes, with the associated third-order consequences.

Research on the effect of these and other potential determinants will fill out the large white area in Figure 8.1 and help map the connections between the different forms of money in politics. Importantly, it will not be necessary to start from scratch. A large amount of high-quality research has already examined the determinants of specific forms of money, which can be used as a starting point: When thinking about money in politics as a system, how can the independent variables analyzed in these studies be expected to affect the other forms?

Other Third-Order Consequences

Another key finding of this book is that a change in one form of money, and the associated second-order effects this has on other types, has third-order implications on how democracies function. In Chapter 7, I showed that such changes affect what voters think about politicians and who wins elections. But there are likely other third-order consequences.

For example, how money is used in politics may shape politicians' *time horizons*. If money in politics primarily entails "smash and grab" self-enrichment without regards for the potential impacts on one's reelection chances, legislators' political time horizons will be limited. The same is true if politicians use their office as a stepping stone to a career in the private sector. Past research shows that legislators with limited time horizons put less effort into their job. For example, they are less likely to collaborate on legislative initiatives, develop less expertise, and are less inclined to represent their constituents.[2] Thus, how money enters politics potentially affects all of these factors.

A limited time horizon has also been shown to have implications for *democratic accountability*. One of the key characteristics of a democratic system is that it allows voters to throw their representatives out of office

---

[2] On the effect of time horizons in general, see Linz (1998). For evidence that they lead to less effort, see Rothenberg and Sanders (2000); Samuels (2003); Sarbaugh-Thompson et al. (2006); Cho and Fowler (2010); Dal Bó and Rossi (2011); Titiunik (2016). On the effect of time horizons on expertise, see Carey, Niemi, and Powell (2000); Moncrief and Thompson (2001); Jones et al. (2002); Samuels (2003). For studies showing that legislators with limited time horizons are less representative of their constituents, see Carey (1998); Rothenberg and Sanders (2000); Tien (2001); Samuels (2003); Uppal (2011); Uppal and Glazer (2015); Egerod (2019).

if they are not satisfied with them. For this to work, incumbents need to be interested in getting reelected. If money in politics comes in the form of self-enrichment or golden parachute jobs, politicians may not seek to stay in office. If this is the case, voters cannot hold them accountable for their actions, which has dire consequences for the functioning of democracy.

In addition to these immediate consequences, how money enters politics may also have long-term implications for *political selection*. Past research has shown that the characteristics of current representatives shape the pool of future candidates. For example, when women or ethnic minorities are elected, this can motivate other women or minorities to be more politically engaged, and the presence of ideological extremists discourages moderates from running for office.[3] It is plausible, and indeed likely, that how office holders use money has a similar effect. For example, if self-enrichment in or after office is the norm, this may discourage public-spirited individuals from considering a career in politics, and encourage those who are primarily interested in rent seeking. Thus, how money enters politics likely plays an important role in creating and sustaining vicious or virtuous cycles by influencing whether people with desirable or undesirable qualities run for office.

Connection to Whether Money Enters Politics

In this book, I have deliberately focused on how money enters politics, and have bracketed the question of *whether* and *how much* of it does. However, the connections between these two deserve further research: Once we take the partial fungibility of different forms into account, the straightforward argument that stricter regulation should get money out of politics becomes a lot more complicated.

In the theoretical setup in Chapter 3, the politician had a choice between two policy options. One was popular among the electorate, whereas the other opened the door for money to flow to the politician. I assumed that they chose the latter and then focused on the ways in which the money would be used. This is the case if two conditions are met. First, the incumbent needs to be better off accepting money from the financier and implementing the less popular policy than not taking the money and choosing the more popular option. This will be the case if the amount of money the incumbent receives is above a certain threshold. The second

---

[3] See e.g. Mansbridge (1999); Campbell and Wolbrecht (2006); Bhavnani (2009); Alexander (2012); Shah (2014); Gilardi (2015); Thomsen (2017); Hall (2019).

condition is that those who provide the money also need to be better off in a situation in which their preferred policy becomes law and they pay money to the politician, than in one in which they do not pay and the policy they dislike is implemented. This will be the case if the amount of money they have to pay is less than some threshold. Taken together, this means that there is a window in which it is feasible for money to enter: If the politician cannot get enough money, or if a financier has to pay too much, there is no money in politics.[4]

Suppose we are in a situation in which this condition is met, so money enters politics in some combination of the different types. A new restriction, let's say a more stringent law against enrichment in office, comes into force. This regulation will increase the threshold at which the incumbent is indifferent between taking and not taking money. This is because they move toward soliciting more money in the form of campaign contributions (which they valued marginally less than self-enrichment before the introduction of new restrictions) or a golden parachute job (for which they have to give up being in office, put in work effort, and wait for the payout). However, because the incumbent changes how they solicit money, the indifference point rises less than it would if there were no fungibility between the different types.

The increase in the indifference point, however, does not automatically mean that there will be less money in politics. Instead, because money can enter politics in different forms, stricter or better enforced laws can have a negative, neutral, or positive effect on how much money enters politics. First, if the new indifference point remains below the amount that entered politics before the reform, it only changes *how* money enters politics, but not *how much*. In this case, the reform is not stringent enough to reduce the overall amount of money in politics. Second, if the new indifference point is above the amount of money that entered politics before the reform, but below the financier's indifference point, the reform may actually have the perverse consequence of *increasing* the amount of money in politics. This is because it makes it untenable for the incumbent to implement the unpopular policy for relatively little money. At the same time, the amount that it now costs the financier is still low enough to be worth it. Finally, the legislation will only be successful at reducing the

---

[4] In the Appendix, I discuss endogenizing the size of the amount of money in politics, which can be done by imposing whether the politician or the financier has the bargaining power and thus gets to make the other party indifferent between having and not having money in politics. See Footnote [5] for the implications for the argument in this section.

amount of money in politics if the incumbent's new indifference point is higher than the financier's indifference point.[5]

The expected effect of restrictions on how much money enters politics in this account is starkly different from what we would expect if the types of money are considered in isolation. When treating different forms separately, we would predict that stricter regulation reduces the total amount of money in politics if it is effective, or has a null effect if it is not. When using the proposed system framework to assess this question, we would instead expect a non-linear relationship between the strength of laws regulating money in politics and how much of it there is. This, of course, also has important policy implications, as limited reforms that make laws only marginally stricter may not successfully remove money from politics, and may in fact do the opposite.[6]

This example makes clear that *how* and *whether* money enters politics are connected in nonobvious ways. Going forward, their relationship should be investigated in more detail. Doing so will help us better understand the conditions under which money can influence politics, and help clarify whether reforms designed to reduce money in politics fall short or succeed.

Research on and Measurement of "Corruption"

The book's findings also have implications for research on corruption writ large. In particular, they call into question the common definition of corruption – the abuse of public office for private or political gain. There are several possible definitions of abuse (Scott, 1972), although most studies have adopted a legal standard – something is corrupt if it is against the law (Fisman and Golden, 2017a). But I have shown in this book that a country's legal environment exerts a considerable influence on how money enters politics. Therefore, if we define corruption based on what is legal, then what is considered corrupt changes across time and space, which has paradoxical consequences: If the same special interest group tries to influence politicians in two different ways, one might be considered corrupt and the other one not, even though they both involve

---

[5] Endogenizing the amount of money in politics by imposing a bargaining power distribution between the politician and the financier alters the space in which the amount of money stays the same after the reform is introduced versus where it increases, but does not change the main insights. See Appendix for details.

[6] This argument parallels the case made by Rothstein (2011) for a "big bang" approach to address corruption.

the same amount of money, have the same goal, and potentially even the same consequences.[7]

This is not a hypothetical concern. Hundreds of studies on corporate campaign contributions in the United States, where the practice is mostly legal, do not mention the word "corruption" at all; nor do they engage the literature on it. Yet studies looking at the same topic in countries such as India, where donations to candidates are illegal, *do* consider it to be corruption and seek to contribute to that literature. Defining corruption as a violation of the law plays a direct role in this.

This problem also affects cross-national measures of the influence of money on politics. Existing measures, from the very broad Corruption Perceptions Index to the more disaggregated Varieties of Democracy indices, focus on *illegal* forms. Of course, this is often of interest. However, in many cases researchers want to focus on the prevalence of both legal and illegal forms of money, which existing measures are ill equipped to do.

We should thus supplement the current definition of corruption with another concept. A good option is provided in the classic contribution by Scott (1972), written before the legalistic standard for corruption became the norm. He refers to transactions for which "without the special consideration of [money], the public official could not have made the same decision" (Scott, 1972, 21). The difference between this definition and the current legalistic one is subtle, but important: The former compares a situation in which money is present to a hypothetical situation in which it is not, rather than to a hypothetical situation in which everyone acts according to the law. Because this definition does not rely on a changing legal standard, it covers self-enrichment, campaign spending, and golden parachute jobs; it applies to legal as well as illegal forms of money; and it does so consistently across space and time.

This definition can also serve as a basis for developing new cross-national measures of money in politics. The argument I have made in this book demonstrates that it would be useful to have separate estimates of (perceptions of) the prevalence of self-enrichment, campaign spending, and golden parachute employment. These can then be aggregated into a measure of money in politics, in all of its legal and illegal forms. Such data would advance our understanding of how (and how much) money enters politics in cross-national perspective.

---

[7] See also Kaufmann and Vicente (2011), Rose-Ackerman and Palifka (2016, ch. 11), and Rothstein and Varraich (2017).

Toward a General Equilibrium Account of Money in Politics

More broadly, I hope this book encourages scholars to think about and situate their research to a greater extent within a framework that treats different types of money in politics as part of a common system. Throughout, I have shown that the system-level framework enriches our understanding of the subject. Considering personal enrichment, campaign spending, and golden parachute employment together can help solve puzzles that have emerged in the literature. For example, it helps us understand why reforms often fail to limit the influence of money on politics; why politicians in some countries leave office to accept lucrative private sector jobs, but those in other countries do not; why incumbency has a large effect on campaign money but a small effect on wealth accumulation and golden parachute jobs; or why voters punish some corrupt incumbents but not others. Examining such puzzles and differing effect sizes using a theoretical framework that incorporates different forms thus helps us better understand how politicians use money, and what consequences this has.

The argument I have made in this book is part of a larger effort to investigate the connections among the various ways in which money influences politics. Other contributions examine the choice between spending money on politicians, lobbying, bribing bureaucrats, influencing the judiciary, and running for office oneself.[8] This book furthers the literature by examining different ways of transferring money *to* politicians. Going forward, and to continue filling in the white space in Figure 8.1, it will be necessary to investigate how self-enrichment, campaign spending, and golden parachute jobs are linked to these other strategies of influencing policy. The more studies that examine the connections between the different modes, the clearer our general equilibrium picture of money in politics will become.

8.2 EVOLVING THE PUBLIC CONVERSATION AND POLICY DESIGN

Given the widespread worry about money in politics, it is no surprise that countries all over the world have made many efforts to try to limit

---

[8] See Rose-Ackerman (1978); Issacharoff and Karlan (1998); Boehmke, Gailmard, and Patty (2005); Campos and Giovannoni (2007); Bennedsen, Feldmann, and Lassen (2009); Naoi and Krauss (2009); Gehlbach, Sonin, and Zhuravskaya (2010); Harstad and Svensson (2011); Kaufmann and Vicente (2011); Bussell (2012); La Raja and Schaffner (2015); You (2017); Szakonyi (2018, 2020); Hou (2019); Ang (2020).

it. The fact that the different forms are part of a common system and partially fungible, and the second- and third-order consequences that this implies, also has important implications for how we should approach the regulation of money in politics. In the remainder of the book, I outline these implications and discuss their ramifications for public conversation and policy design.

Piecemeal Conversations

In many democracies, citizens express concerns about the role that money plays in politics, and various actors advocate reforms to limit it. These reforms typically target *one* specific type of money. For example, during his 2020 presidential campaign, US President Joe Biden vowed to "[r]educe the corrupting influence of money in politics." To do so, he proposed to eliminate private money from elections, require the disclosure of political spending, and introduce a small-donor matching system – all of which target campaign spending.[9] His main primary opponent, Bernie Sanders, struck a similar tone, talking about the need to "get corporate money out of politics." To do so, he declared it essential to overturn *Citizens United*, strengthen and enforce campaign finance regulation, introduce public financing of elections, and eliminate Super PACs.[10] Similarly, American nongovernmental organizations pushing for reforms related to money in politics have names like End Citizens United, Americans for Campaign Reform, or Citizens for Clean Elections, and advocate many of the same policies as Biden and Sanders.

A similar pattern of policy advice can be found elsewhere as well. The India Against Corruption campaign is probably the best-known anti-corruption movement in recent times. One of its key members, Arvind Kejriwal, described the problem it tried to address as follows:

There is endemic corruption rooting out of a basic problem that there is no accountability of a government servant or an elected representatives [sic] of the people. This gives freedom to both elected representatives and government servants to indulge in acts of financial embezzlement of funds that belong to the people (Kejriwal, 2012).

The proposed solution to address personal enrichment among politicians was an independent ombudsman ("Lokpal"), as laid out in the

---

[9] "The Biden Plan to Guarantee Government Works for the People," *joebiden.com*.
[10] "Get Corporate Money Out of Politics," *berniesanders.com*.

first election manifesto of the political party that emanated from the movement:

All public officials ... shall fall within the purview of investigation of the Lokpal. Public officials ... will be required to furnish an annual declaration of assets. Any undeclared assets will be liable for confiscation. Any public official found guilty of corruption would be removed from their position and sentenced to prison. Their property will be confiscated.[11]

And in Britain, the High Pay Centre think tank also worries about the "corporate colonization" of politics, but focuses on a different mechanism: It points out that "[b]etween 2000 and 2014, 600 former ministers and top level civil servants were appointed to over 1,000 different business roles" upon leaving public service:

Ministers and officials have regular and close dealings with commercial companies. This raises the possibility that they will treat a company generously and give it improper preference if there is a prospect of future employment with that company.[12]

As a solution, it proposes introducing cooling off periods, reviewing the suitability of business appointments, and restricting the behavior of former politicians and officials. The German NGO LobbyControl has similar concerns about golden parachute jobs: It calls them "damaging for democracy" and demands cooling off periods as well as an independent panel that reviews and potentially vetoes post-politics employment (Klein and Höntzsch, 2007).

This list could go on at length, but the general pattern is clear: The proposals focus on *one* form of money in politics that is prevalent in a given setting; they propose policies that directly or indirectly limit that particular type; and they claim that this will reduce the amount of money in politics and thus curtail the influence of special interests. Thus, contemporary public conversations about money in politics mirror academic work in that they also tend to focus on one form of money in isolation.

Comprehensive Reforms

Given the piecemeal conversations we have about money in politics, it is perhaps not surprising that existing regulations typically constitute

---

[11] "National Manifesto 2014," *Aam Aadmi Party*, April 4, 2014, p. 4.
[12] "The Revolving Door and the Corporate Colonisation of UK Politics," *High Pay Centre*, March 25, 2015, p. 17.

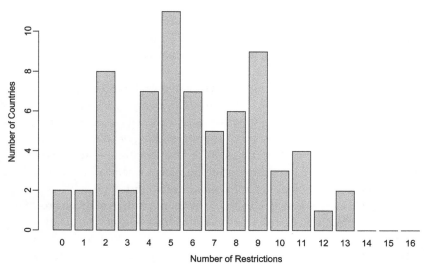

FIGURE 8.2 *Number of restrictions on enrichment in office, campaign spending,
and golden parachute employment in sixty-nine countries.*
Source: Austin and Tjernström (2003) and Djankov et al. (2010).

a patchwork of laws that address some specific forms, but not others.
Figure 8.2 demonstrates this. It uses data from Austin and Tjernström
(2003) and Djankov et al. (2010), who collected information on whether
countries have certain legal restrictions relating to money in politics.
They coded sixteen possible restrictions that cover personal enrichment in
office, campaign finance, and golden parachute employment.[13] The figure
shows a histogram of the number of restrictions that sixty-nine democratic countries have. Almost all countries prohibit at least some forms
of money. However, the median number of restrictions is only six, out of

[13] Djankov et al. (2010) code the regulation of enrichment in office and the revolving door.
For personal enrichment in office, the coded restrictions are: Members of Parliament
(MPs) prohibited from all paid employment, MPs prohibited from holding stock, MPs
prohibited from being members of boards of directors, MPs prohibited from being officers (CEO, CFO), MPs prohibited from being an adviser, MPs have other restrictions
on activities in private sector, MPs have restrictions on accepting gifts, MPs required to
disclose sponsored travel. For the revolving door, they code whether MPs have restrictions on post-tenure agreements. Austin and Tjernström (2003) code the regulation of
campaign finance. The coded laws are: System of regulation for financing of political
parties, provision for disclosure of contributions to political parties, ceiling on contributions to political parties, ban on corporate donations to political parties, ceiling on party
election expenditure, direct public funding for political parties, indirect public funding
for political parties.

a possible sixteen. And even the states that are the most restrictive only have a maximum of thirteen prohibitions. Thus, while countries typically close some avenues through which money may enter politics, many others are left open.

This book has made abundantly clear that such piecemeal approaches are unlikely to be effective. Reductions in campaign spending lead to more golden parachute employment. A crackdown on self-enrichment in office opens the door to more campaign spending, or to more enrichment after leaving public service. Changes in how common golden parachute employment is have implications for campaign finance, and so on. As a consequence, fragmented reforms only have a limited impact.

An obvious policy implication of this book is therefore that to maximize their effectiveness, reforms should address *multiple* forms of money in politics in a *coordinated* manner. For example, a country that contemplates introducing stricter and better enforced penalties for enrichment in office should also think about campaign finance reforms and restrictions on golden parachute employment. Similarly, discussions about changes to a campaign finance regime should be paired with the introduction of cooling off periods for post-politics employment and, if necessary, tougher rules against self-enrichment. Such comprehensive approaches should help avoid the "whack-a-mole" effects demonstrated in this book to a certain extent.

However, such wide-ranging reforms are extremely hard to achieve, since a majority of actors at all potential veto points need to find it in their interest to do so (Tsebelis, 2002). Yet many of those in the majority typically think the rules are fine as they are, in part because they helped them rise to power. It is difficult to even enact reforms that address just one form of money. For example, two-thirds to three-quarters of American citizens have supported greater restrictions on campaign donations for years.[14] However, stricter campaign finance laws have not been passed, and are unlikely to be in the near future. Therefore it seems fanciful to expect a reform that not just limits campaign spending, but also places new restrictions on self-enrichment and golden parachute employment.

There is another barrier that is perhaps even more difficult to overcome: Once politicians leave public office, they become private citizens again. And a central tenet of free and democratic societies is that private

---

[14] "Americans' Views on Money in Politics," *New York Times*, June 2, 2015; "Most Americans Want to Limit Campaign Spending, Say Big Donors Have Greater Political Influence," *Pew Research Center*, May 8, 2018.

citizens have the right to pursue a job of their choosing. For instance, the European Union's Charter of Fundamental Rights states that "[e]veryone has the right to engage in work and to pursue a freely chosen or accepted occupation."[15] To be sure, countries have introduced restrictions and cooling off periods. However, these limitations on post-politics employment tend to be quite narrow and focus on prohibiting former legislators from directly lobbying their former colleagues for a certain period of time. Existing rules do *not* prevent them from taking up *any* position in the private sector. For example, they are free to work as advisers, board members, or nonexecutive directors, which are very prominent among high-profile ex-politicians (cf. Palmer and Schneer, 2019; Weschle, 2021*b*). But prohibiting former politicians from holding *any* job in the private sector would almost surely violate their fundamental rights, and is unlikely to hold up in constitutional courts. Thus, as long as those post-political jobs do not come about through obvious quid pro quo agreements, democratic societies will find it difficult to ever close down this form of money in politics. In other words, a certain level of golden parachute employment may be unavoidable if other forms of money in politics are tightly regulated.

Anticipating and Weighting Trade-Offs

Given these difficulties, comprehensive legislation that simultaneously targets all forms of money in politics is likely a pipe dream. Piecemeal approaches remain the most realistic option. In this case, the book's main policy implication is that it is important to think beyond the first-order effects of money in politics to anticipate second- and third-order implications, and to weigh their benefits and drawbacks ex ante.

This is typically not done. For example, US Senator Tom Udall argued for extensive campaign finance reforms that would limit donations in an essay titled "Amend the Constitution to Restore Public Trust in the Political System: A Practitioner's Perspective on Campaign Finance Reform" (Udall, 2010). And given how many Americans mistrust politics precisely because of the outsize influence that wealthy campaign donors are thought to have, this is not an unreasonable argument. However, as this book has shown, the first-order effect of limiting campaign money likely has the downstream effect of increasing the prevalence of enrichment in office or, more relevant in this particular context, golden parachute jobs.

---

[15] "EU Charter of Fundamental Rights," *European Commission*.

And, as demonstrated in Chapter 7, ordinary voters consider these forms of money to be more problematic than campaign spending. It is thus not clear that campaign finance restrictions would increase public trust. And if politics increasingly serves as a stepping stone to lucrative private sector jobs, this could also have negative long-term effects by decreasing the probability that public-spirited individuals will choose to run for office. At the same time, limiting campaign spending may level the playing field between parties that have access to a lot of money and those that do not.

Another example is the debate on whether to introduce stricter laws that better prohibit golden parachute employment. Because such employment is more common among right-of-center legislators, the main advocates of tougher regulations tend to be left-leaning. For instance, Jon Trickett, a Labour MP in the United Kingdom, assailed members of the Conservative government in 2018 by stating that:

Ministers and special advisers are able to take up jobs in the private sector lobbying on behalf of firms and sectors they used to be responsible for regulating and overseeing. ... We need a radical overhaul of the system to break open the cosy club of the British elite. Members of parliament and special advisers should not be profiting from the expertise built up whilst working in government and must concentrate on their jobs as public servants.[16]

Similarly, when the German NGO LobbyControl in 2013 asked the major parties about their positions on cooling off periods, the three left-leaning parties were broadly in favor, whereas the three right-leaning parties were less supportive or even opposed them.[17] However, such restrictions on post-politics jobs would lead to an increase in campaign money. And given that left-leaning parties typically have less access to money, this may well skew elections in favor of conservatives – hardly a positive outcome for the parties proposing tougher restrictions.

If we do not think through such higher-order implications of a change to one form of money in politics in advance, unpleasant surprises in the form of unintended consequences are bound to occur. Campaign finance reform may inadvertently channel more money into politicians' pockets, in turn leading to a further decrease of the public's trust in politics. An increase in golden parachute employment as a consequence of reforms to

---

[16] "Labour Calls for Overhaul of 'Revolving Door' System of Former Government Ministers Taking High Profile Jobs," *The Independent*, June 28, 2018.

[17] Left parties: SPD, Grüne, Linke. Right parties: CDU, CSU, FDP. See "Wahlprüfsteine: Wie wollen die Parteien Lobbyismus kontrollieren?," *LobbyControl*, September 12, 2013.

one of the other two forms may turn politics into a stepping stone, where legislators are not interested in remaining in office for very long, which could have troubling implications for electoral accountability. Reforms to self-enrichment or golden parachute jobs can affect the pattern of campaign spending, which may tilt election outcomes systematically in the direction of one end of the political spectrum. And so on.

This is not to suggest that policies designed to curb the influence of money in politics are a useless exercise because every normatively positive effect is counterbalanced by a host of negative ones. However, any partial reform involves trade-offs, and these are more consequential than previously thought. Thus it is important to carefully consider them in advance. The insights I have provided in this book can help us think through the entire chain of events that a reform of the regulation of one type of money would set into motion. This, in turn, enables all stakeholders to weigh the pros and cons, and to come to an informed opinion about the overall consequences of a given proposal.

In some instances, this would result in abandoning partial reform proposals because the negative effects outweigh the positive ones. In other instances, reforms would move forward because the positive consequences are substantial enough that it is worth putting up with some side effects. Either way, decisions about whether to pursue a reform will be better informed if we can anticipate downstream effects and judge their consequences. This will also enable activists and policy-makers to propose smarter reforms by prioritizing proposals that have a better balance of trade-offs.

This, of course, requires a discourse that is not just black and white, but that recognizes shades of gray. Without a doubt, this is harder than the debates we currently tend to have. However, considering the direct and indirect effects of a reform *before* implementing it will enable us to make more conscious decisions about which undesirable side effects we are willing to tolerate in order to reap the benefits of a given policy. And that, ultimately, means that a policy – once all its effects and knock-on effects have played out – has a better chance of improving the quality of our democracies.

Appendix: *Formalization of the Argument*

Here, I provide a simple decision-theoretic model in which an incumbent decides how to solicit money. This model underlies the theoretical argument made in Chapter 3 and I provide formal derivations of all implications discussed there.

MODEL SETUP

The basic structure of the model is as follows: There is an incumbent politician (the active player), a financier (a passive player), and a mass of voters (passive as well). They interact over two periods, as shown in Figure 3.1.

The incumbent cares about being in office as well as about their financial situation. In the first period, they decide on a single policy $x \in \{0,1\}$. They know that the electorate prefers $x = 0$, whereas $x = 1$ is preferred by the financier. The financier has instrumental interests in the policy and is willing to spend a certain amount of money M, but only if the policy they prefer is passed. Since I am interested in *how* money enters politics, I assume that the incumbent choses to engage with the financier, so they set $x = 1$ and special interest money M (which I normalize to 1) enters politics. They can solicit this money for their personal enrichment (R), as a campaign contribution (C), in the form of a golden parachute job salary (S), or any mixture of the three, subject to the condition $R + C + S = M$.

At the end of the first period, there is an election whose outcome probabilistically depends on, among other things, the amount of campaign spending. If the incumbent is reelected, they are in office for a second period (during which, for simplicity, they do not decide on a policy). The other options for the second period are retirement or working in a golden

204

parachute job. Next, I describe the actors and their payoffs in more detail. I begin with voters, followed by the financier, and finally the incumbent politician.

Voters

Following the seminal model by Grossman and Helpman (2001), voters care about policy, but are also influenced by campaign spending. They reelect the incumbent if

$$\alpha C - x \geq \theta$$

C captures the effect of campaign spending, weighted by $\alpha > 0$. The larger α, the more important campaigning is for voters, and the less they care about policy. The second term is the effect of policy, so $x = 0$ is more popular than $x = 1$.

The incumbent is confirmed in office if the utility that the electorate gets from their policy choice and their campaign spending exceeds a threshold θ. This threshold is unknown to the candidate ex ante, so they have no way of knowing for sure whether they will be reelected. I model this through a move by nature, which draws θ from a commonly known distribution.

For convenience, I assume that $\theta \sim \text{Triangular}(-h, h, 0)$, where $h > 0$ and the three parameters describe the minimum, maximum, and mode of the distribution. Using this, the probability p that the incumbent wins reelection is

$$p(C) = \begin{cases} \frac{1}{2h^2}(\alpha C - x + h)^2 & \text{if} \quad -h \leq \theta \leq 0 \\ 1 - \frac{1}{2h^2}(h - \alpha C + x)^2 & \text{if} \quad 0 < \theta \leq h \end{cases}$$

Given that θ is equally likely to be positive or negative, this simplifies in expectation to

$$p(C) = \frac{1}{2} + \frac{1}{h}(\alpha C - x)$$

As mentioned earlier, I only consider the case where $x = 1$ here, so

$$p(C) = \frac{1}{2} + \frac{1}{h}(\alpha C - 1)$$

The condition $h > \min\{2, 2(\alpha - 1)\}$ ensures $0 < p(C) < 1$.[1]

Financier

The financier is a passive actor who is willing to pay $M = 1$ to the politician, as long as $x = 1$. This assumes that the benefit that the financier

---

[1] This condition makes use of the fact that M is normalized to 1, so $0 \leq C \leq 1$.

TABLE A1 *Incumbent's payoffs*. Incumbent's payoffs for the four paths shown in Figure 3.1

	Path	Utility
u_1	Run, GP if Lose	$\log(1+R+\delta(1-p(C))S)+\delta p(C)\phi-k-\delta(1-p(C))e$
u_2	Run, Retire if Lose	$\log(1+R)+\delta p(C)\phi-k$
u_3	Not Run, GP	$\log(1+R+\delta S)-\delta e$
u_4	Not Run, Retire	$\log(1+R)$

derives from having $x=1$ instead of $x=0$ is greater or equal to M. Since I assume here that the incumbent chooses $x=1$, the financier simply pays M to the politician in whatever form(s) the latter desires.

Incumbent

The incumbent is the active player in this decision-theoretic model. First, they care about holding office and about their material wealth. I capture the former through a term $\phi > 0$, which can be interpreted as an ego rent or as a more altruistic motivation to do good in office. Second, the incumbent cares about their material wealth. Following standard practice, utility is increasing in the amount of money but with a decreasing marginal effect. For simplicity, I assume a logarithmic functional form, so the amount $A \geq 0$ provides the incumbent with utility $\log(1+A)$.

The incumbent's utility depends on which of the four paths shown in Figure 3.1 they take. Table A1 lists each of them. For the first path, the incumbent runs for reelection and takes up a golden parachute job if they lose. The first term $\log(\cdot)$ is the utility the incumbent receives from material gains. They are twofold. First, there is their personal enrichment R in the first period. Second, with probability $1-p(C)$ they lose the election, which means they receive the golden parachute salary S. Note that since this payment accrues only in the second period, it is discounted by δ, where $0 < \delta < 1$. In addition to those monetary payoffs, the incumbent wins reelection with probability $p(C)$, in which case they receive utility ϕ from being in office for another term, discounted by δ. They pay the cost $k > 0$ for running for reelection, and, if they take a private sector job (with probability $1-p(C)$), they have to make work effort $e > 0$ in the second period, again discounted by δ.

When taking the second path, the incumbent runs for reelection, but retires in case they lose. Benefits of retirement are normalized to zero. The incumbent's monetary benefits come from personal enrichment R. Their non-monetary benefits are the utility from holding office ϕ, which happens with probability $p(C)$ and is discounted by δ. In case of an election loss, they retire and have no payoff in the second period. The incumbent again pays a cost k for running.

For the third path, the incumbent does not run for reelection and instead takes up a golden parachute job for sure. In this case, they receive utility from money used for personal enrichment R as well as from the salary for the golden parachute employment S (discounted by δ), for which they have to make effort e (also discounted by δ).

Finally, the fourth path is to not run for reelection and retire. In this case, the only benefit the incumbent receives is in the form of R.

The incumbent thus has multiple decisions to make. There are four possible paths that differ in whether the incumbent runs for reelection or not, and what career options are available to them in the second period. Along all of the paths, the incumbent can solicit money in a combination of the different types. They solve an optimization problem and choose the combination of career path and money allocation that gives them the highest utility.

"STATE OF NATURE" BENCHMARK

I begin by deriving the optimal course of action for the incumbent in a "state of nature" without any restrictions or constraints on how money can enter politics. The first insight is that Paths 1 and 3 are not viable. Looking at u_3, it is clear that any constrained maximization will result in $S = 0$, since $0 < \delta < 1$ and $e > 0$, which means that Path 4 is preferable. Looking at u_1, a similar logic applies when comparing it to u_2.[2]

We therefore have to find the optimal allocation between R and C for Path 2 (resulting in u_2^*), and then compare that to $u_4^* = \log(2)$ (since $R = 1$). The constrained optimization problem for Path 2 (Run, Retire if Lose) is:

$$\max_{R,C} \quad \log(1+R) + \delta p(C)\phi - k \quad \text{s.t.} \quad R+C = 1$$

The solution to which is:

$$C_2 = \begin{cases} 0 & \text{if} & \phi \leq \frac{h}{2\alpha\delta} \\ 2 - \frac{h}{\alpha\delta\phi} & \text{if} & \frac{h}{2\alpha\delta} < \phi < \frac{h}{\alpha\delta} \\ 1 & \text{if} & \phi \geq \frac{h}{\alpha\delta} \end{cases}$$

Naturally, $R_2 = 1 - C_2$.

---

[2] Since $0 < \delta < 1$, $e > 0$, and $0 < p(C) < 1$.

For the interior solution, it is straightforward to show that $\frac{\partial C_2}{\partial \phi} = \frac{h}{\alpha \delta \phi^2} > 0$, $\frac{\partial C_2}{\partial \delta} = \frac{h}{\alpha \delta^2 \phi} > 0$, and $\frac{\partial C_2}{\partial k} = 0$. The partial derivatives for R_2 have the opposite signs.

For utility u_2, it holds that:

- For the lower corner solution, $\frac{\partial u_2}{\partial \phi} = \frac{\delta(h-2)}{2h} > 0$, since $h > 2$; $\frac{\partial u_2}{\partial \delta} = \frac{\phi(h-2)}{2h} > 0$; and $\frac{\partial u_2}{\partial k} = -1 < 0$.

- For the interior solution, $\frac{\partial u_2}{\partial \phi} = \frac{\delta(4\alpha+h-2)}{2h} - \frac{1}{\phi} > 0$ if $\phi > \frac{2h}{\delta(4\alpha+h-2)}$. This condition holds since $\frac{2h}{\delta(4\alpha+h-2)} < \frac{h}{2\alpha\delta}$, where the latter is the lower boundary for the interior solution. Furthermore, $\frac{\partial u_2}{\partial \delta} = \frac{\phi(4\alpha+h-2)}{2h} - \frac{1}{\delta} > 0$ if $\phi > \frac{2h}{\delta(4\alpha+h-2)}$, which holds by the same argument. Finally, $\frac{\partial u_2}{\partial k} = -1 < 0$.

- For the upper corner solution, $\frac{\partial u_2}{\partial \phi} = \delta(\frac{1}{2} + \frac{\alpha-1}{h}) > 0$ if $\frac{1}{2} + \frac{\alpha-1}{h} > 0$. This condition holds when $h > 2(1-\alpha)$, which is true because $2(1-\alpha) < 2$ (since $\alpha > 0$ and $h > 2$ by assumption). Furthermore, $\frac{\partial u_2}{\partial \delta} = \phi(\frac{1}{2} + \frac{\alpha-1}{h}) > 0$ by the same argument, and $\frac{\partial u_2}{\partial k} = -1 < 0$.

Thus, $\frac{\partial u_2}{\partial \phi} > 0$, $\frac{\partial u_2}{\partial \delta} > 0$, and $\frac{\partial u_2}{\partial k} < 0$.

Since $u_4 = \log(2)$, it follows with respect to ϕ:

- At low levels of ϕ Path 4 is preferred, but at higher levels Path 2 is preferred (since $\frac{\partial u_2}{\partial \phi} > 0$ and $\frac{\partial u_4}{\partial \phi} = 0$).
- As ϕ increases, C weakly increases (since $\frac{\partial C_2}{\partial \phi} \geq 0$ and $\frac{\partial C_4}{\partial \phi} = 0$).

With respect to δ:

- At low levels of δ Path 4 is preferred, but at higher levels Path 2 is preferred (since $\frac{\partial u_2}{\partial \delta} > 0$ and $\frac{\partial u_4}{\partial \delta} = 0$).
- As δ increases, C weakly increases (since $\frac{\partial C_2}{\partial \delta} \geq 0$ and $\frac{\partial C_4}{\partial \delta} = 0$).

Finally, with respect to k:

- At low levels of k Path 2 is preferred, but at higher levels Path 4 is preferred (since $\frac{\partial u_2}{\partial k} < 0$ but $\frac{\partial u_4}{\partial k} = 0$).

LEGAL ENVIRONMENT

Punishing Self-Enrichment

Now, a penalty for self-enrichment is introduced. If the incumbent accepts R, they can now only expect to keep $(1 - \sigma)R$. This means that σ

TABLE A2 *Incumbent's payoffs, with penalty for self-enrichment.*
Incumbent's Payoffs for the four paths shown in Figure 3.1 with penalty for
self-enrichment σ highlighted in gray

	Path	Utility
$u_{1\sigma}$	Run, GP if Lose	$\log(1+\delta(1-p(C))S)+\delta p(C)\phi-k-\delta(1-p(C))e$
$u_{2\sigma}$	Run, Retire if Lose	$\log(1+(1-\sigma)R)+\delta p(C)\phi-k$
$u_{3\sigma}$	Not Run, GP	$\log(1+\delta S)-\delta e$
$u_{4\sigma}$	Not Run, Retire	$\log(1+(1-\sigma)R)$

represents the proportion of the money that the politician anticipates to
pay as a fine. It can be thought of as the monetary value of the penalty
times the probability of getting caught, so it captures both the strictness
of the rules as well as their enforcement. If $\sigma > 1$, the combination of
enforcement and penalty is so severe that in expectation, the incumbent
loses more than they gain. Since this trivially leads to $R = 0$, I will focus
the discussion on cases where $0 < \sigma < 1$. Table A2 shows how this affects
the utilities that the incumbent derives from the four possible paths, with
the newly added term $1-\sigma$ highlighted. Because Paths 2 and 4 now also
have losses, Paths 1 and 3 are potentially viable, so we have to consider all
four options. I first discuss each path separately and then put everything
together to demonstrate the insights shown in Figure 3.2.

Path 1 (Run for Reelection, Golden Parachute if Lose)
If choosing this path, the incumbent optimally allocates campaign spending C and golden parachute salary S by solving the following constrained
maximization problem:

$$\max_{S,C} \quad \log(1+\delta(1-p(C))S)+\delta p(C)\phi-k-\delta(1-p(C))e \quad \text{s.t.} \quad S+C=1$$

The solution to this is:

$$C_{1\sigma} = \begin{cases} 0 & \text{if} \quad \phi \leq \frac{h(2+h)-\alpha(2(e-1)h+\delta e(2+h))}{\alpha(2h+\delta(2+h))} \\[2ex] \frac{1}{4\alpha^2\delta(e+\phi)} & \text{if} \quad \frac{h(2+h)-\alpha(2(e-1)h+\delta e(2+h))}{\alpha(2h+\delta(2+h))} \\[1ex] (\alpha\eta_\sigma-\sqrt{\alpha^2(\zeta_\sigma+\eta_\sigma)}) & < \phi < \frac{2-2\alpha(1+e)+h}{2\alpha} \\[2ex] 1 & \text{if} \quad \phi \geq \frac{2-2\alpha(1+e)+h}{2\alpha} \end{cases}$$

with

$$\eta_\sigma = \delta(2+2\alpha+h)(e+\phi)-4h$$

and

$$\zeta_\sigma = -8\delta(e+\phi)(2\alpha h(e+\phi-1) - h(2+h) + \alpha\delta(2+h)(e+\phi))$$

Of course, $S_{1\sigma} = 1 - C_{1\sigma}$.

For the interior solutions, it holds that $\frac{\partial C_{1\sigma}}{\partial \phi} = \frac{h(4\alpha h + \sqrt{\alpha^2(\zeta_\sigma + \eta_\sigma^2)})}{\alpha\delta(e+\phi)^2\sqrt{\alpha^2(\zeta_\sigma+\eta_\sigma^2)}} > 0$.

For the cutpoints $\underline{\phi}_{1\sigma}$ and $\overline{\phi}_{1\sigma}$ above and below which the corner solution applies, it holds that $\frac{\partial \underline{\phi}_{1\sigma}}{\partial \sigma} = 0$ and $\frac{\partial \overline{\phi}_{1\sigma}}{\partial \sigma} = 0$.

For $u_{1\sigma}$, it holds that $\frac{\partial u_{1\sigma}}{\partial \phi} = \frac{\delta}{2h}(h + 2\alpha C_{1\sigma} - 2) > 0$ since $h > 2$ and $\alpha C_{1\sigma} \geq 0$. It also holds that $\frac{\partial u_{1\sigma}}{\partial \sigma} = 0$.

Path 2 (Run for Reelection, Retire if Lose)

If choosing this path, the incumbent optimally allocates campaign spending C and enrichment in office R as follows:

$$C_{2\sigma} = \begin{cases} 0 & \text{if} & \phi \leq \frac{h(1-\sigma)}{\alpha\delta(2-\sigma)} \\ 1 + \frac{1}{1-\sigma} - \frac{h}{\alpha\delta\sigma} & \text{if} & \frac{h(1-\sigma)}{\alpha\delta(2-\sigma)} < \phi < \frac{h(1-\sigma)}{\alpha\delta} \\ 1 & \text{if} & \phi \geq \frac{h(1-\sigma)}{\alpha\delta} \end{cases}$$

and $R_{2\sigma} = 1 - C_{2\sigma}$.

For the interior solution, it holds that $\frac{\partial C_{2\sigma}}{\partial \phi} = \frac{h}{\alpha\delta\sigma^2} > 0$ and $\frac{\partial C_{2\sigma}}{\partial \sigma} = \frac{1}{(1-\sigma)^2} > 0$.

For the cutpoints $\underline{\phi}_{2\sigma}$ and $\overline{\phi}_{2\sigma}$ above and below which the corner solution applies, it holds that $\frac{\partial \underline{\phi}_{2\sigma}}{\partial \sigma} = -\frac{h}{\alpha\delta} < 0$ and $\frac{\partial \overline{\phi}_{2\sigma}}{\partial \sigma} = -\frac{h}{\alpha\delta(2-\sigma)^2} < 0$, which means that the cutpoints shift to the left as σ increases.

For utility $u_{2\sigma}$, it holds that with respect to ϕ:

- For the lower corner solution, $\frac{\partial u_{2\sigma}}{\partial \phi} = \frac{\delta(h-2)}{2h} > 0$ because $h > 2$.
- For the interior solution, $\frac{\partial u_{2\sigma}}{\partial \phi} = \frac{\delta}{2h}(h + \frac{2\alpha(2-\sigma)}{1-\sigma} - 2) - \frac{1}{\phi} > 0$ if $\phi < \frac{2h(1-\sigma)}{\delta(2\alpha(2-\sigma)+(h-2)(1-\sigma))}$. This condition holds since $\frac{2h(1-\sigma)}{\delta(2\alpha(2-\sigma)+(h-2)(1-\sigma))} < \frac{h(1-\sigma)}{\alpha\delta(2-\sigma)}$, where the latter is the lower boundary for the interior solution.
- For the upper corner solution, $\frac{\partial u_{2\sigma}}{\partial \phi} = \delta(\frac{1}{2} + \frac{\alpha-1}{h}) > 0$ if $h > -2(\alpha-1)$, which is true.

Thus, $\frac{\partial u_{2\sigma}}{\partial \phi} > 0$.

For utility $u_{2\sigma}$, it holds that with respect to σ:

- For the lower corner solution, $\frac{\partial u_{2\sigma}}{\partial \sigma} = -\frac{1}{2-\sigma} < 0$ since $\sigma < 1$.
- For the interior solution, $\frac{\partial u_{2\sigma}}{\partial \sigma} = \frac{\alpha \delta \phi - h(1-\sigma)}{h(1-\sigma)^2} < 0$ if $\phi < \frac{h(1-\sigma)}{\alpha \delta}$. This condition holds since the latter is the upper boundary for the interior solution.
- For the upper corner solution, $\frac{\partial u_{2\sigma}}{\partial \sigma} = 0$.

Thus, $\frac{\partial u_{2\sigma}}{\partial \sigma} \leq 0$.

Path 3 (Not Run for Reelection, Golden Parachute)
Since $S = 1$, $u_{3\sigma} = \log(1+\delta) - \delta e$, so it follows that $\frac{\partial u_{3\sigma}}{\partial \phi} = 0$ and $\frac{\partial u_{3\sigma}}{\partial \sigma} = 0$.

Path 4 (Not Run for Reelection, Retire)
Since $R = 1$, $u_{4\sigma} = \log(2-\sigma)$, so it follows that $\frac{\partial u_{4\sigma}}{\partial \phi} = 0$ and $\frac{\partial u_{4\sigma}}{\partial \sigma} = -\frac{1}{2-\sigma} < 0$.

Putting Things Together
The overall picture of how money enters politics is as follows: At low levels of σ, Path 4 is the preferred option for small values of ϕ and Path 2 for larger values of ϕ, per the argument made in the benchmark case. Since $\frac{\partial u_{2\sigma}}{\partial \sigma} \leq 0$ and $\frac{\partial u_{4\sigma}}{\partial \sigma} < 0$, but $\frac{\partial u_{1\sigma}}{\partial \sigma} = 0$ and $\frac{\partial u_{3\sigma}}{\partial \sigma} = 0$, it follows that at higher levels of σ, Paths 1 and 3 are preferred. Because $\frac{\partial u_{3\sigma}}{\partial \phi} = 0$ but $\frac{\partial u_{1\sigma}}{\partial \phi} > 0$, Path 3 is preferred for small values of ϕ and Path 4 for larger values of ϕ.

From this, these insights shown in Figure 3.2 follow:

- First panel: We start with Path 2, with low R and high C. As σ increases, C increases (since $\frac{\partial C_{2\sigma}}{\partial \sigma} \geq 0$).
- Second panel: We start with Path 2, but a higher R and lower C than in the first panel. As σ increases, C increases (since $\frac{\partial C_2}{\partial \sigma} \geq 0$). In addition, if σ is high enough, Path 1 is preferred (per the argument in the earlier paragraph). Once Path 1 is taken, C and S do not react to σ, since $\frac{\partial C_{1\sigma}}{\partial \sigma} = 0$.
- Third panel: We start with Path 4, so $R = 1$. Once σ is high enough, Path 3 is preferred (per the argument in the above paragraph).

Campaign Finance Regulation

Next, I consider campaign finance legislation. I incorporate this in a similar way as the regulation of enrichment in office: Using money for campaigning purposes is now illegal, and if the incumbent accepts it

TABLE A3 *Incumbent's payoffs, with campaign finance regulation.*
Incumbent's Payoffs for the four paths shown in Figure 3.1 with penalty for
campaign spending τ highlighted in gray

	Path	Utility
$u_{1\sigma}$	Run, GP if Lose	$\log(1+\delta(1-p(\ (1-\tau)\ C))S)+\delta p(\ (1-\tau)\ C)\phi$
		$-k-\delta(1-p(\ (1-\tau)\ C))e$
$u_{2\sigma}$	Run, Retire if Lose	$\log(1+(1-\sigma)R)+\delta p(\ (1-\tau)\ C)\phi-k$
$u_{3\sigma}$	Not Run, GP	$\log(1+\delta S)-\delta e$
$u_{4\sigma}$	Not Run, Retire	$\log(1+(1-\sigma)R)$

nevertheless, then τ represents the share of it that they expect to pay as a fine and are therefore unable to use.[3] If the incumbent takes a campaign contribution, they can anticipate to only keep $(1-\tau)$ C. I again assume that $0 < \tau < 1$. The penalty for self-enrichment and for campaign spending are set separately, since there need to be different laws dealing with the two types of money, and they are typically overseen and prosecuted by different agencies.[4] Table A3 shows the utilities for the four possible paths, with changes highlighted in gray.

Path 1 (Run for Reelection, Golden Parachute if Lose)
With the introduction of τ, the optimal allocation between C and S becomes:

$$
C_{1\tau}=\begin{cases} 0 & \text{if } \phi \leq \frac{h(2+h)-\alpha(1-\tau)(2(e-1)h+\delta e(2+h))}{\alpha(1-\tau)(2h+\delta(2+h))} \\[2ex] \frac{1}{4\alpha^2\delta(e+\phi)(1-\tau)^2}\Big(\alpha(1-\tau)\eta_\tau- & \text{if } \frac{h(2+h)-\alpha(1-\tau)(2(e-1)h+\delta e(2+h))}{\alpha(1-\tau)(2h+\delta(2+h))} \\[2ex] \sqrt{\alpha^2(1-\tau)^2(\zeta_\tau+\eta_\tau)}\Big) & < \phi < \frac{2-2\alpha(1-\tau)(1+e)+h}{2\alpha(1-\tau)} \\[2ex] 1 & \text{if } \quad \phi \geq \frac{2-2\alpha(1-\tau)(1+e)+h}{2\alpha(1-\tau)} \end{cases}
$$

[3] Note that this means the incumbent is at risk of being penalized from the first dollar they use for campaigning purposes. Most countries allow campaign spending and donations up to a certain amount. I focus on the case where there is a complete ban to contrast with the model discussed so far where all spending is legal. Real-world regulation with a partial ban falls somewhere in between the two extremes.

[4] Of course, it may be that a politician accepts money and then decides themself whether to use it for personal enrichment or for their reelection campaign. In this case, either $\sigma = \tau$, or the penalty depends on the timing of the discover relative to the election. If the violation is discovered while the money is spent during the campaign then τ applies, whereas σ applies if it is discovered while stashed away somewhere in the politician's home or office.

with

$$\eta_\tau = \delta(2 + 2\alpha(1 - \tau) + h)(e + \phi) - 4h$$

and

$$\zeta_\tau = -8\delta(e+\phi)(2\alpha(1-\tau)h(e+\phi-1) - h(2+h) + \alpha(1-\tau)\delta(2+h)(e+\phi))$$

Of course, $S_{1\tau} = 1 - C_{1\tau}$.

First, for the interior solution, it holds that $\frac{\partial C_{1\tau}}{\partial \phi} = \frac{h(4\alpha h(1-\tau) + \sqrt{\alpha^2(1-\tau)^2(\eta_\tau^2 + \zeta_\eta)})}{\alpha\delta(e+\phi)^2(1-\tau)\sqrt{\alpha^2(1-\tau)^2(\eta_\tau^2 + \zeta_\eta)}}$

> 0, so $C_{1\tau}$ increases in ϕ.

Second, for the cutpoints $\underline{\phi}_{1\tau}$ and $\overline{\phi}_{1\tau}$ above and below which the corner solution applies, it holds that $\frac{\partial \underline{\phi}_{1\tau}}{\partial \tau} = \frac{h(2+h)}{\alpha(2h+\delta(2+h))(1-\tau)^2} > 0$ and $\frac{\partial \overline{\phi}_{1\tau}}{\partial \tau} = \frac{2+h}{2\alpha(1-\tau)^2} > 0$. Thus, as τ increases, the cutpoints move to the right.

For the corner solutions, where $C_{1\tau} = 0$ or $C_{1\tau} = 1$, it is clear that increasing τ has no effect (other than shifting the cutpoints). Taken together, this means that $C_{1\tau}$ must be at or below C_1, so $\frac{\partial C_{1\tau}}{\partial \tau} \leq 0$.

For $u_{1\tau}$, the following holds with respect to ϕ:

- For the lower corner solution, $\frac{\partial u_{1\tau}}{\partial \phi} = \frac{\delta(h-2)}{2h} > 0$.
- For the interior solution, $\frac{\partial u_{1\tau}}{\partial \phi} = \frac{\delta}{2h}(h - 2 + 2\alpha(1-\tau)C_{1\tau}) > 0$ since $0 < C_{1\tau} < 1$.
- For the upper corner solution, $\frac{\partial u_{1\tau}}{\partial \phi} = \frac{\delta}{2h}(h - 2 + 2\alpha(1-\tau)) > 0$.

Thus, $\frac{\partial u_{1\tau}}{\partial \phi} > 0$.

For $u_{1\tau}$, the following holds with respect to τ:

- For the lower corner solution, $\frac{\partial u_{1\tau}}{\partial \tau} = 0$.
- For the upper corner solution, $\frac{\partial u_{1\tau}}{\partial \tau} = -\frac{\alpha\delta(e+\phi)}{h} < 0$.
- For the interior solution, note that because $\frac{\partial u_{1\tau}}{\partial \phi} > 0$ as well as $\frac{\partial u_{1\tau}}{\partial \tau} = 0$ for the lower corner solution and $\frac{\partial u_{1\tau}}{\partial \tau} < 0$ for the upper corner solution, it must be that $\frac{\partial u_{1\tau}}{\partial \tau} < 0$.

Thus, $\frac{\partial u_{1\tau}}{\partial \tau} \leq 0$.

Path 2 (Run for Reelection, Retire if Lose)

When choosing this path, the optimal allocation is:

$$C_{2\tau} = \begin{cases} 0 & \text{if} & \phi \leq \frac{h(1-\sigma)}{\alpha\delta(2-\sigma)(1-\tau)} \\ 1 + \frac{1}{1-\sigma} - \frac{h}{\alpha\delta\phi(1-\tau)} & \text{if} & \frac{h(1-\sigma)}{\alpha\delta(2-\sigma)(1-\tau)} < \phi < \frac{h(1-\sigma)}{\alpha\delta(1-\tau)} \\ 1 & \text{if} & \phi \geq \frac{h(1-\sigma)}{\alpha\delta(1-\tau)} \end{cases}$$

and $R_{2\tau} = 1 - C_{2\tau}$.

For the interior solution, it holds that $\frac{\partial C_{2\tau}}{\partial \phi} = \frac{h}{\alpha\delta\sigma^2(1-\tau)} > 0$ and $\frac{\partial C_{2\tau}}{\partial \tau} = -\frac{h}{\alpha\delta\phi(1-\tau)^2} < 0$. Comparing $C_{2\tau}$ to C_2, it holds that $C_{2\tau} > C_2$ if $\sigma > \frac{h\tau}{\alpha\delta\phi(1-\tau)+h\tau}$. Thus, if σ is large relative to τ, then $C_{2\tau}$ is larger than C_2. If σ is small relative to τ, then $C_{2\tau}$ is smaller than C_2.

For the cutpoints $\underline{\phi}_{1\tau}$ and $\overline{\phi}_{1\tau}$ above and below which the corner solution applies, it holds that $\frac{\partial \underline{\phi}_{1\tau}}{\partial \tau} = \frac{h(1-\tau)}{\alpha\delta(2-\sigma)(1-\tau)^2} > 0$ and $\frac{\partial \overline{\phi}_{1\tau}}{\partial \tau} = \frac{h(1-\tau)}{\alpha\delta(1-\tau)^2} > 0$. Thus, as τ increases, the cutpoints move to the right.

For utility $u_{2\tau}$, it holds that with respect to ϕ:

- For the lower corner solution, $\frac{\partial u_{2\tau}}{\partial \phi} = \frac{\delta(h-2)}{2h} > 0$.
- For the interior solution, $\frac{\partial u_{2\tau}}{\partial \phi} = \frac{\delta}{2} - \frac{1}{\phi} + \frac{\delta}{h(1-\sigma)}(\alpha(2-\sigma)(1-\tau)+\sigma-1) > 0$ if $\phi > \frac{2h(1-\sigma)}{\delta(2\alpha(2-\sigma)(1-\tau)+(h-2)(1-\sigma))}$. This condition holds since $\frac{2h(1-\sigma)}{\delta(2\alpha(2-\sigma)(1-\tau)+(h-2)(1-\sigma))} < \frac{h(1-\sigma)}{\alpha\delta(2-\sigma)(1-\tau)}$, where the latter is the lower boundary for the interior solution.
- For the upper corner solution, $\frac{\partial u_{2\tau}}{\partial \phi} = \frac{\delta(h-2+2\alpha(1-\tau))}{2h} > 0$.

Thus, $\frac{\partial u_{2\tau}}{\partial \phi} > 0$.

For utility $u_{2\tau}$, it holds that with respect to τ:

- For the lower corner solution, $\frac{\partial u_{2\tau}}{\partial \tau} = 0$.
- For the interior solution, $\frac{\partial u_{2\tau}}{\partial \tau} = \frac{h(1-\sigma)-\alpha\delta\phi(2-\sigma)(1-\tau)}{h(1-\sigma)(1-\tau)} < 0$ if $\phi > \frac{h(1-\sigma)}{\alpha\delta(2-\sigma)(1-\tau)}$. This condition holds since the latter is the lower boundary for the interior solution.
- For the upper corner solution, $\frac{\partial u_{2\tau}}{\partial \tau} = -\frac{\alpha\delta\phi}{h} < 0$.

Thus, $\frac{\partial u_{2\tau}}{\partial \tau} \leq 0$.

Path 3 (Not Run for Reelection, Golden Parachute)
Since $u_{3\tau} = \log(1+\delta) - \delta e$, it follows that $\frac{\partial u_{3\tau}}{\partial \phi} = 0$ and $\frac{\partial u_{3\tau}}{\partial \tau} = 0$.

Path 4 (Not Run for Reelection, Retire)
Since $u_{4\tau} = \log(2-\sigma)$, it follows that $\frac{\partial u_{4\tau}}{\partial \phi} = 0$ and $\frac{\partial u_{4\tau}}{\partial \tau} = 0$.

Putting Things Together
From this, for a case with a low σ, the following insights shown in Figure 3.3 follow:

TABLE A4 *Incumbent's payoffs, with golden parachute restrictions.* Incumbent's Payoffs for the four paths shown in Figure 3.1 with additional work effort x as the result of a cooling off law highlighted in gray

	Path	Utility
u_{1x}	Run, GP if Lose	$\log(1+\delta(1-p((1-\tau)C))S)+\delta p((1-\tau)C)\phi$ $-k-\delta(1-p((1-\tau)C))(e+x)$
u_{2x}	Run, Retire if Lose	$\log(1+(1-\sigma)R)+\delta p((1-\tau)C)\phi-k$
u_{3x}	Not Run, GP	$\log(1+\delta S)-\delta(e+x)$
u_{4x}	Not Run, Retire	$\log(1+(1-\sigma)R)$

- All panels: We start with Path 2. As τ increases, C decreases (since $\frac{\partial C_{2\tau}}{\partial \tau} \leq 0$).
- All panels: In addition, if τ is high enough, Path 4 is preferred since $\frac{\partial u_{2\tau}}{\partial \tau} \leq 0$ but $\frac{\partial u_{4\tau}}{\partial \tau} = 0$.

For a case with a high σ, the following insights shown in Figure 3.4 follow:

- First and second panel: We start with Path 1. As τ increases, C decreases (since $\frac{\partial C_{1\tau}}{\partial \tau} \leq 0$).
- First and second panel: In addition, if τ is high enough, Path 3 is preferred since $\frac{\partial u_{1\tau}}{\partial \tau} \leq 0$ but $\frac{\partial u_{3\tau}}{\partial \tau} = 0$.
- Third panel: We start with Path 2 and $C_{2\tau} = 1$. Once τ is high enough, Path 1 is preferred since τ affects $C = 1$ for Path 2, but $C < 1$ for Path 1. Path 3 is not an option since this is someone with high ϕ.

Golden Parachute Restrictions

As I have argued in Chapter 3, cooling off laws are best thought of as increasing the perceived work effort that the former politician has to make for their salary S. I model this through a term $x > 0$ that denotes this additional effort. Table A4 shows how this affects the utilities for the four possible paths.

Path 1 (Run for Reelection, Golden Parachute if Lose)
If we define $\eta_\tau = \delta(2+2\alpha(1-\tau)+h)(e+\phi+x)$ and $\zeta_\tau = -8\delta(e+\phi+x)$ $(2\alpha(1-\tau)h(e+\phi+x-1)-h(2+h)+\alpha(1-\tau)\delta(2+h)(e+\phi+x))$ then for the interior solution, it holds that $\frac{\partial C_{1x}}{\partial x} = \frac{h(4\alpha h(1-\tau)+\sqrt{\alpha^2(1-\tau)^2(\eta_x^2+\zeta_x)})}{\alpha\delta(e+\phi+x)^2(1-\tau)\sqrt{\alpha^2(1-\tau)^2(\eta_x^2+\zeta_x)}} >$

0. For the cutoffs, it holds that $\frac{\partial \phi_{1x}}{\partial x} = -1 < 0$ and $\frac{\partial \bar{\phi}_{1x}}{\partial x} = -1 < 0$, so they move to the left as x increases. Thus, it follows that $\frac{\partial C_{1x}}{\partial x} \geq 0$.
For u_{1x}, it holds that:

- For the lower corner solution, $\frac{\partial u_{1x}}{\partial x} = -\delta(\frac{1}{2} + \frac{1}{h}) < 0$.
- For the interior solution, $\frac{\partial u_{1x}}{\partial x} = -\frac{\delta}{2h}(2 + h - 2\alpha C(1 - \tau)) < 0$ if $h > 2(\alpha C(1 - \tau) - 1)$. This is true since $2(\alpha C(1 - \tau) - 1) < 2(\alpha - 1)$ and $h > 2(\alpha - 1)$ by definition.
- For the upper corner solution, $\frac{\partial u_{1x}}{\partial x} = -\frac{\delta}{2h}(2 + h - 2\alpha(1 - \tau)) < 0$ if $h > 2(\alpha(1 - \tau) - 1)$. This is true since $2(\alpha(1 - \tau) - 1) < 2(\alpha - 1)$ and $h > 2(\alpha - 1)$ by definition.

Thus, $\frac{\partial u_{1x}}{\partial x} < 0$.

Path 2 (Run for Reelection, Retire if Lose)
Since this path does not involve golden parachute employment, $\frac{\partial C_{2x}}{\partial x} = 0$ and $\frac{\partial u_{2x}}{\partial x} = 0$.

Path 3 (Not Run for Reelection, Golden Parachute)
Since $C_{3x} = 0$, it follows that $\frac{\partial C_{3x}}{\partial x} = 0$. Since $u_{3x} = \log(1 + \delta) - \delta(e + x)$, it follows that $\frac{\partial u_{3x}}{\partial x} = -\delta < 0$.

Path 4 (Not Run for Reelection, Retire)
Since this path does not involve golden parachute employment, $\frac{\partial C_{4x}}{\partial x} = 0$ and $\frac{\partial u_{4x}}{\partial x} = 0$.

Putting Things Together
The following insights follow:

- For Path 1, as x increases, C weakly increases (since $\frac{\partial C_{1x}}{\partial x} \geq 0$).
- If x is high enough, Paths 2 and 4 are preferred to Paths 1 and 3 (since $\frac{\partial u_{1x}}{\partial x} < 0$ and $\frac{\partial u_{3x}}{\partial x} < 0$ but $\frac{\partial u_{2x}}{\partial x} = \frac{\partial u_{4x}}{\partial x} = 0$).

ELECTORAL CAMPAIGN ENVIRONMENT

Effectiveness of Campaign Technology

Recall that the probability of winning an election was defined as

$$p(C) = \frac{1}{2} + \frac{1}{h}(\alpha(1 - \tau)C - 1)$$

The effectiveness of the campaign technology can be incorporated by changing the value of α, where a higher value means that a given amount of campaign spending goes further in persuading voters.

Path 1 (Run for Reelection, Golden Parachute if Lose)

First, for the cutpoints $\underline{\phi}_{1\alpha}$ and $\overline{\phi}_{1\alpha}$, above and below which the corner solution applies, it holds that $\frac{\partial \underline{\phi}_{1\alpha}}{\partial \alpha} = -\frac{h(2+h)}{\alpha^2(1-\tau)(2h+\delta(2+h))} < 0$ and $\frac{\partial \overline{\phi}_{1\alpha}}{\partial \alpha} = -\frac{2+h}{2\alpha^2(1-\tau)} < 0$. Thus, as α increases, the cutpoints move to the left.

We know from earlier that $\frac{\partial C_{1\alpha}}{\partial \phi} > 0$, so $C_{1\alpha}$ increases in ϕ. It follows that for the interior solution, $C_{1\alpha}$ must be above C_1.

For the corner solutions, where $C_{1\alpha} = 0$ or $C_{1\alpha} = 1$, it is clear that increasing α has no effect (other than shifting the cutpoints). Taken together, this means that $\frac{\partial C_{1\alpha}}{\partial \alpha} \geq 0$.

For $u_{1\alpha}$, we know from earlier that $\frac{\partial u_{1\alpha}}{\partial \phi} > 0$. With respect to α, it holds that:

- For the lower corner solution, $\frac{\partial u_{1\alpha}}{\partial \alpha} = 0$.
- For the upper corner solution, $\frac{\partial u_{1\alpha}}{\partial \alpha} = \frac{\delta(e+\phi)(1-\tau)}{h} > 0$.
- For the interior solution, note that because $\frac{\partial u_{1\alpha}}{\partial \phi} > 0$ as well as $\frac{\partial u_{1\alpha}}{\partial \alpha} = 0$ for the lower corner solution and $\frac{\partial u_{1\alpha}}{\partial \alpha} > 0$ for the upper corner solution, it must be that $\frac{\partial u_{1\alpha}}{\partial \alpha} > 0$.

Thus, $\frac{\partial u_{1\alpha}}{\partial \alpha} \geq 0$.

Path 2 (Run for Reelection, Retire if Lose)

For $C_{2\alpha}$, it holds that with respect to α:

- For the lower corner solution, $\frac{\partial C_{2\alpha}}{\partial \alpha} = 0$.
- For the interior solution, $\frac{\partial C_{2\alpha}}{\partial \alpha} = \frac{h}{\alpha^2 \delta \phi(1-\tau)} > 0$.
- For the upper corner solution, $\frac{\partial C_{2\alpha}}{\partial \alpha} = \frac{1}{h}(\delta\phi(1-\tau)) > 0$.

Thus, $\frac{\partial C_{2\alpha}}{\partial \alpha} \geq 0$.

For $u_{2\alpha}$, it holds that with respect to α:

- For the lower corner solution, $\frac{\partial u_{2\alpha}}{\partial \alpha} = 0$.
- For the interior solution, $\frac{\partial u_{2\alpha}}{\partial \alpha} = \frac{\alpha\delta\phi(2-\sigma)(1-\tau)-h(1-\sigma)}{\alpha h(1-\sigma)} > 0$ if $\phi > \frac{h(1-\sigma)}{\alpha\delta(2-\sigma)(1-\tau)}$, which is true since the latter is the lower boundary.
- For the upper corner solution, $\frac{\partial u_{2\alpha}}{\partial \alpha} = \frac{1}{h}(\delta\phi(1-\tau)) > 0$.

Thus, $\frac{\partial u_{2\alpha}}{\partial \alpha} \geq 0$.

Path 3 and 4 (Not Run for Reelection)
Since Paths 3 and 4 do not involve running for reelection, it holds that $\frac{\partial C_{3\alpha}}{\partial \alpha} = \frac{\partial C_{4\alpha}}{\partial \alpha} = 0$ and $\frac{\partial u_{3\alpha}}{\partial \alpha} = \frac{\partial u_{4\alpha}}{\partial \alpha} = 0$.

Putting Things Together
The following insights shown in Figures 3.5 and 3.6 follow from the above discussion:

- For Paths 1 and 2, as α increases, C increases weakly (since $\frac{\partial C_{1\alpha}}{\partial \alpha} \geq 0$ and $\frac{\partial C_{2\alpha}}{\partial \alpha} \geq 0$).
- If α is high enough, Paths 1 and 2 are preferred to Paths 3 and 4 (since $\frac{\partial u_{1\alpha}}{\partial \alpha} \geq 0$ and $\frac{\partial u_{2\alpha}}{\partial \alpha} \geq 0$ but $\frac{\partial u_{3\alpha}}{\partial \alpha} = \frac{\partial u_{4\alpha}}{\partial \alpha} = 0$).

Electoral Competitiveness

Finally, I model the effect of differences in the a priori competitiveness of an election. I do so through two terms. First, I shift the baseline probability of winning for the incumbent upwards by adjusting it as follows:

$$p(C) = \frac{1}{\gamma} + \frac{1}{h}(\alpha(1-\tau)C - 1)$$

where $\gamma < 2$. Thus, the lower γ, the more likely the incumbent is to be reelected. To ensure $p(C) < 1$, I also impose $\gamma > 1$.

Second, as γ decreases (so the a priori chance of winning increases), the marginal effectiveness of campaign spending decreases. This is because someone who starts out with, say, 50 percent support can still convince half the electorate to vote for them. Someone who starts out with 75 percent already has the easily convertible voters on their side, and the quarter of voters left are harder to win over. In other words, as γ decreases, so does α. The impact of the latter has been discussed in the previous section. I first discuss the comparative statics for γ and then consider the impact of γ and α together.

Path 1 (Run for Reelection, Golden Parachute if Lose)
First, for the cutpoint $\underline{\phi}_{1\gamma}$, it holds that $\frac{\partial \underline{\phi}_{1\gamma}}{\partial \gamma} = \frac{h^2(h - \alpha\delta(1-\tau))}{\alpha(1-\tau)(h\gamma + \delta(\gamma - h(1-\gamma)))^2} > 0$ if $\alpha < \frac{h}{\delta(1-\tau)}$. For $p(C) < 1$, it needs to hold that $\alpha < \frac{1 + h - \frac{h}{\gamma}}{1-\tau}$. Thus, if we

establish that $\frac{h}{\delta(1-\tau)} > \frac{1+h-\frac{h}{\gamma}}{1-\tau}$, then $\alpha < \frac{h}{\delta(1-\tau)}$ as well. The former is true since $\frac{h}{\delta} > 2$ (as $h > 2$ and $0 < \delta < 1$) and $1 + h - \frac{h}{\gamma} < 2$ (as $\gamma < h$).

For the cutpoint $\overline{\phi}_{1\gamma}$, $\frac{\partial \overline{\phi}_{1\gamma}}{\partial \gamma} = \frac{h}{\alpha \gamma^2 (1-\tau)} > 0$. Thus, as γ increases, the cutpoints move to the right.

We know from earlier that $\frac{\partial C_{1\gamma}}{\partial \phi} > 0$, so $C_{1\gamma}$ increases in ϕ. It follows that for the interior solution, $C_{1\gamma}$ must be below C_1. Taken together, this means that $\frac{\partial C_{1\gamma}}{\partial \gamma} \leq 0$.

For $u_{1\gamma}$, we know from above that $\frac{\partial u_{1\gamma}}{\partial \phi} > 0$. With respect to γ, it holds that:

- For the lower corner solution, $\frac{\partial u_{1\gamma}}{\partial \gamma} = -\frac{\delta(h\gamma(e+\phi-S)+\delta(e+\phi)S(h(\gamma-1)+\gamma))}{\gamma^2(h\gamma+\delta S(h(\gamma-1)+\gamma))} < 0$ since $\gamma > 1$ and $\phi > S - e$. The latter must be true since otherwise a strategy in which a golden parachute job is the backup option in case of an election loss is not optimal.

- For the upper corner solution, $\frac{\partial u_{1\gamma}}{\partial \gamma} = -\frac{\delta(e+\phi)}{\gamma^2} < 0$.

- For the interior solution, note that because $\frac{\partial u_{1\gamma}}{\partial \phi} > 0$ as well as $\frac{\partial u_{1\gamma}}{\partial \gamma} < 0$ for the lower and upper corner solutions, it must be that $\frac{\partial u_{1\gamma}}{\partial \gamma} < 0$ for the interior solution.

Thus, $\frac{\partial u_{1\gamma}}{\partial \gamma} < 0$.

Path 2 *(Run for Reelection, Retire if Lose)*

Since γ does not affect the marginal utility of either C or R, $\frac{\partial C_{2\gamma}}{\partial \gamma} = 0$. With respect to $u_{2\gamma}$,

$$\frac{\partial u_{2\gamma}}{\partial \gamma} = -\frac{\delta \phi}{\gamma^2} < 0$$

Path 3 and 4 *(Not Run for Reelection)*

Since Paths 3 and 4 do not involve running for reelection, it holds that $\frac{\partial C_{3\gamma}}{\partial \gamma} = \frac{\partial C_{4\gamma}}{\partial \gamma} = 0$ and $\frac{\partial u_{3\gamma}}{\partial \gamma} = \frac{\partial u_{4\gamma}}{\partial \gamma} = 0$.

Putting Things Together

These insights shown in Figure 3.7 follow from the previous discussion:

- If γ is low enough (so the a priori chance of winning is high enough), Path 2 is preferred to Path 4 (since $\frac{\partial u_{2\gamma}}{\partial \gamma} < 0$ but $\frac{\partial u_{4\gamma}}{\partial \gamma} = 0$).

TABLE A5 *Incumbent's payoffs, with financier's electoral/expressive campaign contribution.* Incumbent's Payoffs for the four paths shown in Figure 3.1 with expressive campaign contribution C_E highlighted in gray

	Path	Utility
u_1	Run, GP if Lose	$\log(1 + \delta(1 - p((1-\tau)(C + C_E)))S) + \delta p((1-\tau)$ $(C + C_E))\phi - k - \delta(1 - p((1-\tau)(C + C_E)))(e + x)$
u_2	Run, Retire if Lose	$\log(1 + (1-\sigma)R) + \delta p((1-\tau)(C + C_E))\phi - k$
u_3	Not Run, GP	$\log(1 + \delta S) - \delta(e + x)$
u_4	Not Run, Retire	$\log(1 + (1-\sigma)R)$

- If the incumbent takes Path 2, a smaller γ leads to less C and more R. This is because while $\frac{\partial C_{2\gamma}}{\partial \gamma} = 0$, α decreases as γ decreases, and $\frac{\partial C_{2\alpha}}{\partial \alpha} \geq 0$.

For Figure 3.8, these insights follow:

- If γ is low enough (so the a priori chance of winning is high enough), Path 1 is preferred to Path 3 (since $\frac{\partial u_{1\gamma}}{\partial \gamma} < 0$ but $\frac{\partial u_{3\gamma}}{\partial \gamma} = 0$).
- If γ is low enough, Path 1 can also be preferred to Path 2. It is the case that both $\frac{\partial u_{1\gamma}}{\partial \gamma} < 0$ and $\frac{\partial u_{2\gamma}}{\partial \gamma} < 0$. However, α decreases when γ decreases, so the campaign spending ($C = 1$) in Path 2 becomes less effective. Of course, campaign spending also becomes less effective in Path 1, but the impact is less strong since $C < 1$ in that case.
- When Path 1 is chosen, the impact of γ on C and S is indeterminate since $\frac{\partial C_{1\gamma}}{\partial \gamma} \leq 0$ but $\frac{\partial C_{1\gamma}}{\partial \alpha} \geq 0$.

ROBUSTNESS AND EXTENSIONS

Electoral or Expressive Motives for Campaign Contributions

Table 3.2 laid out the motivations that financiers have for the different forms of money in politics. While an instrumental motivation is common to all of them, there are also motivations specific to certain forms. For campaign contributions, financiers may also have an electoral motive (cf. Grossman and Helpman, 2001). That is, they want to boost the chances that their preferred candidate is elected. Or, alternatively, they may simply express their preference in the same way that small-scale donors do. I incorporate this motivation through an exogenous parameter C_E, which is the amount of money the financier gives for electoral or expressive reasons.

TABLE A6 *Incumbent's payoffs, with human capital motivation for golden parachute.* Incumbent's payoffs with earnings for their human capital S_H and human capital work effort e_H highlighted in gray

	Path	Utility
u_{1a}	Run, GP if Lose	$\log(1+\delta(1-p((1-\tau)C))S)+\delta p((1-\tau)C)\phi$ $-k-\delta(1-p((1-\tau)C))(e+x)$
u_{1b}	Run, GP + HC if Lose	$\log(1+\delta(1-p((1-\tau)C))(S+S_H))+\delta p((1-\tau)$ $C)\phi-k-\delta(1-p((1-\tau)C))(e+x+e_H)$
u_{2a}	Run, Retire if Lose	$\log(1+(1-\sigma)R)+\delta p((1-\tau)C)\phi-k$
u_{2b}	Run, HC if Lose	$\log(1+(1-\sigma)R+\delta(1-p((1-\tau)C))S_H)$ $+\delta p((1-\tau)C)\phi-k-\delta(1-p((1-\tau)C))(e_H+x)$
u_{3a}	Not Run, GP	$\log(1+\delta S)-\delta(e+x)$
u_{3b}	Not Run, GP + HC	$\log(1+\delta(S+S_H))-\delta(e+x+e_H)$
u_{4a}	Not Run, Retire	$\log(1+(1-\sigma)R)$
u_{4b}	Not Run, HC	$\log(1+(1-\sigma)R+\delta S_H)-\delta(e_H+x)$

It is clear from Table A5 that this additional campaign money enters u_1 and u_2 as an additive term. Its presence does not meaningfully change the comparative statics described earlier for σ, τ, x, α, and γ, so the main implications discussed in Chapter 3 are robust when the financier has electoral or expressive motivations.

Human Capital Motivation for Golden Parachute Employment

As Table 3.2 made clear, financiers can have a couple of motivations for making golden parachute hires. Besides an instrumental motivation, they may also be interested in employing former politicians because they bring valuable human capital to their company. This means that the incumbent can use their human capital to get a job independent of their decisions in office. The salary that they receive for their human capital is denoted by the exogenous parameter S_H, for which they have to make effort e_H. For any path where they retired before (Paths 2 and 4), they now also have the option of taking a private sector job in the second period due to their human capital. Similarly, for any path where they used to take a golden parachute job (Paths 1 and 3) with (endogenous) salary S and effort e, they now have the additional option of taking a job with salary $S+S_H$ and work effort $e+e_H$.

Adding this possibility provides a couple of insights (see Table A6). First, there now is the possibility for the incumbent to enrich themselves in office and then take up a job in the private sector (see u_{2b} and u_{4b}). However, they get that job purely for their human capital and not because of their actions in office.

Second, whether the incumbent chooses to put their human capital to use in the private sector depends on the relative size of S_H and e_H. For example, comparing u_{4a} and u_{4b}, in which $R = 1$, it is straightforward that the incumbent will work for a company if

$$e_H \leq \frac{1}{\delta}(\log(2 - \sigma + \delta S_H) - \log(2 - \sigma) - \delta x)$$

so if the efforts they have to make using their human capital are lower than what the salary they receive for it adds to their utility. Similar arguments can be made for the other paths. The relation between S_H and e_H depends on the individual-specific factors that the existing literature on the revolving door has highlighted, such as a politicians' connections and expertise.

However, note that because the human capital motivation enters as additive terms, it does not substantially alter the comparative statics of the impact of σ, τ, x, α, and γ. Thus, the insights and empirical implications of the model remain the same when introducing a human capital motivation for golden parachute hires. By normalizing the costs and benefits of a job based on human capital to zero, as I have implicitly done earlier, the model is much simpler and little insight is lost.

How Much Money Enters Politics

In the model here as well as in Chapter 3, I have assumed that money enters politics, and have set its amount M exogenously. This was appropriate since my interest in this book is to examine how money enters politics, and the results of the constrained maximization I have discussed previously hold for any M. Here, I briefly discuss how to endogenize M and how that has implications for the connection between *how* and *whether* money enters politics, which I mention as an area for future research in Chapter 8.

Money enters politics only if both the incumbent and the financier are better off that way. We therefore have to discuss the utilities of the incumbent and financier when they choose not to engage with each other. The incumbent then has two options. First, they can run for reelection without financial backing by the financier, but with the benefit of having pursued the popular policy $x = 0$. Their utility then is

$$u_5 = \frac{\delta \phi}{\gamma} - k$$

which makes use of the fact that their probability of winning office when $C = 0$ and $x = 0$ is $\frac{1}{\gamma}$. Second, the incumbent can simply not run again and retire, in which case

$$u_6 = 0$$

Thus, the incumbent only engages with the financier if the highest utility from Paths 1 to 4 is larger than the larger utility from Paths 5 and 6. Obviously, they will do so if M is high and will not do so if M is low. Denote the point at which the incumbent is indifferent between taking and not taking money by $\underline{M}$.

For the financier, denote their benefits from having $x = 1$ instead of $x = 0$ by β. This might be a monetary benefit, or it could capture internal satisfaction about having one's favorite policy become law. A high β might mean that the financier's fortune depends heavily on having policy go their way, for example if they are exposed to more regulation or depend on government contracts. The term could also vary depending on which politician the financier is dealing with. For example, a minister, party leader, or a chair of a powerful committee has a lot of power over policy, so their decisions are more consequential for the financier (high β). A backbench member of parliament has much less influence over policy and the fate of the financier (low β). If M is low the financier will not spend money on politics, and if it is high they will. The point at which they are indifferent is $\overline{M}$.

Therefore, if $M < \underline{M}$, the politician is better off not engaging with the financier, and if $M > \overline{M}$, it is too expensive for the financier to influence policy. Any M that satisfies $\underline{M} \leq M \leq \overline{M}$ means that both actors are better off by engaging with each other.

Without further assumptions, there is no way to determine where within this range the actual M falls. Ultimately, it depends on the bargaining power between the incumbent and the financier. If the financier group has all the bargaining power, they will want to set $M = \underline{M}$, so that the incumbent is indifferent between setting $x = 1$ and taking the money and setting $x = 0$ and not taking it.[5] If the incumbent has all the bargaining power, they will want to set $M = \overline{M}$, making the financier indifferent between paying up and living with the unfavorable policy. There is no work that I am aware of that identifies the bargaining power balance between politicians and financiers. In particular, it may well be that this

---

[5] This would result in relatively little money entering politics. Indeed, given the benefits that special interest can potentially reap from favorable policy, the amount of money in politics is often considered to be quite small (Tullock, 1972; Ansolabehere, de Figueiredo, and Snyder, 2003).

balance depends on both structural factors of the country as well as the specifics of particular politician-financier dyads.

As mentioned, the argument on *how* money enters politics is unaffected by this ambiguity. However, it does have implications for the connection between how and whether money enters politics discussed in Chapter 8. There, I argue that stricter regulation of some type of money will push up the indifference point of the incumbent, so $\underline{M}_{New} > \underline{M}$. If $\underline{M}_{New} \leq M$, the amount of money will be the same as before. If $M < M_{New} < \overline{M}$, the reform leads to *more* money in politics. Only if $\underline{M}_{New} \geq \overline{M}$ is there no more money in politics.

Where M lies within the interval $[\underline{M}, \overline{M}]$ affects the space in which the amount of money stays the same after the reform is introduced versus where it increases. At one extreme, if $M = \underline{M}$ then penalizing one form of money will lead to *more* money if $\underline{M}_{New} \geq \overline{M}$. In contrast, if $M = \overline{M}$, then a reform will have *no* effect if $\underline{M}_{New} \geq \overline{M}$. The closer M is to $\underline{M}$, the larger the space in which a reform leads to more money, and the closer it is to $\overline{M}$ the larger the space in which it has no effect on the amount of money in politics.

References

Abdul-Razzak, Nour, Carlo Prato, and Stephane Wolton. 2020. "After *Citizens United*: How Outside Spending Shapes American Democracy." *Electoral Studies* 67: 102190.

Abel van Es, Andrea. 2016. Why Regulate Political Finance? In *Checkbook Elections? Political Finance in Comparative Perspective*, ed. Pippa Norris and Andrea Abel van Es. Oxford University Press. pp. 199–226.

Adams, James and Samuel Merrill. 2009. "Policy-Seeking Parties in a Parliamentary Democracy with Proportional Representation: A Valence-Uncertainty Model." *British Journal of Political Science* 39(3):539–558.

Adams, James, Samuel Merrill, and Bernard Grofman. 2005. *A Unified Theory of Party Competition: A Cross-National Analysis Integrating Spatial and Behavioral Factors*. Cambridge University Press.

Ades, Alberto and Rafael Di Tella. 1999. "Rents, Competition, and Corruption." *American Economic Review* 89(4):982–993.

Adolph, Christopher. 2013. *Bankers, Bureaucrats, and Central Bank Politics: The Myth of Neutrality*. Cambridge University Press.

Adonis, Andrew. 1997. The UK: Civic Virtue Put to the Test. In *Democracy and Corruption in Europe*, ed. Donatella Della Porta and Yves Mény. Pinter. pp. 103–117.

Adsera, Alicia, Carles Boix, and Mark Payne. 2003. "Are You Being Served? Political Accountability and Quality of Government." *Journal of Law, Economics, & Organization* 19(2):445–490.

Advisory Committee on Business Appointments. 2011. "Twelfth Annual Report 2010–2011." https://assets.publishing.service.gov.uk/government/uploads/system/uploads/attachment_data/file/396938/Twelfth_Annual_Report_2010-2011.pdf.

Advisory Committee on Business Appointments. 2012. "Thirteenth Annual Report 2011–2012." https://assets.publishing.service.gov.uk/government/uploads/system/uploads/attachment_data/file/396936/ACOBA_Thirteenth_Annual_Report_2011-12.pdf.

Advisory Committee on Business Appointments. 2016. "Seventeenth Annual Report 2015–2016." https://assets.publishing.service.gov.uk/government/

uploads/system/uploads/attachment_data/file/539186/ACOBA_2015-16_Annual_Report_final.pdf.

Advisory Committee on Business Appointments. 2017. "Eighteenth Annual Report 2016–2017." https://assets.publishing.service.gov.uk/government/uploads/system/uploads/attachment_data/file/632627/170720_ACOBA_2016-17_Annual_Report_ACOBA.pdf.

Aidt, Toke, Miriam A. Golden, and Devesh Tiwari. 2015. "Criminal Candidate Selection for the Indian National Legislature." Unpublished manuscript. https://174bd2f8-f704-43a0-9e18-c9e6852c61c3.filesusr.com/ugd/02c1bf_b515ef1dc03b4f00a58a6b4c48043f38.pdf.

Akey, Pat. 2015. "Valuing Changes in Political Networks: Evidence from Campaign Contributions to Close Congressional Elections." *Review of Financial Studies* 28(11):3188–3223.

Alexander, Amy C. 2012. "Change in Women's Descriptive Representation and the Belief in Women's Ability to Govern: A Virtuous Cycle." *Politics & Gender* 8(4):437–464.

Alt, James E. and David Dreyer Lassen. 2003. "The Political Economy of Institutions and Corruption in American States." *Journal of Theoretical Politics* 15(3):341–365.

Anderson, Christopher J. and Yuliya Tverdova. 2003. "Corruption, Political Allegiances, and Attitudes toward Government in Contemporary Democracies." *American Journal of Political Science* 47(1):91–109.

Ang, Yuen Yuen. 2020. *China's Gilded Age: The Paradox of Economic Boom and Vast Corruption.* Cambridge University Press.

Angrist, Joshua D. and Jörn-Steffen Pischke. 2009. *Mostly Harmless Econometrics: An Empiricist's Companion.* Princeton University Press.

Angrist, Joshua D. and Jörn-Steffen Pischke. 2010. "The Credibility Revolution in Empirical Economics: How Better Research Design is Taking the Con Out of Econometrics." *Journal of Economic Perspectives* 24(2):3–30.

Ansolabehere, Stephen and James M. Snyder, Jr. 2002. "The Incumbency Advantage in US Elections: An Analysis of State and Federal Offices, 1942–2000." *Election Law Journal* 1(3):315–338.

Ansolabehere, Stephen, John M. de Figueiredo, and James M. Snyder, Jr. 2003. "Why Is There so Little Money in U.S. Politics?" *Journal of Economic Perspectives* 17(1):105–130.

Ares, Macarena and Enrique Hernández. 2017. "The Corrosive Effect of Corruption on Trust in Politicians: Evidence from a Natural Experiment." *Research and Politics* 4(2):1–8.

Asher, Sam and Paul Novosad. 2020. "Rent-Seeking and Criminal Politicians: Evidence from Mining Booms." Unpublished manuscript. https://paulnovosad.com/pdf/asher-novosad-mining-politics.pdf.

Ashworth, Scott. 2006. "Campaign Finance and Voter Welfare with Entrenched Incumbents." *American Political Science Review* 100(1):55–68.

Austen-Smith, David. 1987. "Interest Groups, Campaign Contributions, and Probabilistic Voting." *Public Choice* 54(2):123–139.

Austin, Reginald and Maja Tjernström, eds. 2003. "Funding of Political Parties and Election Campaigns." International Institute for Democracy and Electoral Assistance.

Avis, Eric, Claudio Ferraz, Frederico Finan, and Carlos Varjão. 2021. "Money and Politics: The Effects of Campaign Spending Limits on Political Entry and Competition." Unpublished manuscript. https://eml.berkeley.edu/ ffinan/Finan_Limits.pdf.

Banerjee, Abhijit V., Rema Hanna, and Sendhil Mullainathan. 2012. Corruption. In *The Handbook of Organizational Economics*, ed. Robert Gibbons and John Roberts. Princeton University Press. pp. 1109–1147.

Banfield, Edward. 1958. *The Moral Basis of a Backward Society*. The Free Press.

Barber, Michael. 2016. "Donation Motivations: Testing Theories of Access and Ideology." *Political Research Quarterly* 69(1):148–159.

Baron, David P. 1994. "Electoral Competition with Informed and Uninformed Voters." *American Political Science Review* 88(1):33–47.

Baturo, Alexander. 2017. "Democracy, Development, and Career Trajectories of Former Political Leaders." *Comparative Political Studies* 50(8):1023–1054.

Baturo, Alexander and Jonathan Arlow. 2018. "Is There a 'Revolving Door' to the Private Sector in Irish Politics?" *Irish Political Studies* 33(3):381–406.

Baturo, Alexander and Slava Mikhaylov. 2016. "Blair Disease? Business Careers of the Former Democratic Heads of State and Government." *Public Choice* 166(3–4):335–354.

Bauhr, Monika and Marcia Grimes. 2017. "Transparency to Curb Corruption? Concepts, Measures and Empirical Merit." *Crime, Law and Social Change* 68(4):431–458.

Bauhr, Monika and Nicholas Charron. 2018. "Insider or Outsider? Grand Corruption and Electoral Accountability." *Comparative Political Studies* 51(4):415–446.

Bauhr, Monika, Nicholas Charron, and Lena Wängnerud. 2019. "Exclusion or Interests? Why Females in Elected Office Reduce Petty and Grand Corruption." *European Journal of Political Research* 58(4):1043–1065.

Baumgartner, Frank R., Jeffrey M. Berry, Marie Hojnacki, David C. Kimball, and Beth L. Leech. 2009. *Lobbying and Policy Change: Who Wins, Who Loses, and Why*. University of Chicago Press.

Bayley, David H. 1966. "The Effects of Corruption in a Developing Nation." *Western Political Quarterly* 19(4):719–732.

Ben-Zion, Uri and Zeev Eytan. 1974. "On Money, Votes, and Policy in a Democratic Society." *Public Choice* 17:1–10.

Bennedsen, Morten, Sven E. Feldmann, and David Dreyer Lassen. 2009. "Strong Firms Lobby, Weak Firms Bribe: A Survey-Based Analysis of the Demand for Influence and Corruption." Unpublished manuscript. https://papers .ssrn.com/sol3/papers.cfm?abstract_id=1503028.

Benoit, Kenneth and Michael Marsh. 2010. "Incumbent and Challenger Campaign Spending Effects in Proportional Electoral Systems: The Irish Elections of 2002." *Political Research Quarterly* 63(1):159–173.

Bental, Benjamin and Uri Ben-Zion. 1975. "Political Contribution and Policy: Some Extensions." *Public Choice* 24:1–12.

Berg, Heléne. 2020a. "On the Returns to Holding Political Office (Is it Worth it?)." *Journal of Economic Behavior and Organization* 178:840–865.

Berg, Heléne. 2020b. "Politicians' Payments in a Proportional Party System." *European Economic Review* 128: 103504.

Berliner, Daniel. 2014. "The Political Origins of Transparency." *Journal of Politics* 76(2):479–491.

Bertrand, Marianne, Matilde Bombardini, and Francesco Trebbi. 2014. "Is it Whom You Know or What You Know? An Empirical Assessment of the Lobbying Process." *American Economic Review* 104(12):3885–3920.

Besley, Timothy. 2004. "Paying Politicians: Theory and Evidence." *Journal of the European Economic Association* 2(2–3):193–215.

Besley, Timothy. 2005. "Political Selection." *Journal of Economic Perspectives* 19(3):43–60.

Besley, Timothy and Stephen Coate. 2001. "Lobbying and Welfare in a Representative Democracy." *Review of Economic Studies* 68(1):67–82.

Bhatti, Yosef, Jens Olav Dahlgaard, Jonas Hedegaard Hansen, and Kasper M. Hansen. 2019. "Is Door-to-Door Canvassing Effective in Europe? Evidence from a Meta-Study across Six European Countries." *British Journal of Political Science* 49(1):279–290.

Bhavnani, Rikhil R. 2009. "Do Electoral Quotas Work after They Are Withdrawn? Evidence from a Natural Experiment in India." *American Political Science Review* 103(1):23–35.

Bhavnani, Rikhil R. 2012. "Using Asset Disclosures to Study Politicians' Rents: An Application to India." Unpublished manuscript. https://pdfs.semantic-scholar.org/a6ac/e55dfd4cb25ba8fa46e33b88968d5ccd82a3.pdf.

Bhavnani, Rikhil R. 2018. "The Effects of Malapportionment on Cabinet Inclusion: Subnational Evidence from India." *British Journal of Political Science* 48(1):69–89.

Bhavnani, Rikhil R. and Noam Lupu. 2016. "Oil Windfalls and the Political Resource Curse: Evidence from a Natural Experiment in Brazil." Unpublished manuscript. https://rbhavnani.github.io/files/BhavnaniLupuOil.pdf.

Björkman, Lisa. 2014. "'You Can't Buy a Vote': Meanings of Money in a Mumbai Election." *American Ethnologist* 41(4):617–634.

Black, Gordon S. 1972. "A Theory of Political Ambition: Career Choices and the Role of Structural Incentives." *American Political Science Review* 66(1):144–159.

Blanes i Vidal, Jordi, Mirko Draca, and Christian Fons-Rosen. 2012. "Revolving Door Lobbyists." *American Economic Review* 102(7):3731–3748.

Boas, Taylor C., F. Daniel Hidalgo, and Neal P. Richardson. 2014. "The Spoils of Victory: Campaign Donations and Government Contracts in Brazil." *Journal of Politics* 76(2):415–429.

Boehmke, Frederick J., Sean Gailmard, and John W. Patty. 2005. "Whose Ear to Bend? Information Sources and Venue Choice in Policy Making." *Quarterly Journal of Political Science* 1(2):139–169.

Bombardini, Matilde and Francesco Trebbi. 2020. "Empirical Models of Lobbying." *Annual Review of Economics* 12:391–413.

Bonica, Adam. 2016. "Database on Ideology, Money in Politics, and Elections: Public Version 2.0." Stanford University Libraries. http://data.stanford.edu/dime.

Booysen, Susan. 2011. *The African National Congress and the Regeneration of Political Power*. Wits University Press.

Borchert, Jens. 2011. "Individual Ambition and Institutional Opportunity: A Conceptual Approach to Political Careers in Multi-Level Systems." *Regional and Federal Studies* 21(2):117–140.

Brierley, Sarah. 2020. "Unprincipled Principals: Co-opted Bureaucrats and Corruption in Ghana." *American Journal of Political Science* 64(2):209–222.

Brollo, Fernanda. 2013. "Why Do Voters Punish Corrupt Politicians? Evidence from the Brazilian Anti-Corruption Program." Unpublished manuscript. https://pdfs.semanticscholar.org/9220/oaf3df45250fe7d179aa0e58025a2a72d154.pdf.

Brusco, Valeria, Marcelo Nazareno, and Susan C. Stokes. 2004. "Vote Buying in Argentina." *Latin America Research Review* 39(2):66–88.

Bryan, Shari and Denise Baer, eds. 2005. *Money in Politics: A Study of Party Financing Practices in 22 Countries*. National Democratic Institute for International Affairs.

Bueno, Natália S. and Thad Dunning. 2017. "Race, Resources, and Representation: Evidence from Brazilian Politicians." *World Politics* 69(2):327–365.

Burleigh, Tyler, Ryan Kennedy, and Scott Clifford. 2018. "How to Screen Out VPS and International Respondents Using Qualtrics: A Protocol." Unpublished manuscript. https://ssrn.com/abstract=3265459.

Bussell, Jennifer. 2012. *Corruption and Reform in India: Public Services in the Digital Age*. Cambridge University Press.

Bussell, Jennifer. 2018. Whose Money, Whose Influence? Multi-Level Politics and Campaign Finance in India. In *Costs of Democracy: Political Finance in India*, ed. Devesh Kapur and Milan Vaishnav. Oxford University Press. pp. 232–272.

Cain, Bruce E. and Lee Drutman. 2014. "Congressional Staff and the Revolving Door: The Impact of Regulatory Change." *Election Law Journal* 13(1):27–44.

Calland, Richard. 2016. South Africa. In *Checkbook Elections? Political Finance in Comparative Perspective*, ed. Pippa Norris and Andrea Abel van Es. Oxford University Press. pp. 141–158.

Calonico, Sebastian, Matias D. Cattaneo, and Rocío Titiunik. 2014. "Robust Nonparametric Confidence Intervals for Regression-Discontinuity Designs." *Econometrica* 82(6):2295–2326.

Calvo, Ernesto and Maria Victoria Murillo. 2004. "Who Delivers? Partisan Clients in the Argentine Electoral Market." *American Journal of Political Science* 48(4):742–757.

Campante, Filipe R. 2011. "Redistribution in a Model of Voting and Campaign Contributions." *Journal of Public Economics* 57(7):646–656.

Campbell, David E. and Christina Wolbrecht. 2006. "See Jane Run: Women Politicians as Role Models for Adolescents." *Journal of Politics* 68(2):233–247.

Campos, Nauro F. and Francesco Giovannoni. 2007. "Lobbying, Corruption and Political Influence." *Public Choice* 131:1–21.

Carey, John M. 1998. *Term Limits and Legislative Representation*. Cambridge University Press.

Carey, John M. 2009. *Legislative Voting and Accountability*. Cambridge University Press.

Carey, John M., Richard G. Niemi, and Lynda W. Powell. 1998. "The Effects of Term Limits on State Legislatures." *Legislative Studies Quarterly* 23(2):271–300.

Carey, John M., Richard G. Niemi, and Lynda W. Powell. 2000. *Term Limits in the State Legislatures*. University of Michigan Press.

Chandra, Kanchan. 2004. *Why Ethnic Parties Succeed: Patronage and Ethnic Head Counts in India*. Cambridge University Press.

Chang, Eric C. C. 2005. "Electoral Incentives for Political Corruption under Open-List Proportional Representation." *Journal of Politics* 67(3):716–730.

Chang, Eric C. C. and Miriam A. Golden. 2010. "Sources of Corruption in Authoritarian Regimes." *Social Science Quarterly* 91(1):1–20.

Chang, Eric C. C. and Nicholas N. Kerr. 2017. "An Insider–Outsider Theory of Popular Tolerance for Corrupt Politicians." *Governance* 30(1):67–84.

Chang, Eric C. C. and Yun-han Chu. 2006. "Corruption and Trust: Exceptionalism in Asian Democracies?" *Journal of Politics* 68(2):259–271.

Chauchard, Simon. 2018. "Electoral Handouts in Mumbai Elections: The Cost of Political Competition." *Asian Survey* 58(2):341–364.

Che, Yeon-Koo. 1995. "Revolving Doors and the Optimal Tolerance for Agency Collusion." *RAND Journal of Economics* 26(3):378–397.

Chen, Jowei. 2017. "The Impact of Political Geography on Wisconsin Redistricting: An Analysis of Wisconsin's Act 43 Assembly Districting Plan." *Election Law Journal* 16(4):1–10.

Chen, Jowei and David Cottrell. 2016. "Evaluating Partisan Gains from Congressional Gerrymandering: Using Computer Simulations to Estimate the Effect of Gerrymandering in the U.S. House." *Electoral Studies* 44:329–340.

Chen, Jowei and Jonathan Rodden. 2015. "Cutting Through the Thicket: Redistricting Simulations and the Partisan Gerrymanders." *Election Law Journal* 14(4):331–345.

Chislett, William. 2013. *Spain: What Everyone Needs to Know*. Oxford University Press.

Cho, Wendy K. Tam and James H. Fowler. 2010. "Legislative Success in a Small World: Social Network Analysis and the Dynamics of Congressional Legislation." *Journal of Politics* 72(1):124–135.

Chong, Alberto, Ana de la O, Dean Karlan, and Leonard Wantchekon. 2015. "Does Corruption Information Inspire the Fight or Quash the Hope? A Field Experiment in Mexico on Voter Turnout, Choice, and Party Identification." *Journal of Politics* 77(1):55–71.

Chong, Dennis and James N. Druckman. 2013. "Counterframing Effects." *Journal of Politics* 75(1):1–16.

Chowdhury, Javid. 2012. *The Insider's View: Memoirs of a Public Servant*. Penguin Books.

Cirone, Alexandra, Gary W. Cox, and Jon H. Fiva. 2020. "Seniority-Based Nominations and Political Careers." *American Political Science Review* 115(1):234–251.

Claessen, Clint, Stefanie Bailer, and Tomas Turner-Zwinkels. 2021. "The Winners of Legislative Mandate: An Analysis of Post-Parliamentary Career Positions in Germany and the Netherlands." *European Journal of Political Research* 60(1):25–45.

Claessens, Stijn, Erik Feijen, and Luc Laeven. 2008. "Political Connections and Access to Finance: The Role of Campaign Contributions." *Journal of Financial Economics* 88(3):554–580.

Clarke, Kevin A. and David M. Primo. 2012. *A Model Discipline: Political Science and the Logic of Representations*. Oxford University Press.

Clift, Ben and Justin Fisher. 2004. "Comparative Party Finance Reform: The Cases of France and Britain." *Party Politics* 10(6):677–699.

Coate, Stephen. 2004a. "Pareto-Improving Campaign Finance Policy." *American Economic Review* 94(3):628–655.

Coate, Stephen. 2004b. "Political Competition with Campaign Contributions and Informative Advertising." *Journal of the European Economic Association* 2(5):772–804.

Cooper, Michael J., Huseyin Gulen, and Alexei V. Ovtchinnikov. 2010. "Corporate Political Contributions and Stock Returns." *Journal of Finance* 65(2):687–724.

Corbacho, Ana, Daniel W. Gingerich, Virginia Oliveros, and Mauricio Ruiz-Vega. 2016. "Corruption as a Self-Fulfilling Prophecy: Evidence from a Survey Experiment in Costa Rica." *American Journal of Political Science* 60(4):1077–1092.

Cox, Gary W. and Michael F. Thies. 2000. "How Much Does Money Matter? 'Buying' Votes in Japan, 1967–1990." *Comparative Political Studies* 33(1):37–57.

Crespin, Michael H. 2005. "Using Geographic Information Systems to Measure District Change, 2000–2002." *Political Analysis* 13(3):253–260.

Crespin, Michael H. 2010. "Serving Two Masters: Redistricting and Voting in the U.S. House of Representatives." *Political Research Quarterly* 63(4):850–859.

Dal Bó, Ernesto. 2006. "Regulatory Capture: A Review." *Oxford Review of Economic Policy* 22(2):203–225.

Dal Bó, Ernesto and Frederico Finan. 2018. "Progress and Perspectives in the Study of Political Selection." *Annual Review of Economics* 10:541–575.

Dal Bó, Ernesto and Martín Rossi. 2011. "Term Length and the Effort of Politicians." *Review of Economic Studies* 78(4):1237–1263.

Dal Bó, Ernesto, Pedro Dal Bó, and Rafael Di Tella. 2006. "'Plata o Plomo?': Bribe and Punishment in a Theory of Political Influence." *American Political Science Review* 100(1):1–13.

Dalton, Russell J. and Martin P. Wattenberg, eds. 2002. *Parties Without Partisans: Political Change in Advanced Industrial Democracies*. Oxford University Press.

Dawood, Yasmin. 2015. "Campaign Finance and American Democracy." *Annual Review of Political Science* 18:329–348.

de Figueiredo, John M. and Brian Kelleher Richter. 2014. "Advancing the Empirical Research on Lobbying." *Annual Review of Political Science* 17:163–185.

de Figueiredo, Rui J. P., Jr. and Geoff Edwards. 2007. "Does Private Money Buy Public Policy? Campaign Contributions and Regulatory Outcomes in Telecommunications." *Journal of Economics & Management Strategy* 16(3):547–576.

De Vries, Catherine E. and Hector Solaz. 2017. "The Electoral Consequences of Corruption." *Annual Review of Political Science* 20:391–408.

Debroy, Bibek and Laveesh Bhandari. 2012. *Corruption in India: The DNA and the RNA*. Konark.

Dekel, Eddie, Matthew O. Jackson, and Asher Wolinsky. 2009. "Vote Buying: Legislatures and Lobbying." *Quarterly Journal of Political Science* 4(2):103–128.

Delimitation Commission of India. 2008. "Changing Face of Electoral India: Delimitation 2008." https://www.elections.tn.gov.in/Web/forms/int1.pdf.

Della Porta, Donatella. 2000. Social Capital, Beliefs in Government, and Political Corruption. In *Disaffected Democracies: What's Troubling the Trilateral Countries*, ed. Susan S. Pharr and Robert D. Putnam. Princeton University Press. pp. 202–230.

Denzau, Arthur T. and Michael C. Munger. 1986. "Legislators and Interest Groups: How Unorganized Interest Gets Represented." *American Political Science Review* 80(1):89–106.

Di Tella, Rafael and Federico Weinschelbaum. 2008. "Choosing Agents and Monitoring Consumption: A Note on Wealth as a Corruption-Controlling Device." *The Economic Journal* 118(532):1552–1571.

Diermeier, Daniel, Michael Keane, and Antonio Merlo. 2005. "A Political Economy Model of Congressional Careers." *American Economic Review* 95(1):347–373.

Dixit, Avinash, Gene M. Grossman, and Elhanan Helpman. 1997. "Common Agency and Coordination: General Theory and Application to Government Policy Making." *Journal of Political Economy* 105(4):752–769.

Djankov, Simeon, Rafael La Porta, Florencio Lopez-de Silantes, and Andrei Shleifer. 2010. "Disclosure by Politicians." *American Economic Journal: Applied Economics* 2(2):179–209.

Dollar, David, Raymond Fisman, and Roberta Gatti. 2001. "Are Women Really the 'Fairer' Sex? Corruption and Women in Government." *Journal of Economic Behavior & Organization* 46(4):423–429.

Dörrenbächer, Nora. 2016. "Patterns of Post-Cabinet Careers: When One Door Closes another Door Opens?" *Acta Politica* 51(4):472–491.

Duch, Raymond M. and Randolph T. Stevenson. 2008. *The Economic Vote: How Political and Economic Institutions Condition Election Results*. Cambridge University Press.

Dunning, Thad. 2012. *Natural Experiments in the Social Sciences: A Design-Based Approach*. Cambridge University Press.

Edinger, Michael and Bertram Schwarz. 2009. "Wohin nach dem Mandat? Zum Beruflichen Verbleib der Ausgeschiedenen." *SFB 580* 35:26–36.

Egerod, Benjamin C. K. 2019. "Voting for a Career: The Revolving Door Moderates the US Senate." Unpublished manuscript. https://github.com/BCEgerod/BCEgerod.github.io/blob/master/papers/VotingForACareer.pdf.

Eggers, Andrew C. 2014. "Partisanship and Electoral Accountability: Evidence from the UK Expenses Scandal." *Quarterly Journal of Political Science* 9(4):441–472.

Eggers, Andrew C. and Arthur Spirling. 2014. "Guarding the Guardians: Legislative Self-Policing and Electoral Corruption in Victorian Britain." *Quarterly Journal of Political Science* 9(3):337–370.

Eggers, Andrew C. and Jens Hainmueller. 2009. "MPs for Sale? Returns to Office in Postwar British Politics." *American Political Science Review* 103(4):1–21.

Eggers, Andrew C. and Jens Hainmueller. 2013. "Capitol Losses: The Mediocre Performance of Congressional Stock Portfolios." *Journal of Politics* 75(2):535–551.

Eggers, Andrew C. and Jens Hainmueller. 2014. "Political Capital: Corporate Connections and Stock Investments in the U.S. Congress, 2004–2008." *Quarterly Journal of Political Science* 9(2):169–202.

Erikson, Robert S. and Thomas R. Palfrey. 2000. "Equilibria in Campaign Spending Games: Theory and Data." *American Political Science Review* 94(3):595–609.

Esarey, Justin and Leslie A. Schwindt-Bayer. 2018. "Women's Representation, Accountability and Corruption in Democracies." *British Journal of Political Science* 48(3):659–690.

Esarey, Justin and Leslie A. Schwindt-Bayer. 2019. "Estimating Causal Relationships between Women's Representation in Government and Corruption." *Comparative Political Studies* 52(11):1713–1741.

Esterling, Kevin M. 2004. *The Political Economy of Expertise: Information and Efficiency in American National Politics*. University of Michigan Press.

Etzion, Dror and Gerald F. Davis. 2008. "Revolving Doors? A Network Analysis of Corporate Officers and U.S. Government Officials." *Journal of Management Inquiry* 17(3):157–161.

Ewing, Keith D. and Jacob Rowbottom. 2012. The Role of Spending Controls: New Electoral Actors and New Campaign Techniques. In *The Funding of Political Parties: Where Now?*, ed. Keith D. Ewing, Jacob Rowbottom, and Joo-Cheong Tham. Routledge. pp. 77–91.

Falguera, Elin, Samuel Jones, and Magnus Ohman, eds. 2014. "Funding of Political Parties and Election Campaigns. A Handbook on Political Finance." International Institute for Democracy and Electoral Assistance.

Felli, Leonardo and Antonio Merlo. 2006. "Endogenous Lobbying." *Journal of the European Economic Association* 4(1):180–215.

Fernández-Vázquez, Pablo, Pablo Barberá, and Gonzalo Rivero. 2016. "Rooting Out Corruption or Rooting for Corruption? The Heterogeneous Electoral Consequences of Scandals." *Political Science Research and Methods* 4(2):379–397.

Ferraz, Claudio and Frederico Finan. 2008. "Exposing Corrupt Politicians: The Effects of Brazil's Publicly Released Audits on Electoral Outcomes." *Quarterly Journal of Economics* 123(2):703–745.

Ferraz, Claudio and Frederico Finan. 2011. "Electoral Accountability and Corruption: Evidence from the Audits of Local Governments." *American Economic Review* 101(4):1274–1311.

Fink, Alexander. 2012. "The Effects of Party Campaign Spending under Proportional Representation: Evidence from Germany." *European Journal of Political Economy* 28(4):574–592.

Fisher, Justin. 2016. Britain. In *Checkbook Elections? Political Finance in Comparative Perspective*, ed. Pippa Norris and Andrea Abel van Es. Oxford University Press. pp. 45–63.

Fisher, Justin. 2018. "Party Finance." *Parliamentary Affairs* 71(1):171–188.

Fisher, Justin and Todd A. Eisenstadt. 2004. "Introduction: Comparative Party Finance." *Party Politics* 10(6):619–626.

Fisman, Raymond, Florian Schulz, and Vikrant Vig. 2014. "The Private Returns to Public Office." *Journal of Political Economy* 122(4):806–862.

Fisman, Raymond, Florian Schulz, and Vikrant Vig. 2019. "Financial Disclosure and Political Selection: Evidence from India." Unpublished manuscript. https://sites.bu.edu/fisman/files/2019/05/Disclosure-v043rf.pdf.

Fisman, Raymond and Miriam A. Golden. 2017a. *Corruption: What Everyone Needs to Know*. Oxford University Press.

Fisman, Raymond and Miriam A. Golden. 2017b. "How to Fight Corruption: Anticorruption Efforts Must Minimize Unintended Effects." *Science* 356(6340):803–804.

Fleischer, David. 1996. "Political Corruption in Brazil: The Delicate Connection with Campaign Finance." *Crime, Law and Social Change* 25(4):297–321.

Fong, Christian, Chad Hazlett, and Kosuke Imai. 2018. "Covariate Balancing Propensity Score for a Continuous Treatment: Application to the Efficacy of Political Advertisements." *Annals of Applied Statistics* 12(1):156–177.

Fouirnaies, Alexander. 2018. "When Are Agenda Setters Valuable?" *American Journal of Political Science* 62(1):176–191.

Fouirnaies, Alexander. 2021. "How Do Campaign Spending Limits Affect Elections? Evidence from the United Kingdom 1885–2019." *American Political Science Review* 115(2):395–411.

Fouirnaies, Alexander and Andrew B. Hall. 2014. "The Financial Incumbency Advantage: Causes and Consequences." *Journal of Politics* 76(3):711–724.

Fouirnaies, Alexander and Andrew B. Hall. 2016. "The Exposure Theory of Access: Why Some Firms Seek More Access to Incumbents Than Others." Unpublished manuscript. https://papers.ssrn.com/sol3/papers.cfm?abstract_id=2652361.

Fouirnaies, Alexander and Andrew B. Hall. 2018. "How Do Interest Groups Seek Access to Committees?" *American Journal of Political Science* 62(1):132–147.

Fouirnaies, Alexander and Anthony Fowler. 2022. "Do Campaign Contributions Buy Favorable Policies? Evidence from the Insurance Industry." *Political Science Research and Methods* 10(1): 18–32.

Fowler, Anthony and Andrew B. Hall. 2014. "Disentangling the Personal and Partisan Incumbency Advantages: Evidence from Close Elections and Term Limits." *Quarterly Journal of Political Science* 9(4):501–531.

Fowler, Anthony, Haritz Garro, and Jörg L. Spenkuch. 2020. "Quid Pro Quo? Corporate Returns to Campaign Contributions." *Journal of Politics* 82(3):844–858.

Fox, Justin and Lawrence Rothenberg. 2011. "Influence without Bribes: A Non-contracting Model of Campaign Giving and Policymaking." *Political Analysis* 19(3):325–341.

Franco, Annie, Neil Malhotra, Gabor Simovits, and L. J. Zigerell. 2017. "Developing Standards for Post-Hoc Weighting in Population-Based Survey Experiments." *Journal of Experimental Political Science* 4(2):161–172.

French, Patrick. 2011. *India: A Portrait*. Knopf.

Gaddie, Ronald Keith and Charles S. Bullock, III. 2000. *Elections to Open Seats in the U.S. House: Where the Action Is*. Rowman & Littlefield.

Gaikwad, Nikhar. 2013. "Presidential Prospects, Political Support, and Stock Market Performance." *Quarterly Journal of Political Science* 8(4):451–464.

Gans-Morse, Jordan, Sebastian Mazzuca, and Simeon Nichter. 2014. "Varieties of Clientelism: Machine Politics during Elections." *American Journal of Political Science* 58(2):415–532.

García Viñuela, Enrique and Carmen González de Aguilar. 2011. "Reforming Party Finance in Spain." *International Journal of Iberian Studies* 24(1):3–16.

García Viñuela, Enrique and Joaquín Artés. 2008. "Reforming Campaign Finance in the Nineties: A Case Study of Spain." *European Journal of Law and Economics* 25(3):177–190.

Gehlbach, Scott, Konstantin Sonin, and Ekaterina Zhuravskaya. 2010. "Businessman Candidates." *American Journal of Political Science* 54(3):718–736.

Gelman, Andrew and Gary King. 1990. "Estimating Incumbency Advantage without Bias." *American Journal of Political Science* 34(4):1142–1164.

Gerber, Alan. 1998. "Estimating the Effect of Campaign Spending on Senate Election Outcomes Using Instrumental Variables." *American Political Science Review* 92(2):401–411.

Gerber, Alan S., James S. Gimpel, Donald P. Green, and Daron R. Shaw. 2011. "How Large and Long-Lasting Are the Persuasive Effects of Televised Campaign Ads? Results from a Randomized Field Experiment." *American Political Science Review* 105(1):135–150.

Giere, Ronald N. 1990. *Explaining Science: A Cognitive Approach*. University of Chicago Press.

Gilardi, Fabrizio. 2015. "The Temporary Importance of Role Models for Women's Political Representation." *American Journal of Political Science* 59(4):957–970.

Gingerich, Daniel W. 2013. *Political Institutions and Party-Directed Corruption in South America: Stealing for the Team*. Cambridge University Press.

Gingerich, Daniel W. 2014a. "Brokered Politics in Brazil: An Empirical Analysis." *Quarterly Journal of Political Science* 9(3):269–300.

Gingerich, Daniel W. 2014b. "Yesterday's Heroes, Today's Villains: Ideology, Corruption, and Democratic Performance." *Journal of Theoretical Politics* 26(2):249–282.

Gingerich, Daniel W. and Luis Fernando Medina. 2013. "The Endurance and Eclipse of the Controlled Vote: A Formal Model of Vote Brokerage under the Secret Ballot." *Economics & Politics* 25(3):453–480.

Glaeser, Edward L. and Claudia Goldin, eds. 2006. *Corruption and Reform: Lessons from America's Economic History*. University of Chicago Press.

Golden, Miriam A. 2010. Puzzles of Political Corruption in Modern Advanced Democracies. In *Democracy and Accountability: Globalized Political Responsibility*, ed. Hideko Magara. Fukosha. pp. 184–199.

Golden, Miriam A. 2012. "Corruption in the Wealthy World." *Brown Journal of World Affairs* 18(2):75–84.

Golden, Miriam A. and Eric C. C. Chang. 2001. "Competitive Corruption: Factional Conflict and Political Malfeasance in Postwar Italian Christian Democracy." *World Politics* 53(4):588–622.

Golden, Miriam A. and Lucio Picci. 2005. "Proposal for a New Measure of Corruption, Illustrated with Italian Data." *Economics & Politics* 17(1):37–75.

Golden, Miriam A. and Paasha Mahdavi. 2015. The Institutional Components of Political Corruption. In *Routledge Handbook of Comparative Political Institutions*, ed. Jennifer Gandhi and Rubén Ruiz-Rufino. Routledge. pp. 204–220.

Goldman, Eitan, Jörg Rocholl, and Jongil So. 2009. "Do Politically Connected Boards Affect Firm Value?" *Review of Financial Studies* 22(6):2331–2360.

González-Bailon, Sandra, Will Jennings, and Martin Lodge. 2013. "Politics in the Boardroom: Corporate Pay, Networks and Recruitment of Former Parliamentarians, Ministers and Civil Servants in Britain." *Political Studies* 61(4):850–873.

Gowda, M. V. Rajeev and Eswaran Sridharan. 2012. "Reforming India's Party Financing and Election Expenditure Laws." *Election Law Journal* 11(2):226–240.

GRECO. 2009. "Evaluation Report on Spain Transparency of Party Funding." Council of Europe.

GRECO. 2013. "Second Compliance Report on Spain: Transparency of Party Funding." Council of Europe.

Green, Donald P. and Alan S. Gerber. 2015. *Get Out the Vote: How to Increase Voter Turnout*, 3rd ed. Brookings Institution Press.

Green, Donald P., Mary C. McGrath, and Peter M. Aronow. 2013. "Field Experiments and the Study of Voter Turnout." *Journal of Elections, Public Opinion and Parties* 23(1):27–48.

Gromley, William T., Jr. 1979. "A Test of the Revolving Door Hypothesis at the FCC." *American Journal of Political Science* 23(4):665–683.

Groseclose, Tim and Jeffrey Milyo. 1999. "Buying the Bums Out: What's the Dollar Value of a Seat in Congress?" Unpublished manuscript. www.gsb.stanford.edu/faculty-research/working-papers/buying-bums-out-whats-dollar-value-seat-congress.

Groseclose, Tim and Keith Krehbiel. 1994. "Golden Parachutes, Rubber Checks, and Strategic Retirements from the 102nd House." *American Journal of Political Science* 38(1):75–99.

Grossman, Gene M. and Elhanan Helpman. 1994. "Protection for Sale." *American Economic Review* 84(4):833–850.

Grossman, Gene M. and Elhanan Helpman. 2001. *Special Interest Politics*. MIT Press.

Grzymala-Busse, Anna. 2007. *Rebuilding Leviathan: Party Competition and State Exploitation in Post-Communist Democracies*. Cambridge University Press.

Gulzar, Saad, Miguel R. Rueda, and Nelson A. Ruiz. 2021. "Do Campaign Contribution Limits Curb the Influence of Money in Politics?" *American Journal of Political Science.* https://doi.org/10.1111/ajps.12596.

Hainmueller, Jens. 2012. "Entropy Balancing for Causal Effects: A Multivariate Reweighting Method to Produce Balanced Samples in Observational Studies." *Political Analysis* 20(1):25–46.

Hall, Andrew B. 2014. "Partisan Effects of Legislative Term Limits." *Legislative Studies Quarterly* 39(3):407–429.

Hall, Andrew B. 2016. "Systemic Effects of Campaign Spending: Evidence from Corporate Contribution Bans in US State Legislatures." *Political Science Research and Methods* 4(2):343–359.

Hall, Andrew B. 2019. *Who Wants to Run? How the Devaluing of Political Office Drives Polarization.* University of Chicago Press.

Hall, Richard L. and Robert P. van Houweling. 1995. "Avarice and Ambition in Congress: Representatives' Decisions to Run or Retire from the U.S. House." *American Political Science Review* 89(1):121–136.

Hansen, Wendy L. and Michael S. Rocca. 2019. "The Impact of *Citizens United* on Large Corporations and Their Employees." *Political Research Quarterly* 72(2):403–419.

Hansen, Wendy L., Michael S. Rocca, and Brittany Leigh Ortiz. 2015. "The Effects of *Citizens United* on Corporate Spending in the 2012 Presidential Election." *Journal of Politics* 77(2):535–545.

Harstad, Bard and Jakob Svensson. 2011. "Bribes, Lobbying, and Development." *American Political Science Review* 105(1):46–63.

Healy, Kieran. 2017. "Fuck Nuance." *Sociological Theory* 35(2):118–127.

Heidenheimer, Arnold J., Michael Johnston, and Victor T. LeVine, eds. 1989. *Political Corruption: A Handbook.* Transaction.

Heinz, John P., Edward O. Laumann, Robert L. Nelson, and Robert H. Salisbury. 1993. *The Hollow Core: Private Interest in National Policy Making.* Harvard University Press.

Helpman, Elhanan and Torsten Persson. 2001. "Lobbying and Legislative Bargaining." *B.E. Journal of Economic Analysis & Policy* 1(1):1–33.

Hersh, Eitan D. 2015. *Hacking the Electorate: How Campaigns Perceive Voters.* Cambridge University Press.

Heywood, Paul. 1997. From Dictatorship to Democracy: Changing Forms of Corruption in Spain. In *Democracy and Corruption in Europe*, ed. Donatella Della Porta and Yves Mény. Pinter. pp. 65–84.

Hicken, Allen. 2011. "Clientelism." *Annual Review of Political Science* 14:289–310.

Hidalgo, F. Daniel, Júlio Canello, and Renato Lima-de-Oliveira. 2016. "Can Politicians Police Themselves? Natural Experimental Evidence From Brazil's Audit Courts." *Comparative Political Studies* 49(13):1739–1773.

High Pay Center. 2015. "The Revolving Door and the Corporate Colonisation of UK Politics." https://highpaycentre.org/wp-content/uploads/2020/09/FINAL_REVOLVING_DOOR.pdf.

Hill, Stuart. 2005. "Review of: The Political Economy of Expertise: Information and Efficiency in American National Politics by Kevin M. Esterling." *Perspectives on Politics* 3(4):899–900.

Hillman, Amy J. 2005. "Politicians on the Board of Directors: Do Connections Affect the Bottom Line?" *Journal of Management* 31(3):464–481.

Hillman, Amy J., Asghar Zardkoohi, and Leonard Bierman. 1999. "Corporate Political Strategies and Firm Performance: Indications of Firm-Specific Benefits from Personal Service in the U.S. Government." *Strategic Management Journal* 20(1):67–81.

Ho, Daniel E., Kosuke Imai, Gary King, and Elizabeth A. Stuart. 2007. "Matching as Nonparametric Preprocessing for Reducing Model Dependence in Parametric Causal Inference." *Political Analysis* 15(3):199–236.

Hogan, Robert E. 2000. "The Costs of Representation in State Legislatures: Explaining Variations in Campaign Spending." *Social Science Quarterly* 81(4):941–956.

Hollyer, James R., B. Peter Rosendorff, and James Raymond Vreeland. 2011. "Democracy and Transparency." *Journal of Politics* 73(4):1191–1205.

Hollyer, James R., B. Peter Rosendorff, and James Raymond Vreeland. 2014. "Measuring Transparency." *Political Analysis* 22(4):413–434.

Hollyer, James R. and Leonard Wantchekon. 2015. "Corruption and Ideology in Autocracies." *Journal of Law, Economics, & Organization* 31(3):499–544.

Hou, You. 2019. *The Private Sector in Public Office: Selective Property Rights in China*. Cambridge University Press.

Huber, Gregory A. and Kevin Arceneaux. 2007. "Identifying the Persuasive Effects of Presidential Advertising." *American Journal of Political Science* 51(4):961–981.

Huber, John. 2013. "Is Theory Getting Lost in the 'Identification Revolution'?" *The Political Economist* (Summer):1–3.

Huber, Jürgen and Michael Kirchler. 2013. "Corporate Campaigns and Abnormal Stock Returns after Presidential Elections." *Public Choice* 156:285–307.

Hunter, Wendy and Timothy J. Power. 2019. "Bolsonaro and Brazil's Illiberal Backlash." *Journal of Democracy* 30(1):68–82.

Hyslop, Jonathan. 2005. "Political Corruption: Before and After Apartheid." *Journal of Southern African Studies* 31(4):773–789.

Imai, Kosuke and Marc Ratkovic. 2014. "Covariate Balancing Propensity Score." *Journal of the Royal Statistical Society, Series B (Statistical Methodology)* 76(1):243–263.

Issacharoff, Samuel and Pamela S. Karlan. 1998. "The Hydraulics of Campaign Finance Reform." *Texas Law Review* 77(7):1705–1738.

Issacharoff, Samuel and Pamela S. Karlan. 2004. "Where to Draw the Line?: Judicial Review of Political Gerrymanders." *University of Pennsylvania Law Review* 153(1):541–578.

Iyer, Lakshmi and Maya Reddy. 2013. "Redrawing the Lines: Did Political Incumbents Influence Electoral Redistricting in the World's Largest Democracy?" *Harvard Business School Working Paper* 14–51.

Jacobson, Gary C. 1978. "The Effects of Campaign Spending in Congressional Elections." *American Political Science Review* 72(2):469–491.

Jacobson, Gary C. 1985. "Money and Votes Reconsidered: Congressional Elections, 1972–1982." *Public Choice* 47:7–62.

Jacobson, Gary C. 2015. "How Do Campaigns Matter?" *Annual Review of Political Science* 18:31–47.

Jacobson, Gary C. and Jamie L. Carson. 2016. *The Politics of Congressional Elections*, 9th ed. Rowman & Littlefield.

Jalan, Bimal. 2007. *India's Politics: A View from the Backbench*. Penguin-Viking.

Jayachandran, Seema. 2006. "The Jeffords Effect." *Journal of Law and Economics* 49(2):397–425.

Jiménez, Fernando. 2014. La corrupción en un país sin corrupción sistémica: Un análisis de los casos Bárcenas, Palau y ERE. In *Informe sobre la Democracia en España 2014: Democracia sin Política*, ed. Joaquín Estefanía. Fundación Alternativas. pp. 165–187.

Jiménez, Fernando and Manuel Villoria. 2012. Political Finance, Urban Development, and Political Corruption in Spain. In *Money, Corruption, and Political Competition in Established and Emerging Democracies*, ed. Jonathan Mendilow. Lexington Books. pp. 115–136.

Jiménez, Fernando and Vicente Carbona. 2012. "'Esto funciona así': Anatomía de la corrupción en España." *Letras Libres* 125:8–19.

Johnson, R. W. 2015. *How Long Will South Africa Survive? The Looming Crisis*. Hurst.

Johnston, Michael. 1979. "Patrons and Clients, Jobs and Machines: A Case Study of the Uses of Patronage." *American Political Science Review* 73(2):385–398.

Johnston, Michael. 2005. *Syndromes of Corruption: Wealth, Power, and Democracy*. Cambridge University Press.

Johnston, Michael. 2014. *Corruption, Contention, and Reform*. Cambridge University Press.

Johnston, Ron and Charles Pattie. 2012. Local Parties, Local Money and Local Campaigns. In *The Funding of Political Parties: Where Now?*, ed. Keith D. Ewing, Jacob Rowbottom, and Joo-Cheong Tham. Routledge. pp. 92–109.

Jones, Mark P., Sebastian Saiegh, Pablo T. Spiller, and Mariano Tommasi. 2002. "Amateur Legislators–Professional Politicians: The Consequences of Party-Centered Electoral Rules in a Federal System." *American Journal of Political Science* 46(3):656–669.

Jucá, Ivan, Marcus André Melo, and Lucio Rennó. 2016. "The Political Cost of Corruption: Scandals, Campaign Finance, and Reelection in the Brazilian Chamber of Deputies." *Journal of Politics in Latin America* 8(2):3–36.

Jung, Hoyong. 2020. "Examining Politicians' Wealth Accumulation in South Korea." *Asian Survey* 60(2):290–322.

Kalla, Joshua L. and David E. Broockman. 2016. "Campaign Contributions Facilitate Access to Congressional Officials: A Randomized Field Experiment." *American Journal of Political Science* 60(3):545–558.

Kapur, Devesh and Milan Vaishnav. 2018. Builders, Politicians, and Election Finance. In *Costs of Democracy: Political Finance in India*, ed. Devesh Kapur and Milan Vaishnav. Oxford University Press. pp. 74–118.

Kaufmann, Daniel and Pedro C. Vicente. 2011. "Legal Corruption." *Economics & Politics* 23(2):195–219.

Keane, Michael P. and Antonio Merlo. 2010. "Money, Political Ambition, and the Career Decisions of Politicians." *American Economic Journal: Microeconomics* 2(3):186–215.

Kejriwal, Arvind. 2012. *Swaraj*. HarperCollins.

Kennedy, Ryan, Scott Clifford, Tyler Burleigh et al. 2020. "The Shape of and Solutions to the MTurk Quality Crisis." *Political Science Research and Methods* 8(4):614–629.

Khatri, Naresh and Abhoy K. Ojha. 2016. Indian Economic Philosophy and Crony Capitalism. In *Crony Capitalism in India: Establishing Robust Conteractive Institutional Frameworks*, ed. Naresh Khatri and Abhoy K. Ojha. Palgrave Macmillan. pp. 61–86.

Kiewiet, D. Roderick and Langche Zeng. 1993. "An Analysis of Congressional Career Decisions, 1947–1986." *American Political Science Review* 87(4):928–941.

Kim, In Song. 2017. "Political Cleavages within Industry: Firm-level Lobbying for Trade Liberalization." *American Political Science Review* 111(1):1–20.

Kim, In Song, Jan Stuckatz, and Lukas Wolters. 2020. "Strategic and Sequential Links between Campaign Donations and Lobbying." Unpublished manuscript. http://web.mit.edu/insong/www/pdf/campaign-lobby.pdf.

Kitschelt, Herbert. 2000. "Linkages between Citizens and Politicians in Democratic Politics." *Comparative Political Studies* 33(6–7):845–879.

Kitschelt, Herbert. 2013. "Democratic Accountability and Linkages Project." Duke University.

Kitschelt, Herbert and Steven I. Wilkinson, eds. 2007. *Patrons, Clients, and Policies: Patterns of Democratic Accountability and Political Competition.* Cambridge University Press.

Klarner, Carl E. 2013. "State Legislative Election Returns Data, 2011–2012." Harvard Dataverse.

Klarner, Carl E., William D. Berry, Thomas M. Carsey et al. 2013. "State Legislative Election Returns (1967–2010)." ICPSR.

Klašnja, Marko. 2015. "Corruption and the Incumbency Disadvantage: Theory and Evidence." *Journal of Politics* 77(4):928–942.

Klašnja, Marko and Rocío Titiunik. 2017. "The Incumbency Curse: Weak Parties, Term Limits, and Unfulfilled Accountability." *American Political Science Review* 111(1):129–148.

Klein, Heidi and Tillmann Höntzsch. 2007. "Fliegende Wechsel – die Drehtür kreist. Zwei Jahre danach – Was macht die Ex-Regierung Schröder II heute?" https://www.lobbycontrol.de/download/drehtuer-studie.pdf.

Klitgaard, Robert E. 1988. *Controlling Corruption.* University of California Press.

Klumpp, Tilman, Hugo M. Mialon, and Michael A. Williams. 2016. "The Business of American Democracy: Citizens United, Independent Spending, and Elections." *Journal of Law and Economics* 59(1):1–43.

Klüver, Heike. 2013. *Lobbying in the European Union: Interest Groups, Lobbying Coalitions, and Policy Change.* Oxford University Press.

Kochanek, Stanley A. 1987. "Briefcase Politics in India: The Congress Party and the Business Elite." *Asian Survey* 27(12):1278–1301.

Korte, Karl-Rudolf. 2017. "Wahlkampfkosten." www.bpb.de/politik/wahlen/wahlen-in-deutschland/335674/wahlkampfkosten.

Kosack, Stephen and Archon Fung. 2014. "Does Transparency Improve Governance?" *Annual Review of Political Science* 17:65–87.

Krasno, Jonathan S., Donald P. Green, and Jonathan A. Cowden. 1994. "The Dynamics of Campaign Fundraising in House Elections." *Journal of Politics* 56(2):459–474.

Krishna, Anirudh. 2007. Politics in the Middle: Mediating Relationships between the Citizens and the State in Rural North India. In *Patrons, Clients, and Policies: Patterns of Democratic Accountability and Political Competition*, ed. Herbert Kitschelt and Steven I. Wilkinson. Cambridge University Press. pp. 141–158.

Kroszner, Randall S. and Thomas Stratmann. 1998. "Interest-Group Competition and the Organization of Congress: Theory and Evidence from Financial Services' Political Action Committees." *American Economic Review* 88(5):1163–1187.

Kunicova, Jana and Susan Rose-Ackerman. 2005. "Electoral Rules and Constitutional Structures as Constraints on Corruption." *British Journal of Political Science* 35(4):573–606.

La Porta, Rafael, Florencio Lopez-de Silantes, Andrei Shleifer, and Robert Vishny. 1999. "The Quality of Government." *Journal of Law, Economics, & Organization* 15(1):222–279.

La Raja, Raymond J. and Brian F. Schaffner. 2014. "The Effects of Campaign Finance Spending Bans on Electoral Outcomes: Evidence from the States about the Potential Impact of Citizens United v. FEC." *Electoral Studies* 33:102–114.

La Raja, Raymond J. and Brian F. Schaffner. 2015. *Campaign Finance and Political Polarization: When Purists Prevail*. University of Michigan Press.

Lambsdorff, Johann Graf. 2006. Causes and Consequences of Corruption: What Do We Know from a Cross-Section of Countries? In *International Handbook on the Economics of Corruption*, ed. Susan Rose-Ackerman. Edward Elgar. pp. 3–52.

Lambsdorff, Johann Graf. 2007. *The Institutional Economics of Corruption and Reform: Theory, Evidence, and Policy*. Cambridge University Press.

LaPira, Timothy M. and Herschel F. Thomas, III. 2014. "Revolving Door Lobbyists and Interest Representation." *Interest Groups & Advocacy* 3(1):4–29.

LaPira, Timothy M. and Herschel F. Thomas, III. 2017. *Revolving Door Lobbying: Public Service, Private Influence, and the Unequal Representation of Interests*. University of Kansas Press.

Law, Marc T. and Cheryl X. Long. 2012. "What Do Revolving-Door Laws Do?" *Journal of Law and Economics* 55(2):421–436.

Lazarus, Jeffrey and Amy McKay. 2012. "Consequences of the Revolving Door: Evaluating the Lobbying Success of Former Congressional Members and the Staff." Unpublished manuscript. https://ssrn.com/abstract=2141416.

Lazarus, Jeffrey, Amy McKay, and Lindsey Herbel. 2016. "Who Walks through the Revolving Door? Examining the Lobbying Activity of Former Members of Congress." *Interest Groups & Advocacy* 5(1):82–100.

Lessig, Lawrence. 2011. *Republic, Lost: How Money Corrupts Congress–and a Plan to Stop It*. Twelve.

Lester, Richard H., Amy J. Hillman, Asghar Zardkoohi, and Albert Al Cannella, Jr. 2008. "Former Government Officials as Outside Directors: The Role of Human and Social Capital." *Academy of Management Journal* 51(5):999–1013.

Li, Zhao. 2018. "How Internal Constraints Shape Interest Group Activities: Evidence from Access-Seeking PACs." *American Political Science Review* 112(4):792–808.

Lindberg, Staffan I., Michael Coppedge, John Gerring et al. 2014. "V-Dem: A New Way to Measure Democracy." *Journal of Democracy* 25(3):159–169.

Linz, Juan J. 1998. "Democracy's Time Constraints." *International Political Science Review* 19(1):19–37.

Lipset, Seymour M. and Stein Rokkan. 1967. *Party Systems and Voter Alignments: Cross-National Perspectives.* The Free Press.

Lodge, Tom. 1998. "Political Corruption in South Africa." *African Affairs* 97(387):157–187.

Lowry, Michael P. 2008. "Legitimizing Elections through the Regulation of Campaign Financing: A Comparative Constitutional Analysis and Hope for South Africa." *Boston College International and Comparative Law Review* 31(2):185–212.

Lucca, David, Amit Seru, and Francesco Trebbi. 2014. "The Revolving Door and Worker Flows in Banking Regulation." *Journal of Monetary Economics* 65:17–32.

Luechinger, Simon and Christoph Moser. 2014. "The Value of the Revolving Door: Political Appointees and the Stock Market." *Journal of Public Economics* 119:93–107.

Maddens, Bart, Bram Wauters, Jo Noppe, and Stefaan Fiers. 2006. "Effects of Campaign Spending in an Open List PR System: The 2003 Legislative Elections in Flanders/Belgium." *West European Politics* 29(1):161–168.

Magee, Christopher S. P. 2012. "The Incumbent Spending Puzzle." *Social Science Quarterly* 93(4):932–949.

Makkai, Toni and John Braithwaite. 1992. "In and Out of the Revolving Door: Making Sense of Regulatory Capture." *Journal of Public Policy* 12(1):61–78.

Makse, Todd. 2017. "A Very Particular Set of Skills: Former Legislator Traits and Revolving Door Lobbying in Congress." *American Politics Research* 45(5):866–886.

Mancuso, Wagner Pralon, Dalson Britto Figueiredo Filho, Bruno Wilhelm Speck, Lucas Emanuel Oliveira Silva, and Enivaldo Carvalho da Rocha. 2016. "Corporate Dependence in Brazil's 2010 Elections for Federal Deputy." *Brazilian Political Science Review* 10(3):1–24.

Manin, Bernard, Adam Przeworski, and Susan C. Stokes. 1999. Elections and Representation. In *Democracy, Accountability, and Representation*, ed. Adam Przeworski, Susan C. Stokes, and Bernard Manin. Cambridge University Press. pp. 29–54.

Mansbridge, Jane. 1999. "Should Blacks Represent Blacks and Women Represent Women? A Contingent 'Yes'." *Journal of Politics* 61(3):628–657.

Manza, Jeff and Clem Brooks. 1997. "The Religious Factor in U.S. Presidential Elections, 1960–1992." *American Journal of Sociology* 103(1):38–81.

Mattozzi, Andrea and Antonio Merlo. 2008. "Political Careers or Career Politicians." *Journal of Public Economics* 92(3–4):597–608.

Mauro, Paolo. 1995. "Corruption and Growth." *Quarterly Journal of Economics* 110(3):681–712.

Mayer, Jane. 2016. *Dark Money: The Hidden History of the Billionaires Behind the Rise of the Radical Right.* Doubleday.

Mayhew, David R. 1974. *Congress: The Electoral Connection.* Yale University Press.

McKay, Amy Melissa. 2018. "Fundraising for Favors? Linking Lobbyist-Hosted Fundraisers to Legislative Benefits." *Political Research Quarterly* 71(4):869–880.

McKay, Joanna. 2003. Political Corruption in Germany. In *Corruption in Contemporary Politics*, ed. Martin J. Bull and James L. Newell. Palgrave Macmillan. pp. 53–65.

McMenamin, Iain. 2012. "If Money Talks, What Does It Say? Varieties of Capitalism and Business Financing of Parties." *World Politics* 64(1):1–38.

McMillan, John and Pablo Zoido. 2004. "How to Subvert Democracy: Montesinos in Peru." *Journal of Economic Perspectives* 18(4):69–92.

Mian, Atif, Amir Sufi, and Francesco Trebbi. 2010. "The Political Economy of the US Mortgage Default Crisis." *American Economic Review* 100(5):1967–1998.

Mian, Atif, Amir Sufi, and Francesco Trebbi. 2013. "The Political Economy of the Subprime Mortgage Credit Expansion." *Quarterly Journal of Political Science* 8(4):373–408.

Milligan, Kevin and Marie Rekkas. 2008. "Campaign Spending Limits, Incumbent Spending, and Election Outcomes." *Canadian Journal of Economics* 41(4):1351–1374.

Mistree, Dinsha. 2015. "Party-Directed Corruption in the Developing World." *Comparative Politics* 47(3):354–374.

Moncrief, Gary and Joel A. Thompson. 2001. "On the Outside Looking in: Lobbyists' Perspectives on the Effects of State Legislative Term Limits." *State Politics & Policy Quarterly* 1(4):394–411.

Montinola, Gabrielle R. and Robert W. Jackman. 2002. "Sources of Corruption: A Cross-Country Study." *British Journal of Political Science* 32(1):147–170.

Mungiu-Pippidi, Alina. 2015. *The Quest for Good Governance: How Societies Develop Control of Corruption.* Cambridge University Press.

Mungiu-Pippidi, Alina. 2017. "The Time has Come for Evidence-Based Anticorruption." *Nature Human Behaviour* 1(1):0011.

Musella, Fortunato. 2015. "Presidents in Business: Career and Destiny of Democratic Leaders." *European Political Science Review* 7(2):293–313.

Mutch, Robert E. 2014. *Buying the Vote: A History of Campaign Finance Reform.* Oxford University Press.

Myerson, Roger B. 1993. "Effectiveness of Electoral Systems for Reducing Government Corruption: A Game-Theoretic Analysis." *Games and Economic Behavior* 5(1):118–132.

Naoi, Megumi and Ellis Krauss. 2009. "Who Lobbies Whom? Special Interest Politics under Alternative Electoral Systems." *American Journal of Political Science* 53(4):874–892.

Naßmacher, Karl-Heinz. 2000. "Parteienfinanzierung in der Bewährung." *Aus Politik und Zeitgeschichte* B 16.

Nichter, Simeon. 2008. "Vote Buying or Turnout Buying? Machine Politics and the Secret Ballot." *American Political Science Review* 102(1):19–31.

Nichter, Simeon. 2018. *Votes for Survival: Relational Clientelism in Latin America*. Cambridge University Press.

Norris, Pippa and Andrea Abel van Es. 2016. Does Regulation Work? In *Checkbook Elections? Political Finance in Comparative Perspective*, ed. Pippa Norris and Andrea Abel van Es. Oxford University Press. pp. 227–253.

Nyblade, Benjamin and Steven R. Reed. 2008. "Who Cheats? Who Loots? Political Competition and Corruption in Japan, 1947–1993." *American Journal of Political Science* 52(4):926–941.

Olken, Benjamin A. 2009. "Corruption Perceptions vs. Corruption Reality." *Journal of Public Economics* 93(7–8):950–964.

Olken, Benjamin A. and Rohini Pande. 2012. "Corruption in Developing Countries." *Annual Review of Economics* 4:479–509.

Palmer, Maxwell and Benjamin Schneer. 2016. "Capitol Gains: The Returns to Elected Office from Corporate Board Directorships." *Journal of Politics* 78(1):181–196.

Palmer, Maxwell and Benjamin Schneer. 2019. "Postpolitical Careers: How Politicians Capitalize on Public Office." *Journal of Politics* 81(2):670–675.

Parker, Glenn R. 2008. *Capital Investments: The Marketability of Political Skills*. University of Michigan Press.

Pattie, Charles and Ron Johnston. 2012. "The Electoral Impact of the UK 2009 MPs' Expenses Scandal." *Political Studies* 60(4):730–750.

Pattie, Charles J., Ronald J. Johnston, and Edward A. Fieldhouse. 1995. "Winning the Local Vote: The Effectiveness of Constituency Campaign Spending in Great Britain, 1983–1992." *American Political Science Review* 89(4):969–983.

Pereira, Carlos and Marcus André Melo. 2015. "Reelecting Corrupt Incumbents in Exchange for Public Goods: Rouba Maz Faz in Brazil." *Latin America Research Review* 50(4):88–115.

Persson, Anna, Bo Rothstein, and Jan Teorell. 2013. "Why Anticorruption Reforms Fail–Systemic Corruption as a Collective Action Problem." *Governance* 26(3):449–471.

Persson, Torsten. 1998. "Economic Policy and Special Interest Politics." *The Economic Journal* 108(447):310–327.

Persson, Torsten, Gerard Roland, and Guido Tabellini. 2000. "Comparative Politics and Public Finance." *Journal of Political Economy* 108(6):1121–1161.

Persson, Torsten and Guido Tabellini. 2000. *Political Economics: Explaining Economic Policy*. MIT Press.

Persson, Torsten, Guido Tabellini, and Francesco Trebbi. 2003. "Electoral Rules and Corruption." *Journal of the European Economic Association* 1(4):958–989.

Petrova, Maria, Andrei Simonov, and James M. Snyder, Jr. 2019. "The Effect of Citizen United on U.S. State and Federal Elections." Unpublished manuscript. https://sites.google.com/site/mariapetrovaphd/Citizens%20United%20draft.pdf.

Pinto-Duschinsky, Michael. 1981. *British Political Finance 1830–1980*. American Enterprise Institute.

Pinto-Duschinsky, Michael. 2002. "Financing Politics: A Global View." *Journal of Democracy* 13(4):69–86.

Potter, Joshua D. and Margit Tavits. 2015. "The Impact of Campaign Finance Laws on Party Competition." *British Journal of Political Science* 45(1):73–95.

Powell, Eleanor Neff and Justin Grimmer. 2016. "Money in Exile: Campaign Contributions and Committee Access." *Journal of Politics* 78(4):974–988.

Power, Greg. 2012. *Global Parliamentary Report: The Changing Nature of Parliamentary Representation*. Inter-Parliamentary Union and United Nations Development Programme.

Praça, Sérgio and Matthew M. Taylor. 2014. "Inching Toward Accountability: The Evolution of Brazil's Anticorruption Institutions, 1985–2010." *Latin American Politics and Society* 56(2):27–48.

Prat, Andrea. 2002. "Campaign Spending with Office-Seeking Politicians, Rational Voters, and Multiple Lobbies." *Journal of Economic Theory* 103(1):162–189.

Public Protector South Africa. 2016. "State of Capture." https://cdn.24.co.za/files/Cms/General/d/4666/3f63a8b78d2b495d88f10ed060997f76.pdf.

Pujas, Véronique and Martin Rhodes. 2002. Party Finance and Political Scandal: Comparing Italy, Spain, and France. In *Political Corruption: Concepts & Contexts*, ed. Arnold J. Heidenheimer and Michael Johnston. Transaction. pp. 739–760.

Querubin, Pablo and James M. Snyder, Jr. 2013. "The Control of Politicians in Normal Times and Times of Crisis: Wealth Accumulation by U.S. Congressmen, 1850–1880." *Quarterly Journal of Political Science* 8(4):409–450.

Razafindrakoto, Mireille and François Roubaud. 2010. "Are International Databases on Corruption Reliable? A Comparison of Expert Opinion Surveys and Household Surveys in Sub-Saharan Africa." *World Development* 38(8):1057–1069.

Robinson, Vicki and Stefaans Brummer. 2006. "SA Democracy Incorporated: Corporate Fronts and Political Party Funding." *Institute for Security Studies Papers* 129.

Roemer, John E. 2006. "Party Competition under Private and Public Financing: A Comparison of Institutions." *Advances in Theoretical Economics* 6(1):1–31.

Rohde, David W. 1979. "Risk-Bearing and Progressive Ambition: The Case of Members of the United States House of Representatives." *American Journal of Political Science* 23(1):1–26.

Rose-Ackerman, Susan. 1978. *Corruption: A Study in Political Economy*. Academic Press.

Rose-Ackerman, Susan and Bonnie J. Palifka. 2016. *Corruption and Government: Causes, Consequences, and Reform*, 2nd ed. Cambridge University Press.

Rothenberg, Lawrence S. and Mitchell S. Sanders. 2000. "Severing the Electoral Connection: Shirking in the Contemporary Congress." *American Journal of Political Science* 44(2):316–325.

Rothstein, Bo. 2011. "Anti-Corruption: The Indirect 'Big Bang' Approach." *Review of International Political Economy* 18(2):228–250.

Rothstein, Bo. 2018. "Fighting Systemic Corruption: The Indirect Strategy." *Daedalus* 147(3):35–49.

Rothstein, Bo and Aiysha Varraich. 2017. *Making Sense of Corruption.* Cambridge University Press.

Ruiz, Nelson A. 2020. "The Power of Money: The Consequences of Electing a Donor Funded Politician." Unpublished manuscript. https://papers.ssrn.com/sol3/papers.cfm?abstract_id=3123592.

Salant, David J. 1995. "Behind the Revolving Door: A New View of Public Utility Regulation." *RAND Journal of Economics* 26(3):362–377.

Salisbury, Robert H., Paul Johnson, John P. Heinz, Edward O. Laumann, and Robert L. Nelson. 1989. "Who You Know versus What You Know: The Uses of Government Experience for Washington Lobbyists." *American Journal of Political Science* 33(1):175–195.

Samii, Cyrus. 2016. "Causal Empiricism in Quantitative Research." *Journal of Politics* 78(3):941–955.

Samuels, David. 2001*a*. "Does Money Matter? Credible Commitments and Campaign Finance in New Democracies: Theory and Evidence from Brazil." *Comparative Politics* 34(1):23–42.

Samuels, David. 2001*b*. "Incumbents and Challengers on a Level Playing Field: Assessing the Impact of Campaign Finance in Brazil." *Journal of Politics* 63(2):569–584.

Samuels, David. 2001*c*. "Money, Elections, and Democracy in Brazil." *Latin American Politics and Society* 43(2):27–48.

Samuels, David. 2002. "Pork Barreling Is Not Credit Claiming or Advertising: Campaign Finance and the Sources of the Personal Vote in Brazil." *Journal of Politics* 64(3):845–863.

Samuels, David. 2003. *Ambition, Federalism, and Legislative Politics in Brazil.* Cambridge University Press.

Santos, Fabiano G. and Fabiano J. H. Pegurier. 2011. "Political Careers in Brazil: Long-Term Trends and Cross-Sectional Variation." *Regional and Federal Studies* 21(2):165–183.

Sarbaugh-Thompson, Marjorie, Lyke Thompson, Charles D. Elder et al. 2006. "Democracy among Strangers: Term Limits' Effects on Relationships between State Legislators in Michigan." *State Politics & Policy Quarterly* 6(4):384–409.

Scarrow, Susan E. 2003. "Party Finance Scandals and their Consequences in the 2002 Election: Paying for Mistakes?" *German Politics & Society* 21(1):119–137.

Scarrow, Susan E. 2007. "Political Finance in Comparative Perspective." *Annual Review of Political Science* 10:193–210.

Schlesinger, Joseph A. 1966. *Ambition and Politics: Political Careers in the United States.* Rand McNally.

Schofield, Norman and Itai Sened. 2006. *Multiparty Democracy: Elections and Legislative Politics.* Cambridge University Press.

Schwindt-Bayer, Leslie A. and Margit Tavits. 2016. *Clarity of Responsibility, Accountability, and Corruption.* Cambridge University Press.

Scott, James C. 1972. *Comparative Political Corruption.* Prentice-Hall.

Seibel, Wolfgang. 1997. Corruption in the Federal Republic of Germany before and in the Wake of Reunification. In *Democracy and Corruption in Europe*, ed. Donatella Della Porta and Yves Mény. Pinter. pp. 85–102.

Shah, Paru. 2014. "It Takes a Black Candidate: A Supply-Side Theory of Minority Representation." *Political Research Quarterly* 67(2):266–279.

Shepherd, Michael E. and Hye Young You. 2020. "Exit Strategy: Career Concerns and Revolving Doors in Congress." *American Political Science Review* 114(1):270–284.

Skocpol, Theda and Alexander Hertel-Fernandez. 2016. "The Koch Network and Republican Party Extremism." *Perspectives on Politics* 14(3):681–699.

Snyder, Jr., James M. and Michael M. Ting. 2008. "Interest Groups and the Electoral Control of Politicians." *Journal of Public Economics* 92(3–4):482–500.

Solaz, Hector, Catherine E. De Vries, and Roosmarijn A. de Geus. 2019. "In-Group Loyalty and the Punishment of Corruption." *Comparative Political Studies* 52(6):896–926.

Solé-Ollé, Albert and Pilar Sorribias-Navarro. 2018. "Trust No More? On the Lasting Effects of Corruption Scandals." *European Journal of Political Economy* 55:185–203.

Sontheimer, Kurt. 2000. "Vom Unheil und Segen einer Affäre." *Aus Politik und Zeitgeschichte* B 16.

Speck, Bruno Wilhelm. 2016. Brazil. In *Checkbook Elections? Political Finance in Comparative Perspective*, ed. Pippa Norris and Andrea Abel van Es. Oxford University Press. pp. 27–44.

Spencer, Douglas M. and Abby K. Wood. 2014. "Citizens United, States Divided: An Empirical Analysis of Independent Political Spending." *Indiana Law Journal* 89(1):315–372.

Sridharan, Eswaran and Milan Vaishnav. 2016. India. In *Checkbook Elections? Political Finance in Comparative Perspective*, ed. Pippa Norris and Andrea Abel van Es. Oxford University Press. pp. 64–83.

Stanig, Piero. 2018. "Regulation of Speech and Media Coverage of Corruption: An Empirical Analysis of the Mexican Press." *American Journal of Political Science* 59(1):175–193.

Stegmueller, Daniel. 2013. "Religion and Redistributive Voting in Western Europe." *Journal of Politics* 75(4):1064–1076.

Stephenson, Matthew C. 2021. "Bibliography on Corruption and Anticorruption." www.law.harvard.edu/faculty/mstephenson.

Stokes, Susan C. 2005. "Perverse Accountability: A Formal Model of Machine Politics with Evidence from Argentina." *American Political Science Review* 99(3):315–325.

Stone, Walter J. and Elizabeth N. Simas. 2010. "Candidate Valence and Ideological Positions in U.S. House Elections." *American Journal of Political Science* 54(2):371–388.

Stratmann, Thomas. 2005. "Some Talk: Money in Politics. A (Partial) Review of the Literature." *Public Choice* 124:135–156.

Sukhtankar, Sandip. 2012. "Sweetening the Deal? Political Connections and Sugar Mills in India." *American Economic Journal: Applied Economics* 4(3):43–63.

Sukhtankar, Sandip and Milan Vaishnav. 2015. "Corruption in India: Bridging Research Evidence and Policy Options." Brookings-NCAER India Policy Forum.

Suttner, Raymond. 2009. "Why Is This Election Different from All Others? ANC, COPE, and the Way Forward." Centre for Policy Studies.

Swamy, Anand, Stephen Knack, Young Lee, and Omar Azfar. 2001. "Gender and Corruption." *Journal of Development Economics* 64(1):25–55.

Szakonyi, David. 2018. "Businesspeople in Elected Office: Identifying Private Benefits from Firm-Level Returns." *American Political Science Review* 112(2):322–338.

Szakonyi, David. 2020. *Politics for Profit: Business, Elections, and Policymaking in Russia*. Cambridge University Press.

Teachout, Zephyr. 2014. *Corruption in America: From Benjamin Franklin's Snuff Box to Citizens United*. Harvard University Press.

Thachil, Tariq. 2014. *Elite Parties, Poor Voters: How Social Services Win Votes in India*. Cambridge University Press.

Thompson, Leonard. 2014. *A History of South Africa*, 4th ed. Yale University Press.

Thomsen, Danielle M. 2017. *Opting Out of Congress: Partisan Polarization and the Decline of Moderate Candidates*. Cambridge University Press.

Tien, Charles. 2001. "Representation, Voluntary Retirement, and Shirking in the Last Term." *Public Choice* 106(1–2):117–130.

Titiunik, Rocío. 2016. "Drawing Your Senator from a Jar: Term Length and Legislative Behavior." *Political Science Research and Methods* 4(2):293–316.

Titl, Vitezslav and Benny Geys. 2018. "Political Donations and the Allocation of Public Procurement Contracts." *European Economic Review* 111:443–458.

Transparency International. 2014. "Cabs for Hire? Fixing the Revolving Door between Government and Business." www.transparency.org.uk/sites/default/files/pdf/publications/Cabs_for_HireY_Fixing_the_Revolving_Door_between_Government_and_Business.pdf.

Treisman, Daniel. 2000. "The Causes of Corruption: A Cross-National Study." *Journal of Public Economics* 76(3):399–457.

Treisman, Daniel. 2007. "What Have We Learned about the Causes of Crossnational Corruption from 10 Years of Empirical Research?" *Annual Review of Political Science* 10:211–244.

Tribe, John. 2010. "The Poulson Affair: Corruption and the Role of Bankruptcy Law Public Examinations in the Early 1970s." *King's Law Journal* 21(3):495–528.

Truex, Rory. 2014. "The Returns to Office in a 'Rubber Stamp' Parliament." *American Political Science Review* 108(2):235–251.

Tsebelis, George. 2002. *Veto Players: How Political Institutions Work*. Princeton University Press.

Tshitereke, Clarence. 2002. "Securing Democracy: Party Finance and Party Donations – the South African Challenge." *Institute for Security Studies Papers* 63.

Tullock, Gordon. 1972. "The Purchase of Politicians." *Western Economic Journal* 10(3):354–355.

Udall, Tom. 2010. "Amend the Constitution to Restore Public Trust in the Political System: A Practitioner's Perspective on Campaign Finance Reform." *Yale Law & Policy Review* 29(1):235–252.

Uppal, Yogesh. 2009. "The Disadvantaged Incumbents: Estimating Incumbency Effects in Indian State Legislatures." *Public Choice* 138(1–2):9–27.

Uppal, Yogesh. 2011. "Does Legislative Turnover Adversely Affect State Expenditure Policy? Evidence from Indian State Elections." *Public Choice* 147(1–2):189–207.

Uppal, Yogesh and Amihai Glazer. 2015. "Legislative Turnover, Fiscal Policy, and Economic Growth: Evidence from U.S. State Legislatures." *Economic Inquiry* 53(1):91–107.

Uslaner, Eric M. 2008. *Corruption, Inequality, and the Rule of Law*. Cambridge University Press.

Uslaner, Eric M. 2017. *The Historical Roots of Corruption: Mass Education, Economic Inequality, and State Capacity*. Cambridge University Press.

Vaishnav, Milan. 2017. *When Crime Pays: Money and Muscle in Indian Politics*. Yale University Press.

Valentino, Nicholas A., Vincent L. Hutchings, and Dmitri Williams. 2004. "The Impact of Political Advertising on Knowledge, Internet Information Seeking, and Candidate Preference." *Journal of Communication* 54(2):337–354.

Van Biezen, Ingrid, Peter Mair, and Thomas Poguntke. 2012. "Going, Going, … Gone? The Decline of Party Membership in Contemporary Europe." *European Journal of Political Research* 51(1):24–56.

Warner, Carolyn M. 2007. *The Best System Money Can Buy: Corruption in the European Union*. Cornell University Press.

Waterbury, John. 1973. "Endemic and Planned Corruption in a Monarchical Regime." *World Politics* 25(4):533–555.

Weitz-Shapiro, Rebecca. 2012. "What Wins Votes: Why Some Politicians Opt Out of Clientelism." *American Journal of Political Science* 56(3):568–583.

Weitz-Shapiro, Rebecca. 2016. *Curbing Clientelism in Argentina: Politics, Poverty, and Social Policy*. Cambridge University Press.

Werner, Timothy. 2011. "The Sound, the Fury, and the Nonevent: Business Power and Market Reactions to the *Citizens United* Decision." *American Politics Research* 39(1):118–141.

Weschle, Simon. 2014. "Two Types of Economic Voting: How Economic Conditions Jointly Affect Vote Choice and Turnout." *Electoral Studies* 34:39–53.

Weschle, Simon. 2016. "Punishing Personal and Electoral Corruption: Experimental Evidence from India." *Research and Politics* 3(2):1–6.

Weschle, Simon. 2021a. "Campaign Finance Legislation and the Supply-Side of the Revolving Door." *Political Science Research and Methods* 9(2):365–379.

Weschle, Simon. 2021b. "Parliamentary Positions and Politicians' Private Sector Earnings: Evidence from the UK House of Commons." *Journal of Politics* 83(2):706–721.

Wilkinson, Steven I. 2004. *Votes and Violence: Electoral Competition and Ethnic Riots in India*. Cambridge University Press.

Wilkinson, Steven I. 2007. Explaining Changing Patterns of Party-Voter Linkages in India. In *Patrons, Clients, and Policies: Patterns of Democratic Accountability and Political Competition*, ed. Herbert Kitschelt and Steven I. Wilkinson. Cambridge University Press. pp. 110–140.

Winters, Matthew S. and Rebecca Weitz-Shapiro. 2013. "Lacking Information or Condoning Corruption: When Do Voters Support Corrupt Politicians?" *Comparative Politics* 45(4):418–436.

Winters, Matthew S. and Rebecca Weitz-Shapiro. 2017. "Can Citizens Discern? Information Credibility, Political Sophistication, and the Punishment of Corruption in Brazil." *Journal of Politics* 79(1):60–74.

Würfel, Maximilian. 2018. "Life after the Bundestag: An Analysis of the Post-Parliamentary Careers of German MPs." *German Politics* 27(3):295–316.

Yadav, Vineeta. 2011. *Political Parties, Business Groups, and Corruption in Developing Countries*. Oxford University Press.

Yadav, Vineeta and Bumba Mukherjee. 2016. *The Politics of Corruption in Dictatorships*. Cambridge University Press.

You, Hye Young. 2017. "Ex Post Lobbying." *Journal of Politics* 79(4):1162–1176.

Zhao, Xinshu and Steven H. Chaffee. 1995. "Campaign Advertisements versus Television News as Sources of Political Issue Information." *Public Opinion Quarterly* 59(1):41–65.

Zitzewitz, Eric. 2012. "Forensic Economics." *Journal of Economic Literature* 50(3):731–769.

Index

Lightning Source UK Ltd.
Milton Keynes UK
UKHW010707010622
403833UK00002B/189

9 781009 054713